To Chan
With compliments of
George and Ta-Chung.

Manufacturing Production Functions
in the United States, 1957

An Interindustry and Interstate Comparison of Productivity

CORNELL STUDIES IN INDUSTRIAL AND LABOR RELATIONS

Cornell Studies in Industrial and Labor Relations and International Reports are research monographs developed by faculty and staff at the New York State School of Industrial and Labor Relations.

I *Wartime Manpower Mobilization: A Study of World War II Experience in the Buffalo-Niagara Area*, by Leonard P. Adams. 184 pp. 50¢.

II *AFL Attitudes toward Production: 1900–1932*, by Jean Trepp McKelvey. 160 pp. $1.00.

III *Sources of Wage Information: Employer Associations*, by N. Arnold Tolles and Robert L. Raimon. 368 pp. $1.00.

IV *The Labor Injunction in New York City, 1935–1950*, by Jacob Seidenberg. 192 pp. $1.00.

V *Nonferrous Metals Industry Unionism, 1932–1954: A Story of Leadership Controversy*, by Vernon H. Jensen. 344 pp. $1.25.

VI *The Industrial Mobility of Labor as a Probability Process*, by Isadore Blumen, Marvin Kogan, and Philip J. McCarthy. 176 pp. $3.00.

VII *Empire in Wood: A History of the Carpenters' Union*, by Robert A. Christie. 376 pp. $2.25.

VIII *Workers and Industrial Change: A Case Study of Labor Mobility*, by Leonard P. Adams and Robert L. Aronson. 224 pp. $3.00.

IX *Hawthorne Revisited:* MANAGEMENT AND THE WORKER, *Its Critics, and Developments in Human Relations in Industry*, by Henry A. Landsberger. 132 pp. $1.75.

X *Conflict Within the AFL: A Study of Craft Versus Industrial Unionism, 1901–1938*, by James O. Morris. 336 pp. $5.00.

XI *Union Democracy: Practice and Ideal—An Analysis of Four Large Local Unions*, by Alice H. Cook. 256 pp. $4.75.

XII *Procedures and Policies of the New York State Labor Relations Board,* by Kurt L. Hanslowe. 224 pp. $4.00.

XIII *Fringe Benefits: Wages or Social Obligation?* by Donna Allen. 288 pp. $4.75; paperback edition, $2.50.

XIV *Teaching Industrial Relations in High Schools: A Survey of Selected Practices in the United States,* by Robert E. Doherty. 108 pp. $2.00.

XV *Manufacturing Production Functions in the United States, 1957: An Interindustry and Interstate Comparison of Productivity,* by George H. Hildebrand and Ta-Chung Liu. 240 pp. $6.00.

CORNELL INTERNATIONAL INDUSTRIAL AND LABOR RELATIONS REPORTS

I *Labor Unions and National Politics in Italian Industrial Plants,* by Maurice F. Neufeld. 160 pp. $2.00.

II *American Labor and the International Labor Movement, 1940–1953,* by John P. Windmuller. (out of print) 260 pp. $3.00.

III *Jobs and Workers in India,* by Oscar A. Ornati. 236 pp. $1.50.

IV *Contemporary Collective Bargaining in Seven Countries,* Adolf Sturmthal, Editor. (out of print) 392 pp. $4.50.

V *Italy: School for Awakening Countries,* by Maurice F. Neufeld. 600 pp. $9.00.

VI *Poor Countries and Authoritarian Rule,* by Maurice F. Neufeld. 256 pp. $5.00.

PUBLISHED BY

THE NEW YORK STATE SCHOOL OF

INDUSTRIAL AND LABOR RELATIONS

A Contract College of the State University

Cornell University, Ithaca, New York

Manufacturing
Production Functions
in the United States, 1957

An INTERINDUSTRY and INTERSTATE
COMPARISON of PRODUCTIVITY

BY

George H. Hildebrand
*Professor of Industrial and Labor
Relations and of Economics*

Ta-Chung Liu
Professor of Economics

New York State School of Industrial and Labor
Relations, Cornell University, Ithaca, New York

Preface

THIS monograph presents estimates of production functions and labor demand functions for fifteen two-digit industries in American maufacturing. The estimates rest upon cross-section analysis of census data for 1957. This was the latest year for which the necessary statistics were available at the time the work was under way.

Readers who are relatively unfamiliar with the field will find it useful to start with Chapter I, which provides both historical perspective about the underlying problem and a brief summary of our major findings. Chapter II contributes to the same end, for it presents a detailed review and evaluation of the contemporary literature of the field. In Chapter III, the theoretical formulation of the present inquiry is fully set forth. In Sections (1) and (2) of Chapter IV, the statistical problems of estimation are discussed. Sections (3) and (4) present in order our estimates for the separate industries and an analysis of our over-all findings. Section (5) reviews and considers the major criticisms that might be made of our approach, and Section (6) compares labor and capital productivities by states and census regions.

The initial plan for the study, devised in the winter of 1960–1961, included an original sample survey of the manufacturing establishments of the State of New York, in addition to the analysis of the 1957 census data. Unfortunately, the response rate for the New York sample was quite disappointing (see Appendix III), although it did throw some light on one of the hypotheses underlying our approach. However, we were able to carry through the census phase of the study as initially planned. The preliminary results obtained were presented at the Econometric Society meeting in Pittsburgh in December 1962.

Because of the keen and sympathetic interest taken by former Dean John W. McConnell, it was possible to launch the inquiry with support provided by the New York State School of Industrial and Labor Relations at Cornell University. The National Science Foundation then awarded us a generous grant, which we gratefully acknowledge.

Many people have made diverse and much needed contributions to the project. We have benefited much from the technical comments and suggestions of Mrs. Irma Adelman, Alfred H. Conrad, Victor R. Fuchs, Zvi Griliches, Howard H. Hines, Edwin S. Mills, Marc Nerlove, Robert W. Kilpatrick, Robert M. Solow, Bernt P. Stigum, Lawrence K. Williams, C. Brian Williams, and of the anonymous specialist who advised on publication. At various stages we have received invaluable assistance from Mo-Hung Che, Alfredo Daniels, Yu-Kange Mao, Mrs. Veronica A. Shaw, and Paul Ming Shiah. We have enjoyed the unstinting cooperation of the Cornell Computing Center in performing the computations. We are also deeply indebted to Mrs. Verma W. McClary for a most painstaking job of typing the manuscript, which she has undertaken with remarkable patience, competence, and equanimity.

G.H.H.
T.C.L.

Ithaca, New York
February 1965

Contents

I *Introduction*... 1

II *A Critical Review of Existing Research on Production Functions for Manufacturing*.. 19

    (1) Literature Prior to 1957............................ 20

    (2) Contributions Published after 1957................. 28

III *A Simultaneous Equation Model: Theoretical Considerations*......... 44

    (1) The Demand Elasticity for Output of "Industry".... 45

    (2) The Treatment of Technological Change............ 49

    (3) The Demand Function for Labor and the Speed of Adjustment................................. 53

    (4) The Complete Model Summarized................ 57

IV *Statistical Findings*....................................... 60

    (1) Decision among Alternative Specifications: The Conventional Practice and Statistical Decision Theory.. 60

    (2) Decision among Alternative Specifications: The Procedure Followed in This Study.................. 62

    (3) Production Functions and Demand Functions for Labor for Individual Industries................. 70

    (4) Industrial Production Functions: Summary and Analysis of Findings............................... 104

    (5) Criticisms of Our Approach...................... 130

    (6) Variations of Labor and Capital Productivities by States.. 138

Appendices

    I: Output-Labor, Capital-Labor, and Certain Other Important Data on Seventeen Manufacturing Industries in 1957.. 160

    II: Estimated Marginal Physical and Revenue Products of Labor and Capital by Industry and by State, 1957.. 187

    III: Results of a Sample Study of Manufacturing Production Functions in New York State.................... 202

    IV: Rejected Estimates for the Textile and the Furniture and Fixture Industries............................ 214

Bibliography.. 217

Index.. 223

Tables

1. Tests of the Empirical Basis of the "New Class of Production Function" Developed by Arrow, Chenery, Minhas, and Solow, Using U.S. Census of Manufacturers, 1957 36

2. Production Functions for 15 Two-Digit Manufacturing Industries, 1957 104

3. Technology-Output and Capital-Output Elasticities 107

4. Measurement of Returns to Scale under Constant Technology . . 109

5. Returns to Scale and Technology Effect 110

6. Input-Output Elasticities and Income Shares 111

7. Analysis of Change in Employment, 1956 to 1960 117

8. Change in Employment of Nonproduction Employees 120

9. Marginal Revenue Product of Capital, 1957 121

10. Deviations from the Optimum in the Allocation of Labor Resources, 1957 124

11. Marginal "Physical" Product of Capital, 1957 125

12. Elasticities of Output with Respect to Production and Nonproduction Employees in Ten Industries as a Whole 128

13. First Computation of Aggregate Input-Output Elasticities 130

14. Second Computation of Aggregate Input-Output Elasticities . . . 131

15. Comparative Efficiencies of Production Workers by State and Region 154

16. Comparative Efficiencies of Capital by State and Region 157

Appendix I: (tabulations of industry input and output data) 160

Appendix II: (Tables 1–6) 187

Manufacturing Production Functions
in the United States, 1957

An Interindustry and Interstate Comparison of Productivity

CHAPTER I

Introduction

THE central problem of this study concerns a theoretical formulation and statistical estimation of production functions in the industries composing the manufacturing sector of the American economy. Viewed in the strict sense of a precise mathematical relationship between output and its associated inputs, the concept of a production function is relatively new, dating from the emergence of the marginal productivity theory in the early nineties. However, every concept has a history, and in this case it is a lengthy one. To appreciate the purpose of this investigation and to give it the necessary perspective, it is therefore worthwhile to present a brief review of the development of the theory of production as one of the foundation stones of modern economics.[1]

The concept of production as such, and attempts to discover the forces governing production itself, have passed through three main stages of thought. The first one begins with the 18th century, which ushered in a long period of fragmentary and unsystematic speculation, reaching its terminus with the 1880's. The second opens with the nineties, in the explicit formulation of the marginal productivity analysis, considered both as a theory of factor service pricing and as a theory of the functional distribution of income among cooperating factors. The final stage begins with the late twenties, and is still in course. It was initiated in 1928 with the publication of the pioneering work of Charles W. Cobb

[1]For a fuller account of this history, see Edwin Cannan, *A History of the Theories of Production and Distribution in English Political Economy from 1776 to 1848,* 3rd ed. (London: P. S. King, 1924); Paul H. Douglas, *The Theory of Wages* (New York: Macmillan, 1934), Ch. I-II; Joseph A. Schumpeter, *History of Economic Analysis,* edited by Elizabeth Boody Schumpeter (New York: Oxford University Press, 1954), pp. 1026–1053; and George J. Stigler, *Production and Distribution Theories: The Formative Period* (New York: Macmillan, 1941), pp. 320–387.

and Paul H. Douglas [12]. With their first of a notable series of studies, which perhaps took some inspiration from collateral attempts to estimate statistical demand functions for commodities, the main thrust of investigation shifted away from the purely abstract side, toward efforts at empirical measurement of both production functions and derivative demand functions for the factors of production.

By the 18th century, the first stage, writers such as Turgot and Smith interested themselves in the forces supposedly determining the output both of the whole economy ("annual revenue of the nation") and of the single unit of enterprise. This was also the time when the trinitarian scheme of land-labor-capital came into being, linking up directly with the idea of diminishing returns, the principle of population, and the subsistence theory of wages. These speculations, however, were both discordant and incomplete. The very notion of diminishing returns turned implicitly upon the imperfect substitutability of productive factors one for another, while the principle of marginal imputation was embedded just beneath the surface of the classical theory of rent. But these nascent ideas were not to be followed up for years to come. In consequence, the theory of production remained separate from the theory of factor valuation, even with the advent of the marginal revolution in the seventies.

With the work of Walras, Wicksteed, Wicksell, Barone, and others in the nineties, these deficiencies were overcome on the purely abstract plane, by diverse formulations of the marginal productivity principle. It is of interest that most of these theorists worked on both the whole economy and the single establishment levels, as did their classical predecessors. Of equal importance, this was the time when the dispute over Euler's theorem broke out, which was essentially a controversy over assumptions, as Stigler has shown. Here the issues turned on whether, at either the aggregative or the firm level, constant returns to scale were a necessary condition if exhaustion of the product was to hold; whether constant returns were a realistic portrayal of production relationships; and whether strict proportionality in these relationships was compatible with perfectly competitive equilibrium.

The last point about this period concerns the peculiar treatment of technological change which then prevailed—one that nonetheless was quite consistent with the ruling premises of the static analysis then in course of formation. The convention introduced at the time was to grant such change as a historical fact, but to construct the production function itself in such a way that the level of technique was taken to be given and fixed. Much later this view was modified to incorporate such change within the function, but to assume at the same time that its impacts were neutral as among factor combinations, in the sense that the elasticity of substitution between capital and labor is taken to be unaffected by changes in technology. The role of technology in production has always been a vexing one for the theorist, because it poses the difficult problem of recognizing technical advances and somehow measuring in explicit fashion their separate effects upon production, as distinguished from those induced by purely quantitative shifts in factor inputs with technique unchanged.

The advent of the present stage in the theory of production was associated with the publication of the first Cobb-Douglas study in 1928. It is to these two men that we owe the inception of the now flourishing interest in inductive studies of the production function. Of particular importance for later inquiries, they based their early investigation upon time series collected for the manufacturing sector as a broad aggregate. More than this, by adopting Euler's theorem as supposedly the best form for estimating an aggregative production function, they introduced some ruling assumptions that have not ceased to exert their influence upon later work: that constant returns to scale and full competitive equilibrium prevail in the aggregate under study, and that technological change could be neglected as an explicit factor affecting the form of the function to be estimated. As his work progressed, Douglas experimented with cross-section studies, and also explored the statistical possibilities of relaxing the assumption that the exponents of the factor inputs must sum to unity. The tradition that he and Cobb introduced in their first work, however, has never been wholly abandoned in the ensuing years.[2]

[2]We present a detailed review of later work in Chapter II.

We ourselves are beneficiaries of that tradition, not only because it has inspired interest in the whole problem, but because of the challenge posed by the difficulties encountered in executing statistical estimates within the framework of these ruling assumptions. What, then, are the basic conceptions guiding the present inquiry?

First, the production function is one of a system of interdependent relationships governing the determination of output, employment, and many other variables. To estimate the production function for a given industry, a theoretical simultaneous equation model must be formulated, and the related functions estimated together with the production function.

Second, the production functions to be formulated and estimated should be free of a priori assumptions that the establishment or the industry is in equilibrium, that its competitive conditions are perfect for both the factor and the product markets, that constant returns to scale prevail, and that technological change is neutral in its impacts upon the ratios of labor to capital inputs.

Third, it should be possible to assign quantitative importance to technological change as a factor affecting the output of an establishment. To do so requires the use of indirect measures that can serve as surrogates or proxy variables most likely to reflect shifts in technology. In our view, three such measures will qualify: the ratio of the value of machinery and equipment to that of plant and structures; the ratio of net depreciated assets to gross assets; and the ratio of technical and professional employees to production workers.

Statistics for value added, employment, capital assets, number of establishments, and other relevant variables are available in the census survey data for 1957 on a state-by-state basis for each of the two-digit industries. For a given industry, the per establishment data of these variables for a given state may be considered as averages for the "representative establishment" in that state, thus permitting a production function to be estimated for the industry on the basis of these observations for the "representative establishments" of the different states. The aggregativeness of the two-digit industries and the undesirableness of using data on book

4

value of assets as a measure of capital are recognized; but closer scrutiny indicates that these weaknesses, especially the latter, are by no means as damaging as they might seem (see Chapter IV, Section (5)).

The main results obtained are the production functions and the demand functions for labor for 15 two-digit industries (Chapter IV, Section (3)); certain data on output-labor and output-capital ratios by industry and by state (Appendix I); estimated marginal physical and revenue products of labor and capital by industry and by state (Appendix II); and the results obtained from a sample for New York State (Appendix III).

Distinct features of this study are the simultaneous equation models formulated and estimated; the inclusion of production workers and nonproduction employees in the production functions as separate variables for ten of the 15 industries examined, the embodiment of technology in the exponent of the capital variables in the production functions; and an attempt to estimate separately the purely quantitative influence of a change of capital on output, the scale effects, and the role of technological change.

For a full account of the manner in which the simultaneous equations model was set up theoretically, and in which the alternative versions of the production functions were estimated and a choice made among the latter in each case, the reader may consult Chapter III and the first three sections of Chapter IV. We turn now to a brief resumé, in nontechnical terms, of the principal findings presented in Sections (4) and (6) of Chapter IV.

The first of these is that, considered by itself, technological change was of high importance to increases in output for most of the industries studied for 1957. The task here is to estimate separately the marginal productivity of a purely quantitative increase in capital stock with technique unchanged; and the marginal productivity of a qualitative change in capital concomitant with a change in its vintage (as a surrogate for technological change), with the gross value of assets held constant. We term the first measure the "capital-output elasticity" and the second the "technology-output elasticity." If, now, we take the ratio of the latter elasticity to the sum of both elasticities together, for

5

each industry, we have a measure of "technology-capital intensity." This indicates the comparative importance of technical change to the change in output arising from a given increase of capital stock in the industry.

As Table 3 in Chapter IV shows, the sum of capital-output and technology-output elasticities obtained range from 1.29 in food and kindred products to 0.20 in leather products, and they exceed 0.50 in 11 out of 15 cases. To illustrate, on our estimate a 1 per cent increase of capital stock in the food and kindred products industry—allowing for the effects both of a purely quantitative increase and of technical improvements—would have yielded a 1.29 per cent increase of output in 1957. Of this composite effect, technology contributed 59 per cent. Given the high values of the technology-capital intensity ratios for most of the industries, ranging from 50 to 72 per cent, the inference is clear: technological change was of great importance to increases in industry outputs.

Our next major finding is that the bulk, if not all, of these industries were experiencing increasing returns to scale in 1957. Strictly defined, increasing returns prevail when output increases in greater proportion to an equi-proportionate increase of all factor inputs together, with technique arbitrarily held constant. In this formulation, the scale effect can be obtained by finding the sum of the labor-output and capital-output elasticities, as estimated for each industry (Table 4, Chapter IV). Where the data permitted, the labor-output elasticity was computed separately for production and nonproduction workers, with both included in the over-all sum measuring the scale effect. Thus for food products in 1957 the output elasticity for production workers was 0.31, for nonproduction workers, 0.40, and for purely quantitative increase of capital (technique unchanged), 0.53. Hence the scale effect was 1.24.

For the 15 industries together, the range of the estimated scale effects extended from 1.24 for food products to 0.92 for leather products. This means that for food products, 1 per cent increases in production workers, nonproduction employees, and in quantity of capital (technique unchanged) would have yielded a 1.24 per cent increase in output in 1957. In only three cases out of 15 was the computed scale effect equal to unity or less. Moreover, these values represent the lower bound of the true scale effects, since the industry production functions do not include land and entrepreneurship as input variables. If the latter also could have been incorporated in the estimating equations and allowed to rise in proportion, the measured scale effects would have been still greater.

The next step in the scale problem is to include the effect of changing technology (Table 5, Chapter IV). This can be measured by taking the sum of the technology-output elasticity and the scale returns cited immediately above, that is, where the last presumes that technology is constant. The scale returns, including technological effects, are, of course, even greater than those without these effects. They range from 2.0 for food products to 1.05 for leather products, and they are greater than 1.4 in 11 of the 15 industries.

The percentage contribution of technical improvements to the over-all increase in output when capital and labor inputs are increased in the same proportions, when their scale effect is included, and when technique itself is now allowed to change, is then computed. For the 15 industries, the share of the increased output attributable to technology alone ranged from 38.0 per cent in food products to 12.4 per cent for leather products. Taking food products as an example, a 1 per cent increase in both capital and labor inputs, with technology also changing, would have yielded a 2 per cent increase in output in 1957, and technology alone would have accounted for 38.0 per cent of this 2 per cent rise in product on our estimates.

Again it should be manifest that improvements in technique were of large importance, contributing over one-fourth of the over-all increase in output in ten out of 15 cases. The ranking of the industries under this measure conforms well to that cited earlier, where the relative contribution of technology-output elasticity was measured against a purely quantitative increase in capital alone (Table 3, Chapter IV). Note also that the generally high relative importance of technological change in the combined measures of the technological and scale effects together requires neither the assumption that the industry was in equilibrium nor that it operated under constant returns to scale. Rather, the ruling presupposition here is that technical improvements find embodiment in accretions to capital that differ qualitatively from the stock to which they are added. On the same ground, improvements will be much less significant without such qualitative changes in capital.

The next inference of importance yielded by this study is that use of factor income shares to measure the respective labor-output and capital-output elasticities, a practice quite prevalent in the literature, is very likely to underestimate seriously the true values of the latter. This can be tested (Table 6, Chapter IV) by computing the relative share of the factor in value added by the industry in 1957, and taking these values in ratio to the factor-output elasticities as found by our method of determination. If the resulting percentages so obtained fall below 100 per cent, this indicates that the income-share method underestimates the true elasticities.

We have made this test for the ten industries in which production and nonproduction labor could be separated, and for five where they could not be. For capital, whose returns were measured as the residual after deduction of labor compensation, business property tax, and depreciation from value added, the test could be applied for all 15 industries. For production workers alone, underestimation is evident in eight out of ten cases. For nonproduction workers, it prevails in all ten, and much more markedly. For the five industries in which all labor is taken together, underestimation exists throughout. Finally, the output elasticity for capital as measured by its relative income share falls below 100 per cent in 12 out of 15 cases, in some by very large amounts. Evidently, then, the income-shares approach has serious weaknesses as a measure of factor-output elasticities.

This brings us to one of the most important findings of the whole study: relative to the private profit-maximizing positions of these industries in 1957, ten of them were employing too many production workers, while the other five were employing too much total labor, and by implication too many production workers as well. In consequence, if our estimated production functions are valid for these industries, all of them should have been reducing employment to reach their best attainable profit levels from the use of labor, where the marginal revenue product per dollar of labor compensation would then equal unity in all cases. This finding is indeed a disturbing one, but it clearly reflects one of the gravest problems of our time: automation of production processes at the expense of production workers.

In obtaining the estimated adjustments in employment required for profit-maximization, the first step was to determine the marginal revenue productivity of labor in each industry in 1957, using marginal physical productivity found from its production function and plausible demand elasticity for its product. The next step was to calculate the change in industry employment required to maximize profits, discussed in detail in Section (3) of Chapter IV and shown in column (1) of Table 7 in Chapter IV. Note that these estimated adjustments required are all high, and all negative, ranging from ⁻64.0 per cent in transportation equipment (production workers) to ⁻9.7 per cent in rubber (total employees).

Obviously it would take some time for the industry to make its indicated reduction in employment even if management were fully aware of the profitability of such action. Estimates of the coefficients of the speed of adjustment in employment during 1956–1957 are derived from the demand functions for labor presented in Section (3) of Chapter IV for the different industries. They are all exceedingly small. Multiplying the required adjustments for profit maximization by the coefficient of the speed of adjustment, we obtain for each industry in Section (3) of Chapter IV the reduction in employment that would take place in a single year. For most industries, these estimated single-year adjustments, all of rather small magnitudes, are fairly consistent with the actual changes in employment from 1956 to 1957.

Since single-year changes may be erratic, a longer term comparison of the estimated required adjustments for profit maximization and the actual changes over 1956–1960 is also attempted in Table 7 in Chapter IV.[3] In column (4) of Table 7, the industries are ranked by the estimated magnitudes of the changes in employment required for profit-maximization during 1956–1960. The array in column (9) gives the actual changes in employment, corrected for changes in output, during the same period. If the figures in column (4) are to be taken as indicating the comparative pressure upon the 15 industries to adjust employment to the profit-maximizing position, then a significant rank correlation should prevail between this array and that for corrected actual changes (column (9)). The coefficient obtained is 0.66. If in fact the two arrays were wholly independent, there is less than a 1 per cent chance of reaching this high a correlation. This strengthens considerably the validity of our estimated employment changes required to overcome deviations from the profit-maximizing position. It suggests also that the underlying industry production

[3]The many conceptional and statistical difficulties in making the longer term comparison will not be repeated in this summary. The essence of the procedure, presented in Table 7, can be shown by taking the food products industry as an example. To maximize its 1957 profits from the use of production workers, it should have reduced employment of this group of employees by 23.2 per cent (column (1) of Table 7). The coefficient of the speed of adjustment from 1956 to 1957, as estimated from the demand function for production labor is 0.16 (see Chapter IV, p. 73). On the assumption that the speed of adjustment over the 4-year span 1956–1960 is equal to 4 times 0.16, or 0.64 (column (2) of Table 7), this industry should, by 1960, have accomplished 64 per cent of the 23.2 per cent adjustment required, or 14.8 percentage points (column (3)). The magnitude of this adjustment puts this industry in the seventh rank (column (4)) for estimated required adjustments. In fact, it reduced employment by 7.3 per cent during 1956–1960 (column (5)). Output, however, increased by 9 per cent in the meantime (column (6)). This influence must be removed to isolate the pure profit-maximizing adjustment in employment as based upon the 1957 equilibrium conditions. We do so by dividing the total change in output for 1960/1956 (+ 9 per cent) by our estimated labor-output elasticity (0.31, presented earlier in Table 6), and regarding the quotient (+ 29 per cent, column (7) of Table 7) as the change in employment associated with the change in output. The corrected profit-maximizing change in employment, −36.3 per cent (column (8)), is obtained by subtracting algebraically the 29 per cent accompanying the output change from the actual decline of 7.3 per cent. This corrected change may be regarded as the upper bound of the industry's adjustment in production workers for profit maximization. For non-production workers and capital, both increased, and part of the increase in output was attributable to these factors. Hence, if we compare the actual changes in employment corrected for output changes (column (8)) with our estimates of the extent to which required changes would have been accomplished by 1960 (column (3)), the actual exceed the required in 11 out of the 15 industries, in spite of the fact that the wage-price ratio increased in most industries. The figures in column (8) are then ranked in column (9).

functions capture fairly well the input-output relations actually prevailing in 1957.

Accordingly, the array of estimated industry employment changes can serve as a good index (column (4) in Table 7) of the comparative pace of automation and mechanization in these same industries. Among these, the leaders would stand in the following order: transportation equipment, instruments, apparel, fabricated metal products, lumber products, petroleum and coal products, and food products. These, then, are the industries whose employment opportunities appear most vulnerable to technological change, granting that all 15 faced significant contractions in employment on the basis of 1957 conditions, assuming also that money wages could not fall thereafter relative to product prices. In fact, money wages rose further in relation to product prices in most industries, exacerbating the actual declines in employment. Also significant, in most cases it would have taken very large increases in the demand for the products of these industries to have offset through larger outputs the labor-displacing effects of their efforts after 1956 to economize on the use of labor in pursuit of maximum profits.

Where the data permitted and where plausible figures could be had, we have also compared estimated with actual changes of employment of nonproduction employees (Table 8, Chapter IV). In all six cases, employment of this group should have been increased to maximize 1957 profits from this source. For 1956–1957, all of these industries did expand this kind of employment, and the two arrays for this group yield a rank correlation coefficient of 0.91, significant at 5 per cent.

There remains the question, to what extent was capital invested in the 15 industries at profit-maximizing levels for 1957? Lacking demand functions for capital, we cannot estimate its adjustment speed by industry, or compare estimated with actual changes. But we have calculated the marginal revenue products of capital MRP_K (before business income tax) per dollar of investment by industry, which indicates the comparative profitability of investment. These results, shown in Table 9, Chapter IV, reveal large diversities in marginal rates of return. This is not surprising. Most investments involve long term commitments. Risks of obsolescence as well as differences in cyclical sensitivity lead to varying adjustment speeds. In consequence, any tendency toward equalization in rates of return would be quite slow and never complete. In our findings, the estimated marginal rates of return on investment by industry vary from $2.44 (before income tax) per dollar invested in transportation equipment to only $0.14 in stone, clay, and glass.

The next step in our inquiry was to measure the deviations of employment in these industries relative to the optimal amounts indicated under conditions of 1957. Here the standard is not that of maximum profits from the input of labor, because none of the industries was operating under conditions of perfect competition in either its product or factor markets. Rather, we are concerned now with the so-called Pareto optimum, that is, with the degree of employment required to yield, in some sense, maximum income and real product, hence welfare, to the economy as a whole.

For such purpose, the appropriate standard is the marginal physical productivity of factor input times the price of the industry's product, per dollar of input compensation. At the optimum, this ratio should be equal to unity. Given negatively sloping product demand curves, standing at unity this ratio will call for larger quantities of factor input than will the profit-maximizing standard, which involves marginal revenue productivity instead. For the same reason, attainment of the Pareto level of input would not maximize profits, although it will effect maximum economic returns from the use of labor or capital in the industry. Obviously, there is a host of profound implications in the adoption of such a standard in actual practice, and we do not wish to be interpreted either as recommending or rejecting its use as a policy. Our sole interest here is in testing the extent to which the manufacturing sector of production was operating at maximum economic efficiency in 1957 in the sense of Pareto optimality.

Not unexpectedly, our estimates under the Pareto standard yield results almost completely at variance with those obtained from the profit-maximizing test. Table 10 in Chapter IV shows these results. In all industries but one (transportation equipment), employment in 1957 was below optimum, meaning that it should have been larger under conditions then existing. In short, the actual ratios for marginal "physical" productivity (strictly, those for "value of marginal product") per dollar of labor compensation almost all exceeded 1.00, for all types of labor. In other words, labor under this standard was underemployed, in many cases substantially so. For production workers only, this holds in eight out of ten industries. For nonproduction employees, it is true for all ten, while it is also true for all of the five in which total labor had to be measured. In interpreting the data, it should be borne in mind that the indicated deviations are not predictions of adjustments in employment to come after 1957. Rather, they reflect the changes called for in 1957 if the Pareto standard had been adopted in practice.

The greatest underemployment of production labor (Table 10) was in stone, clay, and glass; paper products; chemicals; and fabricated metal products. For nonproduction employees, the shortfall was largest in apparel, petroleum and coal products, chemicals, and stone, clay, and glass.

We applied the same standard of optimality to capital in these industries, shown in Table 11 (p. 125). As under the profit-maximizing test, and for the same reasons, the variations among the industries were extremely large. On the Pareto standard, new capital investment under 1957 conditions would have contributed its largest returns to the whole economy if concentrated in two groups—capital equipment (transportation equipment, instruments, electric machinery, and other machinery) and consumers' goods (food products, leather products, rubber, and apparel).

So far, this summary has been confined to findings concerning the 15 industries taken separately and comparatively. Nothing has been said about them collectively, considered as an aggregate. This emphasis upon disaggregated results is deliberate. Any realistic view of a decentralized private enterprise economy, where coordination is achieved through prices, must center upon establishment-by-establishment and industry-by-industry comparisons. These are the levels at which resource flows and input-output relationships take place and are determined. Calculations of these processes at grosser levels of magnitude both sacrifice operational significance and foreclose examination of the extent to which the allocative results of private decisions conform to the criteria for optimum economic efficiency.

Nonetheless, aggregate relationships attract a certain interest of their own, if only because the preponderant tradition in studies of production functions has been to concentrate upon sector and whole economy levels.

Accordingly, we have posed once again the same set of questions for all 15 industries together. To illustrate: what would have been the percentage increase in output in the manufacturing sector in 1957, measured by value added, if all factor inputs had been increased by 1 per cent each? Plainly, the answer rests upon estimations of the factor-output elasticities, the scale effect, and the independent contribution of technological change for the whole manufacturing sector, essentially on the same conceptual basis as for each separate industry. However, having obtained production functions for the separate industries, we should obtain the estimates in the sector case by finding weighted averages, rather than directly by multiple regression.

One of the appropriate procedures for such purpose calls for weighting the respective industry output elasticities by the proportions of total value added contributed by each industry. For the ten cases in which production and nonproduction workers could be treated separately, the respective weighted labor-output elasticities for the whole group are 0.43 and 0.34 for 1957 (Table 12, Chapter IV). Total value added in that year was $102.2 billion, while the wage bill for production workers was $34.4 billion. For nonproduction workers, the salary bill was $16.8 billion.

Presuming that wage and salary rates were fixed and that prices did not change, a 1 per cent ($340 million) increase in employment of production workers in 1957 would have yielded a $440 million increase in value added ($102.2 billion × 0.43). A matching proportionate increase for nonproduction labor would have cost $168 million, and would have enlarged total output by $348 million ($102.2 billion × 0.34). Obviously, nonproduction labor was a "better buy" at the time, in the sense that the increment to value added per dollar of added salary outlay was $2.07, while for production workers it was $1.29, although increased employment of both types of labor would have been profitable under the assumption of constant wages and prices. Bear in mind also that these relationships presuppose no change in production technique.

To extend the analysis to all 15 industries, the total labor-output elasticities for the remaining five were used, and the first ten were put on the same footing by summing the separate elasticities for the two types of labor. Each industry's labor-output elasticity was then weighted by the industry's share in value added, and the sum of these weighted values obtained as a measure of the over-all sector elasticity (Table 12). The same weights were then applied to the separate capital-output (technology fixed) and technology-output elasticities, which, upon summation, provided sector estimates for these variables (Table 13). The results are as follows: 0.80 (total labor), 0.29 (capital in the purely quantitative sense), and 0.45 (technological change).

It turns out that increasing returns to scale held for the whole sector, measured by the sum of the total labor and capital quantity elasticities. Thus a 1 per cent increase in these inputs in 1957 would have yielded a 1.09 per cent increase in product. If technique also were allowed to change, the increase would have risen to 1.54 per cent, of which technical improvements alone (technology intensity as earlier defined) would have accounted for 29 per cent. Moreover, of the composite effect of a purely quantitative 1 per cent increase in capital together with improved technology (technology-capital intensity), 60 per cent would have been imputable to technical advances alone. Clearly, technical improvements dominated capital investment, and exerted considerable leverage upon potential increases in output deriving from increased inputs of all factors together. At the same time, pure scale effects were of some significance.

Turning, now, from sector-wide results back to the separate industry production functions, it must be emphasized that the latter conceal some potentially interesting details. The reason is that these functions actually are industry averages, found by application of the technique of multiple regression to the state-by-state observations for "representative establishments" for all states

15

in which the industry was significant in 1957. It will be recalled that on the Pareto optimum test the industry-wide functions indicated that both types of labor were generally underemployed, while on the profit-maximizing criterion production labor was generally overemployed in 1957.

Two questions are automatically posed. First, for each industry, how well do the general findings yielded by the two tests stand up on a state-by-state basis? Second, what were the comparative efficiencies of each type of labor and of capital by industry and state? In both instances, the task is to descend to the state and regional levels.

Complete matrices of marginal physical and revenue products of labor and capital by state and by industry are presented in Appendix II. In section (6) of Chapter IV, the reader will find a series of six summary tabulations: two for production workers, two for nonproduction labor, and two for total labor. Each is designed to bring out, for each industry, those states and regions in which either the marginal physical or marginal revenue productivity per dollar of compensation diverged significantly from the industry-wide ratios. In other words, these tabulations will reveal the exceptional cases.

The first tabulation (pp. 140–141) shows the deviant states for production workers in ten industries, on the Pareto criterion. Recalling that the industry-wide ratios were all above unity (except transportation equipment, which had a ratio below unity), this breakdown shows that out of 234 observations there were 11 cases with ratios well below 1.00, and 49 close to 1.00. On the profits-maximizing test for production workers, which appears in the second tabulation (pp. 143–145), the industry-wide figures for the ten industries indicated general and substantial overemployment in 1957. On a state-by-state basis, 18 cases out of 260 involved ratios of well over unity, and 77 were very close to 1.00.

The third tabulation (p. 146) deals with nonproduction labor in the same ten industries, on the Pareto criterion. Recall that the industry-wide averages were all well over 1.00 for this type of labor. Here there were but four cases out of 260 where the state ratios were well below 1.00, and only 11 that were close to unity.

The fourth tabulation (pp. 148–149) considers this type of labor on the profits-maximizing test. Here the industry-wide functions all yielded values above 1.00—indicating underemployment of this type of labor. When these marginal revenue products per dollar of compensation are put on a state basis for each industry, there were 25 out of 260 observations in which substantial overemployment was indicated, and 45 in which employment was close to the optimal amounts.

The two remaining tabulations refer to the five industries whose production functions were estimated for total labor. In the first one (p. 150), which applies the Pareto criterion, the over-all functions yielded ratios above 1.00 in four industries, and approximately at 1.00 in the fifth. The tabulation generally confirms these results. Out of 85 observations, there were no instances of ratios well below unity, and only 12 where they were close to 1.00. Of the latter, seven were in the instruments industry, whose over-all function yielded similar results.

On the profits-maximizing criterion, the industry-wide functions indicated that overemployment prevailed in 1957 in all five industries. When segregated and tabulated on a state-by-state basis (p. 151), it turns out that of the 85 observations, nine involved ratios well over 1.00, and 23 involved ratios which were close to 1.00.

This brings us to our second main question: the comparative efficiencies of labor and of capital by states. Table 15 in Chapter IV presents a tabulation of the results for production labor only, for the ten industries where it can be separated, while Table 16 does the same for capital, for all 15 industries. In both tables, the basic procedure was to array the marginal physical products of the productive factor by states for each industry, and to split this array into upper, middle, and lower thirds. As grouped, each such observation is then classed by state and region. For each productive factor, then, in each industry it becomes possible to discover patterns of concentration by states and regions, both by industry and for all industries together.

These geographic distributions of levels of marginal physical productivity for both production labor and capital afford many interesting insights. Only four will be mentioned here, however.

In the regions of early industrialization—New England, the Middle Atlantic, and the East-North Central—one half of the marginal physical productivity figures of production labor for the industries present fall in the middle third, 34 per cent in the lower, and only 17 per cent in the upper. By contrast, for the marginal physical productivities of capital in these regions, 36 per cent of the cases fall in the upper third, and only 28 per cent in the lower.

On the contrary, in the more recently industrialized regions— the South Atlantic, West North Central, Mountain, and Pacific— 45 per cent of the productivity values for production labor are in the upper third, and 29 per cent in the lower. For capital productivities in these regions, only 30 per cent were in the upper third, and 43 per cent were in the lower.

We thus reach the tentative conclusion that production workers were relatively more productive, in the sense of returns per dollar of wage cost, in the newer regions as compared with the older ones, while capital was more efficient in the latter.

The results of our New York sample study are given in Appendix III. The estimated functions appear to be reasonably satisfactory for nine industries. This limited evidence indicates that the ratio of the value of equipment to that of structure would have been a satisfactory proxy variable for the level of technology if a larger number of observations had been available.

This completes a summary review of our findings. In the next chapter we present a review of existing research on production functions.

CHAPTER II

A Critical Review of Existing Research on Production Functions for Manufacturing

SINCE the publication of the pathbreaking work by Cobb and Douglas [12] in 1928, many important attempts have been made to estimate production functions for manufacturing industries in the United States.[1] The present study grows out of a survey of the difficulties besetting these inquiries, and represents an effort to overcome them. No attempt is made here to summarize the results of these investigations nor, with a few exceptions, to describe in detail their methods or approaches.[2]

The purpose of this chapter is to focus on the difficulties encountered by these earlier inquiries. For convenience, we review first those appearing before 1957, following with those published after that date.

[1] Studies of manufacturing production functions of other countries follow the same pattern and will not be cited here.

A substantial volume of literature exists on agricultural production functions. An excellent analysis of this literature has been made by Heady and Dillon [33] who have contributed a large number of original studies themselves. Agricultural economists have the enviable advantage of being able to conduct controlled experiments that would be practically impossible to carry out for manufacturing. Sample studies are also easier to make in agriculture than in manufacturing. The regulated utilities and railroads also have certain institutional features that are conducive to a study of their production and cost functions. For instance, see Klein [43], pp. 226–236, and pp. 265–268, and Nerlove [58]. Studies of agriculture and the regulated industries will not be reviewed here.

[2] A general knowledge of the studies reviewed is therefore assumed on the part of the reader. An excellent survey of the literature by Walters [78] appeared after this part of our study had been completed in the winter of 1961.

(1) *Literature prior to 1957*

Estimates of production functions for manufacturing industries in the United States prior to 1957 are mainly of the following three types:

(a) For manufacturing as a whole fitted to time series data on value added, labor, and capital. The pioneering attempt by Cobb and Douglas [12] belongs to this category, as do the contributions by Edelberg [19] and Wall [77]. Closely related to this group are production functions for the economy as a whole; for instance, those worked out by Klein and Goldberger [45] and Valavanis-Vail [75].

(b) For manufacturing as a whole fitted to cross-section data for the individual industries for the same year. Thus, statistics on value added, labor, and capital for the textile industry constitute one point in a three-dimensional space; those for the iron and steel industry form another point; and so on. A regression plane is then fitted to these points. Douglas and his co-workers have done a large number of studies along this line. (See, for instance, [17] and [29].)

(c) For manufacturing as a whole (and also for a few separate but still highly aggregated industries in manufacturing) fitted to data across the states for the same year. We have been able to find only one study of American manufacturing along this line. It is contributed by Bronfenbrenner and Douglas [4]. Functions fitted to international data for the same year also belong to this category.

All three types have as the primary basis of their statistical estimates the following function:[3]

$$V = aL^bK^c10^{dT}e, \tag{2.1}$$

or $\log V = \log a + b \log L + c \log K + dT + \log e,$ (2.2)

where V, L, K, T, and e represent output, labor, capital, time, and a random disturbance term respectively, and a, b, c, and d are parameters.

---

[3]There are of course many variations from this basic form. Most of the studies are without the time variable, T. Klein and Goldberger [45] use a linear function, instead of a constant elasticity function.

Regarding these studies, the following observations may be made:[4]

(*i*) The time series data on output, labor, and capital all vary with time, and the estimated functions probably provide summary statements of the relationships between historical rates of change in the three variables. That is, they are not the kind of production functions from which the theorist derives marginal productivities of factors of production. Moreover, statistics for labor and capital tend to move closely and to cluster together over time. Thus they do not provide sufficient scatter for estimating the production surface.

The first part of the criticism is valid. The second part is more relevant for type (a) investigations than for the cross-section ones. To illustrate, sufficient scatter apparently exists in most of the industries examined in the present study, which uses cross-section data.

(*ii*) The basic statistics used to estimate manufacturing production functions—essentially, published census data for industrial totals at various levels of aggregation—are inappropriate for this purpose.

The reason is that the production function, as it is understood in economic theory, is, or should be, basically a microeconomic concept having to do with the alternatives open to the individual decision unit (an establishment or a firm) for the allocation of production resources. This is the familiar problem of aggregation found in practically all econometric problems of estimation. In an important early paper, Klein [44] has considered the proper way in which the individual observations should be aggregated so that the production function will satisfy the following criteria:

[handwritten margin notes: (1) Time series all trend together; (2) Cross section; Klein + micro data xys]

(a) If production functions exist for the individual units, a proper functional relationship should exist between the aggregate input and output data.[5] (b) If the familiar profit-maximizing condition (i.e., under perfect competition, values of marginal physical products are equal to the respective factor prices) is fulfilled by the microunits, the same should hold with regard to the marginal products obtained from the functional relationship between the aggregate input and output data. In this connection, Klein has shown that if the production functions for the microunits are of the Cobb-Douglas type, and if the two criteria given above are to be satisfied, the aggregate input and output variables should be represented by the geometric means of the respective micro-variables. For the case where the input-output elasticities are the same for all microunits[6] and where perfect competition prevails, the input-output elasticities are simply estimated from the respective factor shares. While Klein has not explicitly formulated the procedures for estimating the input-output elasticities directly from the aggregate variables, instead of from factor shares, the implication of his analysis appears to be that geometric means of the micro input and output variables should be used.

Nataf [54] has dealt with the problem in a different way, but has reached the same conclusion for the Cobb-Douglas functions. Suppose that for each microunit i, we have the production function:

$$V_i = f_i \ (L_i, \ K_i), \qquad i = 1, \ \ldots, \ N.$$

Suppose, further, we want to construct aggregates:

$$V = V \ (V_1, \ V_2, \ \ldots, \ V_N),$$

$$L = L \ (L_1, \ L_2, \ \ldots, \ L_N),$$

$$K = K \ (K_1, \ K_2, \ \ldots, \ K_N),$$

[5]Klein has demonstrated, for instance, that it is not evident that an acceptable aggregate production function exists if the aggregates are constructed as Divisia indexes. See [44].

[6]When a production function is estimated from a set of data for individual units, or some aggregates of them, we in fact assume that the elasticities are the same for all units. This of course is the reason why one strives to get data from producing units as homogeneous as possible with one another. When the individual elasticities are in fact quite different, Theil [71] has suggested a method of analyzing the biases involved in the aggregate elasticities estimated from aggregate data which are the conventional arithmetic averages. For the method Klein suggested for

such that an exact relation of the following type exists:

$$V = f (L, K).$$

For this to be achieved, Nataf has shown that the function must be of a type that is additively separable. When put in the logarithmic form, the Cobb-Douglas production functions are of this type. Thus,

$$\log V = a \log L + b \log K,$$

where $\log V = \sum_i \log V_i,$

$$\log L = \sum_i \log L_i,$$

$$\log K = \sum_i \log K_i,$$

and $\log V_i = a \log L_i + b \log K_i.$

Thus, the aggregate variables are the geometric averages of the microvariables.

Because the census data are available only in arithmetic sums and averages and have been used in making all three types of Cobb-Douglas estimates, the Klein-Nataf condition of aggregation is not met. It is therefore not clear what correspondence exists between the aggregate functions and the underlying micro-functions, and what is the meaning of the marginal product estimates obtained from them. There does not appear to be a fundamental solution to the problem, unless one can avoid using arithmetic aggregates and substitute individual observations to construct geometric averages. Hopefully, the relationships derived from arithmetic means may not differ significantly from those derived from geometric averages.

If establishment data are lacking, the closest approximation to the required microdata perhaps can be obtained by following the type (c) approach described above; that is, by using census figures for a given industry across the states. The result would presumably be better if the industries are as narrowly defined as possible. The reason for preferring this approach is that statistics for the *average* value added, labor and capital per establishment

deriving aggregate elasticities from different component elasticities, see Chapter IV, Section (4) (vi).

in a given state, then may be taken as a rough indication of the "representative establishment" in that state, and that the observations for such representative establishments in the different states for the same industry furnish a reasonable basis for estimating the production surface for firms in that industry. Since the type (c) approach appears to be the most promising of the three, it is surprising that we have been able to find only one attempt (Bronfenbrenner and Douglas [4]) along this line for manufacturing industries in the United States. Even in this important paper, the advantages of this approach are not fully exploited. First, data for value added, labor, and capital in each state apparently have not been divided by the number of establishments to reveal the influence of the different average sizes of the establishments in different states.[7] Second, instead of fitting the functions for as narrowly defined industries as the data in the 1909 census permit, Bronfenbrenner and Douglas have aggregated the data to obtain estimates for what they have called the "most capitalist," "least capitalist," "monopolistic," and "sweated" industries. Separate functions have been obtained for only three individual industries—in their nomenclature, clothing and textiles, foods and beverages, and metals and machinery—but these are still unnecessarily aggregative.

(iii) The economic meaning of a production function for manufacturing as a whole derived from cross-section data pertaining to industry-to-industry aggregates or averages is obscure.

This criticism, applicable only to type (b) studies, is valid, because it is extremely doubtful whether one can make much sense of a production surface composed of points, each representing a different industry.[8] To be meaningful at all, at the very least the following conditions must be met: (1) labor and capital must be fairly homogeneous across the industries. In fact, factor inputs are not homogeneous even among firms within a given industry.

[7]Marschak and Andrews [48] have corrected the Bronfenbrenner-Douglas estimates for this factor. In addition, they have also weighted the moments by the percentages of establishments in each state; but this refinement does not result in estimates significantly different from those obtained with unweighted moments.

[8]This type of functions is quite different from transformation functions between different outputs produced on common production factors, the latter being homogeneous within each category.

But this condition is more nearly met in type (c) (and even type (a)) studies than in those of (b). (2) For type (b) functions to have either predictive or normative values, it is necessary that, as value added increases from one level to another, the production surface must go through successive industries in the same order and roughly at the same points *in the future* as it did during the sample year. This condition cannot be expected to be met.[9]

In fact, this criticism is also applicable to type (a) studies if the nature of the industry has changed significantly through time, and also to those of type (c) if the cross-section data do not come from a sufficiently homogeneous industry. More precisely, the input-output elasticities of the different years (type (a)) or of the different locations (type (c)) may not really be the same, even if the inputs were sufficiently alike. Theil, [71] and [73], has made an interesting analysis of the relationships between the macro-parameters estimated by regression methods from the aggregate variables conventionally available (i.e., arithmetic sums or averages) and the underlying microparameters. He has shown that the expectations of the least-squares estimates of the macroparameters would involve an "aggregation bias," defined as the difference between this expected value and the arithmetic mean of the underlying microparameters. However, the magnitudes of these biases usually cannot be estimated, because the underlying microparameters are unknown. Even if they can be estimated, it would still be difficult to interpret the meaning of the arithmetic average of the microparameters in economic applications. Theil [71] has also investigated the requirements of "perfect aggregation," meaning the absence of any contradiction between any statement derived from the micro relationships and a corresponding statement for the macro relationships. For the Cobb-Douglas type of production functions, the weights used in the "perfect aggregation" are the same as the Nataf weights for combining different component elasticities.[10]

[9]Bronfenbrenner [3] has defended the usefulness of type (b) studies; and while not defending them, Phelps Brown [59] and Marschak and Andrews [48] have attempted to attribute some economic meaning to them. However, condition (2) has not been mentioned in their contributions.

[10]See Chapter IV, Section (4) (vi).

(iv) The "enterpreneurship" and/or "top management" factor cannot be quantified and included in the function. Hence the estimated coefficients of labor and capital would be biased in some unknown way because of this omission.[11] Moreover, many other variables, such as changing general moral, social, and economic conditions, are also unquantifiable. Their omission would all result in biases in the coefficients of the included variables.

This criticism is valid for all classes of studies, and there does not appear to be any fundamental solution to the problem. If, however, the omitted variables were correlated with the included variables in the future in roughly the same way as in the sample period, the application of the estimated functions may not result in major errors.[12]

(v) Whatever its level of aggregation, the production function is only one of a system of interrelated economic relationships. Estimates of production functions by the single-equation least-squares method are subject to the well-known "simultaneous equation bias."

The nature of this objection is similar to the more familiar criticism of the empirical demand and supply equations estimated

[11]Theil [72] and Griliches [27] have studied the effects of omitted variables. Let us assume that the only explanatory variables included in the production function (2.2) are log L and log K. Let M stand for the omitted factor "entrepreneurship" and/or "management" (or for that matter, any omitted variable). Let r_{VL} be the correlation coefficient between log V and log L, with r_{VK}, r_{KL}, r_{ML}, and r_{MK} similarly interpreted. Denote the standard deviations of the variables M, L, and K as S_M, S_L, and S_K. Let b and c be the least-squares estimates of b and c in equation (2.2) respectively. It can be shown that:

$$b - \hat{b} = -\frac{(r_{ML} - r_{MK}r_{KL})S_M}{(1 - r^2_{KL})S_L}$$

$$c - \hat{c} = -\frac{(r_{MK} - r_{ML}r_{KL})S_M}{(1 - r^2_{KL})S_K}.$$

The omission of log M from the equation (2.2) would result in an upward bias in $\hat{b}$ if $r_{ML} > r_{MK}r_{KL}$, and vice versa. (It may be assumed that b, $\hat{b}$, c and $\hat{c}$ are all positive magnitudes.) An upward bias in $\hat{c}$ would result if $r_{MK} > r_{ML}r_{KL}$, and vice versa. It is possible for both b and c to have upward bias (e.g., when $r_{MK} = r_{ML}$), but is is impossible for them both to have downward bias.

[12]For instance, if $r_{MK} > r_{ML}r_{KL}$ in the future as well as in the past (see n. 11, above), it is true that $\hat{c}$ would remain larger than c. But it also means that if capital increases in the future (while other factors, except M, remain constant), M would also increase so that c would represent the combined effect of both increased K and M.

by the single-equation method. In that case, one is not sure whether the result obtained is a demand equation, a supply equation, or a "mongrel." In the present case, the estimated equation (2.2) may be a production function, a demand function for labor, a demand function for capital, or a "mongrel."[13] This criticism was first put forth in an important paper by Marschak and Andrews [48].

However, the single-equation least-squares estimates are not necessarily inferior to the simultaneous-equation estimates because the relative "sharpness" of the former sometimes more than compensates for their bias. Thus, Theil [72] has found in a number of instances that the bias of the single-equation estimate (in absolute value) plus twice its standard error is smaller than twice the standard error of the corresponding two-stage least-squares estimate. Accordingly, all estimates must be judged on their relative merits in each individual case.

(vi) The treatment of the effects of differences in technology and efficiency is inadequate. Intimately related to this problem is the lack of homogeneity in the labor and capital variables used, whether these are time series or cross section data.

The earlier studies of all three types make no explicit provision for technological change or for the heterogeneity of labor and capital. In the more recent type (a) studies (see, for instance, Wall [77], and Klein and Goldberger [45]), a smooth and neutral technological progress is usually postulated; but this assumption cannot be convincingly rationalized and has not been substantiated. In the simultaneous model worked out by Marschak and Andrews [48], differences in technology and efficiency in effect are treated as random disturbances. Preferably, the influence of technology and efficiency should be brought systematically into the production function without adopting the rigid assumptions of neutral technological improvement and of smooth progress

---

[13] A closely related criticism, advanced by writers before the development of simultaneous-equation estimation, has to do with errors of observation. The question is raised whether, in fitting the least-squares equation, one should minimize the squared errors in the value-added direction or in the direction of labor or capital. Douglas and his co-workers (e.g., [4] and [30]) have advanced a number of reasons why the minimization should be done in the value-added direction. The arguments given are not really completely convincing. Even if they were, they still would not constitute an adequate reply to the allegation of simultaneous-equation bias.

through time. The manner in which these difficult problems are dealt with in the more recent literature will be discussed in Section (2) below.

(vii) The basic measures of capital yield highly misleading indications of the amount actually in use as an input during a given period of time.

This criticism is valid mainly for two reasons. First, data for capital assets are mostly book values, representing historical cumulations of purchases of assets at original costs. Second, capital assets available at a given time are not necessarily the same as the amount of capital actually in use as an input. These difficulties will be discussed again in connection with our own estimates.[14]

(viii) Output and capital are represented in the existing functions respectively by value added and by value of plant and equipment, both in dollar values rather than physical terms. Only L is represented in physical units, by manhours. Under certain conditions, the exponents of L and K in these equations are not measures of output-input elasticities, but rather are these elasticities adjusted by the demand elasticity for output and supply elasticities for inputs.

Marschak and Andrews [48] first pointed this out. Their criticism is valid for time series studies and for cross-section analysis of public utility services where prices in different localities may show substantial differentials in the same year because these services are not transferable. As will be explained in connection with our own estimates, for cross-section data for manufacturing industries in a single year, the use of value figures in making the production function estimates would merely increase the residual variance, but the exponents are estimates of the input-output elasticities. The bearing of the elasticity of demand for the output of the industry on the production function estimates will be discussed in detail in the next two chapters.

(2) *Contributions Published after 1957*

Interest in the estimation of aggregate production functions has been renewed by a stimulating paper by Solow [67] in 1957.

[14]See Chapter IV, Section (5), (iii).

Since that time, many important contributions have appeared in rapid succession.

The central ideas underlying our own work were conceived in 1960. Some preliminary results were obtained in the winter of 1961, and were circulated privately in the spring of 1962. The main part of the review of literature presented here was prepared before our preliminary results were developed, and it has not been possible to include many important papers published or put in private circulation since that time. Among the literature published before the spring of 1962, Solow [67], Arrow, Chenery, Minhas, and Solow [2], Solow [65], and Hoch [36] and [37] occupy uniquely important positions; these will be discussed here. Among those papers of special interest that appeared later, Solow [68] and Frankel [22] made new attempts to estimate aggregate production functions for the whole economy, employing methods different from our own. In our review we have avoided the very large body of literature on agriculture and the regulated industries, because the nature of the problem and of the data is different from that for manufacturing industries in many important respects. However, the methods used in the new studies of Griliches [26] and Nerlove [58], respectively, for agriculture and electric power, may with proper modifications be applied to manufacturing industries. The essays by Mundlak [53] and Walters [78], surveying the literature critically and making new suggestions, do not duplicate all the views presented in this chapter. Other significant contributions, not yet published, include a paper by Nerlove [55] on the problem of estimation and identification of Cobb-Douglas production functions; an attempt by Nerlove [57] to formulate a theoretical approach and a statistical method for measuring relative efficiency; a project by Shen [63] to measure scale, efficiency, and substitution effects by taking principal components; and an attempt by Brown and Conrad [5] to relate input-output elasticities to certain "fundamental parameters" in the economy.

To derive a production function for the private nonfarm sectors in the United States, Solow [67] assumed that markets were competitive, that functional distribution accorded with marginal productivity, and that constant returns to scale prevailed. Although Solow then concluded from the findings that technical change was neutral, later he conceded in a note that the evidence actually was far from conclusive.[15] His main finding is that more than 85 per cent of the rise in output per man-hour is attributable to technical progress. By contrast, he thought that capital per man-hour in the purely quantitative sense was very minor in importance. More disaggregated functions have been estimated by Massell [49] and [50], along the approach developed by Solow. A detailed discussion of the above contributions by Solow and Massell is no longer necessary, since Solow, in collaboration with three other authors, has later developed a more elaborate alternative approach to the problem.

This work by Arrow, Chenery, Minhas, and Solow [2] is so important that it is necessary to review it in some detail. On the basis of the data for twenty-four manufacturing industries in nineteen countries, the authors have observed that a significant relationship existed between value added per unit of labor and the real wage rate in each industry across countries as follows:[16]

$$\log \frac{V}{L} = \log a + b \log w + e \tag{2.3}$$

where

V: value added

L: labor input

w: real wage rate

a, b: parameters

e: a random disturbance term.

On the main assumptions (1) that perfect competition exists both in the product and the factor markets; (2) that the data represent situations in equilibrium; (3) that constant returns to scale prevail; and (4) that prices of products and material inputs did not vary systematically with the wage rate, the authors have shown that the following differential equation (2.4)[17] can be derived from equation (2.3):

[15]See Hogan [38], and Solow's reply [66].
[16]See [2], equation (1b), p. 228.
[17]See [2], equation (9), p. 230.

30

$$\log \frac{V}{L} = \log a + b \log \left(\frac{V}{L} \cdot \frac{K}{L} \cdot \frac{d \frac{V}{L}}{K \, d \frac{V}{L}} \right), \qquad (2.4)$$

where K represents capital.

They have also shown that the parameter b turns out to be the elasticity of substitution between labor and capital,[18] and that the solution of the differential equation (2.4) is the following production function:[19]

$$V = (\beta K^{-\rho} + \alpha L^{-\rho})^{-1/\rho} \qquad (2.5)$$

where

$$\rho = \frac{1}{b} - 1 \qquad (2.6)$$

$$\alpha = a^{-1/b} \qquad (2.7)$$

and β is another parameter.

Estimates of the parameters a and b in equation (2.3) can be obtained by fitting the equation to actual data. Provided that the assumptions underlying the differential equation (2.4) are met, the estimated magnitudes of a and b can be used to derive (through equations (2.6) and (2.7)) the parameters ρ and α in the production function (2.5). β is a constant of integration.

The production function (2.5) can be written in a more meaningful way in (2.8):[20]

$$V = \gamma[\delta K^{-\rho} + (1 - \delta) L^{-\rho}]^{-1/\rho} \qquad (2.8)$$

where

$$\rho = \frac{1}{b} - 1 : \text{the substitution parameter} \qquad (2.9)$$

$$\delta = \frac{\beta}{\alpha + \beta} : \text{the distributive parameter} \qquad (2.10)$$

$$\gamma = (\alpha + \beta)^{-1/\rho} : \text{the efficiency parameter.} \qquad (2.11)$$

ρ is called the substitution parameter because it is derived from parameter b, the elasticity of substitution.

[18]See [2], p. 229, and see n. 25, below.
[19]See [2], equation (11), p. 230.
[20]See [2], equation (13), p. 230.

If the equation 2.3 exists and if the assumptions underlying the differential equation (2.4) are valid, then, for any given value of ρ, the functional distribution of income is determined by δ, as shown in the following formula:[21]

$$\frac{\text{Wage bill}}{\text{Earnings of capital}} = \frac{wL}{rK} = \frac{1-\delta}{\delta}\left(\frac{K}{L}\right)^{\rho} \qquad (2.12)$$

where r is the rate of return on capital.

The equation (2.12) can be written as follows:

$$\frac{\delta}{1-\delta} = \frac{r}{w}\left(\frac{K}{L}\right)^{1+\rho}. \qquad (2.13)$$

Hence, with b (and therefore ρ, see the equation (2.9)) estimated from equation (2.3) fitted to empirical data and with data on K, L, r, and w given, the parameter δ can be derived from (2.13).

Arrow, Chenery, Minhas, and Solow have estimated the values of δ for four industries in five countries.[22] It has been found that the magnitude of δ is fairly stable in each industry across the countries. Since δ bears the following relationship with the parameters α and β,[23] α and β being respectively the labor and capital coefficients in the production function (2.5):

$$\frac{\delta}{1-\delta} = \frac{\beta}{\alpha},$$

the ratio of β to α is therefore considered fairly stable across the countries in each industry. A test has been made that indicates that for each industry, β is unlikely to be the same in different countries.[24] It follows that for each industry, α and β probably vary across the different countries by approximately the same proportion. This equiproportional change in the labor and capital coefficients α and β is taken to represent the change in efficiency, and is considered as an evidence of the "neutrality" of technological change. Since from equation (2.11) the parameter γ will change in proportion to the proportional change in α and β, it is called the efficiency parameter.

[21]See [2], equation (23), p. 233.
[22]See [2], Table 3, p. 235.
[23]Derived from equation (2.10).
[24]See [2], pp. 232–233.

The data for four industries in the five countries analyzed indicate that, for each industry, the substitution and distributive parameters are fairly stable across countries, while the efficiency parameter varies.[25]

This new class of production functions, formulated as in equation (2.5) or (2.8), and fitted to a fairly wide range of empirical data, opens up a new vista for the study of production functions, and is an invaluable contribution. The method by which the authors have derived their functions, however, is subject to a number of criticisms, even though it must be granted that they had to work with the best data they could find.

(i) The assumption of perfect competition is invalid with regard to the product and/or the factor markets in most of the twenty-four industries for which the equation (2.3) has been fitted empirically. To illustrate, of the four industries for which the production function (2.8) has been estimated, three involve basic chemicals, iron and steel, and metal products, all of which are likely to be far short of perfectly competitive.

(ii) The data the authors have used mostly concern unusual years of unstable conditions—e.g., 1954 (a recession year) for the United States and Canada; 1953 (end of the Korean War) for Japan—when it is quite unlikely that equilibrium actually existed.

(iii) Since the single-equation least-squares method is used to fit the functions, an unknown element of bias is admittedly introduced into the estimates.[26]

(iv) The new class of production functions has very attractive theoretical properties, but its empirical starting point appears to be rather weak. It was derived on the "finding that a linear logarithmic function provides a *good* fit to the observations of wages and labor input." (See [2], p. 228, italics added.) The new production function, reproduced here as (2.5) or (2.8), is derived from the linear logarithmic function (reproduced here as (2.3)) on

[25]The parameter b was taken at first to be equal to the elasticity of substitution. The changing magnitude of γ across the countries necessitates a modification of the position; but the modification is of minor importance in terms of its effect on the estimated magnitude of the elasticity of substitution. See [2], p. 237.

[26]See [2], p. 245.

the condition that the latter relationship exists independently of the capital variable.[27] If, however, the capital variable is present in some way in the relationship (2.3), it would no longer be possible to derive the simple differential equation (2.4) from (2.3); and this class of production functions, which is the solution of the differential equation (2.4), would be deprived of its starting empirical basis. Because capital data are not available for the 24 industries in the 19 countries studied, a direct test was not made to determine whether the empirical relationship (2.3) is in fact independent of the capital variable.

We have used the U.S. census data on manufactures for 1957 to make a test of this point. The coefficients of determination between value added per man-hour of all employees (V/L) and the average salary and wage rate of all employees (W) were calculated first. Multiple regressions of value added per man-hour on the wage rate and capital per man-hour (K/L) were then computed. The results are presented in Part (A) of Table 1.[28] The same computations were then repeated, with all employees replaced by production workers (L_p), and the average salary and wage rate (W) replaced by the average wage rate of production workers (W_p). (See Part B of Table 1.) As anticipated by Arrow, Chenery, Minhas, and Solow, V/L and W are significantly related in a great majority of the cases at any reasonable level of significance for which one wishes to make the test. So are V/L_p and W_p. However, the coefficient of determination between V/L and W is below 0.1 for three of the 15 industries, and that between V/L_p and W_p for two of the 15 industries. Moreover, the multiple regressions of V/L on W and K/L show that the relationship between V/L and W is probably not independent of capital per man-hour in at least ten industries, and perhaps not in another three.[29] About the same picture is revealed by data in Part (B) of Table 1 on the relationship among

[27]This point is obvious from the derivation given in [2], pp. 229–230. It is also brought out explicitly by the authors on p. 231, [2], where the authors refer to "the existence of a relationship between V/L and w, independent of the stock of capital."

[28]These computations have been done for the 17 two-digit industries for which production functions have been attempted in this study. For the reason why computations have not been done for the other three of the 20 two-digit industries, see Chapter IV, Section (3).

[29]For the following ten industries, the regression coefficients of K/L (given in

V/L_p, W_p, and K/L_p. It is also interesting to observe that the regression coefficients of K/L and K/L_p tend to be significant in practically all the cases where the coefficients of determination between V/L and W or between V/L_p and W_p are too low for comfort (say, less than 0.2). This empirical evidence casts serious doubt upon the probability that the regression coefficients b obtained by Arrow, Chenery, Minhas, and Solow for the 24 industries (given in [2] Table 2, p. 227) are estimates of the elasticities of substitution between labor and capital in these industries, as they claim.[30] They would be such only if the relationship is independent of capital, but this condition is not met in the majority of the cases tested in Table 1.

If one relies upon the goodness of fit of an empirical relationship as the initial basis for deriving a theoretical one, as Arrow, Chenery, Minhas, and Solow did, one probably would have to consider the three-variable relationship (V/L, W, and K/L) as better established than the two-variable one (V/L and W).[31]

Table 1) are in the neighborhood of twice their respective standard errors or larger: food and kindred products; pulp, paper and products; chemicals and products; stone, clay, and glass products; primary metal products; fabricated metal products; machinery except electrical; electrical machinery; transportation equipment; and instruments. For textile mill products, apparel, and petroleum and coal products, the coefficients of K/L are larger than their respective standard errors.

[30]The modification of the relationship between b and the elasticity of substitution discussed by the authors on p. 237 of their article is irrelevant to the point discussed here.

[31]To pursue the analysis from a theoretical point of view similar to the discussion in n. 5, p. 228 of Arrow, Chenery, Minhas, and Solow [2], the three-variable relationship means that, at a given wage rate, the labor input per unit of output depends upon the labor-capital ratio.

It might be thought that the significance of the K/L variable in the three variable relationship is spurious in the sense that V/L and K/L are correlated, whatever the production function, and hence that K/L could be significant in a multiple regression relationship fitted to a finite size sample for the three variables relationship even if K/L is in fact absent from the V/L and W relationship. This argument appears to be of doubtful validity. If K/L is in fact absent from the true relationship between V/L and W, then the expected value of the regression coefficients of K/L in a fairly large number of the three-variable regressions of a given finite number of observations should be insignificantly different from zero. The regressions in Table 1 are not for the same industry and are not of the same sample size; hence the above defense of our position is not exactly applicable. However, the fact that the coefficients in a majority of the three-variable regressions are significantly different from zero is a good indication that the same would be true if a large number of samples of the same size were available for the same industry, so that the three-variable relationship could be computed from these samples.

Table 1. Tests of the Empirical Basis of the "New Class of Production Function" Developed by Arrow, Chenery, Minhas, and Solow, Using U.S. Census of Manufactures, 1957.

(A) For All Employees

$\dfrac{V}{L}$ = Value added per man-hour of all employees

W = Average Salary and Wage Rate

$\dfrac{K}{L}$ = Capital per man-hour

	No. of observations[a] *(States)*	*Coefficients of determination* $\dfrac{V}{L}$ *between* — *and* W	*Regressions of* $\dfrac{V}{L}$ *on* W *and* $\dfrac{K}{L}$		
			Regression coefficients of W	*Regression coefficients* $\dfrac{K}{L}$ *of* —	*Coefficient of determination*
Food and kindred products..........	35	0.401	0.407 (0.177)	0.446 (0.139)	0.548
Textile mill products	18	0.651	0.975 (0.175)	0.160 (0.109)	0.695
Apparel and related products..........	18	0.641	1.071 (0.263)	0.097 (0.086)	0.669
Lumber and wood products..........	14	0.943	0.990 (0.135)	0.002 (0.070)	0.943
Furniture and fixtures...........	19	0.819	1.258 (0.128)	−0.154 (0.072)	0.859
Pulp, paper and products..........	28	0.253	0.386 (0.322)	0.331 (0.050)	0.730
Chemicals and products..........	31	0.309	0.866 (0.231)	0.201 (0.085)	0.424
Petroleum and coal products..........	18	0.062	0.180 (0.716)	0.282 (0.224)	0.152
Rubber products....	16	0.522	1.278 (0.553)	0.018 (0.217)	0.523

Part A of Table 1 (continued).

	No. of observations[a] (States)	Coefficients of determination between $\frac{V}{L}$ and W	Regressions of $\frac{V}{L}$ on W and $\frac{K}{L}$		
			Regression coefficients of W	Regression coefficients of $\frac{K}{L}$	Coefficient of determination
Leather and leather goods.......	15	0.357	0.890 (0.457)	−0.050 (0.113)	0.368
Stone, clay and glass products.......	25	0.251	0.539 (0.177)	0.295 (0.065)	0.611
Primary metal products...........	28	0.075	0.298 (0.704)	0.321 (0.141)	0.234
Fabricated metal products...........	32	0.180	0.401 (0.207)	0.178 (0.068)	0.336
Machinery except electrical...........	25	0.146	0.222 (0.263)	0.258 (0.100)	0.343
Electrical machinery.	22	0.068	0.300 (0.210)	0.278 (0.071)	0.483
Transportation equipment.........	26	0.234	1.008 (0.448)	0.214 (0.060)	0.504
Instruments and related products.....	12	0.556	0.601 (0.294)	0.217 (0.116)	0.681

(B) For Production Workers only

$\dfrac{V}{L_p}$ value added per manhour of production workers

W_p = average wage rate of production workers

$\dfrac{K}{L_p}$ capital per manhour of production workers

			Regressions of $\dfrac{V}{L}$ on W and $\dfrac{K}{L}$		
	No. of observations[a] (States)	Coefficients of determination between $\dfrac{V}{L}$ and W_p	Regression coefficients of W_p	Regression coefficients of $\dfrac{K}{L}$	Coefficient of determination
Food and kindred products..........	35	0.322	0.282 (0.144)	0.430 (0.148)	0.464
Textile mill products..........	18	0.598	1.427 (0.299)	0.122 (0.156)	0.641
Apparel and related products..........	18	0.508	1.094 (0.374)	0.211 (0.102)	0.617
Lumber and wood products..........	14	0.919	0.989 (0.165)	−0.033 (0.090)	0.920
Furniture and fixtures............	19	0.765	1.402 (0.177)	−0.191 (0.102)	0.807
Pulp, paper and products..........	28	0.390	0.298 (0.340)	0.304 (0.069)	0.657
Chemicals and products..........	31	0.297	0.780 (0.254)	0.076 (0.109)	0.309
Petroleum and coal products..........	18	0.150	−0.027 (0.951)	0.309 (0.283)	0.213
Rubber products....	16	0.734	1.231 (0.286)	−0.052 (0.132)	0.738
Leather and leather goods.......	15	0.434	0.926 (0.528)	0.0003 (0.118)	0.434

Part B of Table 1 (continued).

	No. of observations[a] (States)	Coefficients of determination between $\frac{V}{L}$ and W_p	Regressions of $\frac{V}{L}$ on W and $\frac{K}{L}$		
			Regression coefficients of W_p	Regression coefficients of $\frac{K}{L}$	Coefficient of determination
Stone, clay, and glass products.......	25	0.268	0.568 (0.175)	0.309 (0.069)	0.627
Primary metal products...........	28	−0.073	0.187 (0.683)	0.374 (0.154)	0.250
Fabricated metal products...........	32	−0.074	0.189 (0.208)	0.243 (0.080)	0.298
Machinery except electrical...........	25	0.133	0.222 (0.226)	0.204 (0.104)	0.262
Electrical machinery.	22	0.358	0.606 (0.233)	0.202 (0.089)	0.494
Transportation equipment.........	26	0.248	0.998 (0.545)	0.205 (0.073)	0.441
Instruments and related products.....	12	0.718	0.874 (0.264)	0.196 (0.098)	0.805

Source: Bureau of the Census [7] and [8].
[a]Not all industries are significantly represented in all states; and data on K (capital at the beginning of 1957) are not available for all states.

Granted, the production functions obtained from the three-variable empirical relationship would probably be very complicated. The complexity of a production function, however, is not ground for its rejection, provided that it is a better description of reality than the simpler version. Indeed, the more complex function may be a superior version since its empirical basis is stronger. In any case, more theoretical and empirical work probably can be profitably done on this point.

(v) Since the estimates and tests made by Arrow, Chenery, Minhas, and Solow for the parameters δ and γ (in [2], Table 3, p.

235) all involve the use of the estimated regression coefficients b as the respective elasticities of substitutions in the different industries, and since it is doubtful whether the estimated b can in fact be so used (see (iv) above), the validity of these estimates and tests is also in doubt.

(vi) An important attractive feature of this "new class of production function" is that the elasticity of substitution can be any constant, not necessarily zero or unity.[32] However, the estimated values of b obtained by Arrow, Chenery, Minhas, and Solow for the 24 manufacturing industries are, with a single insignificant exception, in the range from 0.72 to unity, and 19 of them are in the range from 0.80 to unity.[33] We have already explained in point (iv) above why we do not believe that there is sufficient empirical basis to consider these figures as elasticities of substitution. But in order to indicate the kind of difficulties inherent in the particular manner in which estimates of production functions are derived by the authors from data on distributive shares, let us assume for the moment that these figures are in fact estimates of elasticities of substitution. Their magnitudes then would strongly suggest the possibility that these elasticities are all very close to unity, affected by some systematic influence that consistently pulls the estimated b down from the unity level. This hunch easily can be rationalized by removal of the untenable assumption made by the authors (see point (ii) above), that the empirical data represent equilibrium situations. Suppose, for the sake of argument, that the true production function is the standard Douglas relationship $V = bK^aL^{1-a}$. Further, assume that the marginal value product was larger than the wage rate so that equilibrium did not prevail:

$$a \frac{V}{L} > w,$$

or

$$\frac{V}{L} = \frac{1}{a} cw, \text{ and } c > 1.$$

[32] For the linear production function $V = aL + bK + c$, the elasticity of substitution is infinite; for the Douglas function $V = aL^bK^c$, the elasticity of substitution is unity.

[33] See [2], Table 2, p. 227. The modification of the relationship between b and the elasticity of substitution, introduced by the authors on p. 237, would reduce the estimated elasticities of substitution by small amounts.

40

To rationalize the result obtained by Arrow, Chenery, Minhas, and Solow, c may be assumed to be a function of the wage rate,[34] i.e., $c = fw^{-g}$. It follows that:

$$\log \frac{V}{L} = \log \frac{f}{a} + (1 - g)\log w.$$

The parameter g may be a small fraction, and the empirical results obtained by the authors (i.e., all the estimated b's are smaller than, but close to, unity) would be obtained from the Douglas function (with the elasticity of substitution equal to unity) on the plausible assumption that the empirical data do not represent equilibrium situations. We are not saying that this interpretation is necessarily preferable to the Arrow-Chenery-Minhas-Solow position that equilibrium prevailed. This demonstration does, however, bring sharply into focus the possible dangers involved in making rigid assumptions of perfect competition and the actual existence of equilibrium.

In still another attempt that did not come to our notice until some preliminary results of our study had been obtained, Solow [65] has formulated an ingeneous method of estimating the rate of technical progress, which he assumes to be exponentially constant through time, assuming also that technical progress is neutral but that it is embodied in new investment, and that constant returns to scale and competitive equilibrium in the labor market also prevail. The production function is of the following form:

$$Q(t) = Be^{-\delta(1-\alpha)t} L(t)^\alpha J(t)^{1-\alpha}$$

where

$$J(t) = \int_{-\infty}^{t} e^{\delta v} I(v) \, dv$$

and Q, L, I, and t represent respectively output, labor, investment, and time, v denotes a given year, and B is a scale constant. The parameters δ and α represent the inverse of the average length of life of capital goods and the labor-output elasticity respectively. The constant σ is equal to $\delta + \lambda / (1 - \alpha)$, where α is the exponentially constant rate of technical progress.

From this production function, the following equation is obtained, which may be fitted to empirical data:

[34]For a discussion of this hypothesis, see Chapter III, Section (3).

41

$$\frac{\dfrac{dR}{dt} + \delta R}{I(t)} = B^{1/(1-\alpha)}\, e^{\,\lambda t\,(1-\alpha)}$$

where

$$R(t) = \frac{Q(t)^{\frac{1}{1-\alpha}}}{L(t)^{\alpha/(1-\alpha)}}$$

and

$$\frac{dR}{dt} = -\delta R + B^{1/(1-\alpha)}\, e^{(\sigma-\delta)t}\, I(t).$$

On the basis of outside estimates of α and δ, λ can then be estimated with time series data for Q, L, and I. With α and δ assumed at $\frac{2}{3}$ and 0.04 respectively, λ is estimated at 2.5 per cent per year. This is higher than the usual estimates of "technical progress" of around 1.5 per cent per year. Since new technology is embodied in new capital, investment becomes a great deal more important to economic growth in Solow [65] than it is generally taken to be in the recent literature on growth.

We think that Solow's suggestion that technical advance is embodied in new capital is a much more rewarding approach than any other we have seen. If improvement in technology is always so embodied, however, one would be inclined not to introduce the effects of the improvement through a "neutral" term.[35] It is also difficult to apply Solow's method to cross-section data, because time does not enter the relationships explicitly.

Hoch made two important attempts, [36] and [37], to overcome the simultaneous equation complications, in addition to contributing many interesting ideas about other theoretical and estimating problems. However, some of his assumptions are unlikely to be fulfilled except in perfectly competitive industries and in agriculture, with which the quantitative part of his analysis was concerned. For instance, to lessen simultaneous equation bias, Hoch makes the critical assumption that the disturbance term is independent of the input variables, on the ground that the latter are functions of expected rather than actual output. In using annual data on

[35] I.e., the term $e^{\,\lambda v}$ in equation (4), Solow [65].

42

manufacturing industries, one must assume that actual output in the earlier part of the year would affect expected output in the later part of the same year, hence that the error term and inputs cannot be independent of each other. The application of the technique of covariance analysis to production function studies in [36] is very interesting. The nature of the technique, however, is such that differences in efficiency are computed and ranked for different producing units in different time periods, without explanation for these differences. Technical progress is therefore disembodied in this approach, or rather, it is embodied in unknown factors.

This completes our brief review of the literature. In the next chapter we set forth the theoretical principles which underlie our own approach.

CHAPTER III

A Simultaneous Equation Model: Theoretical Considerations

THE production functions presented in this study represent an attempt to overcome some of the difficulties encountered in previous work. Data from the 1957 Census of Manufactures [6], [7], and [8] are used to derive estimates for 17 two-digit industries across states.[1] These cross-section data are free from the time series difficulties discussed in Chapter II, (1), (i). As functions are obtained for each of the 17 industries separately, they are less ambiguous in their economic meaning than those obtained from data across industries (see Chapter II, (1), (iii)). A system of relationships determining production and employment has been formulated; and the two-stage least-squares method, in addition to single-equation least-squares, is used to estimate the functions. The results obtained are thus largely free from the simultaneous equations bias mentioned in Chapter II, (1), (v).[2]

Our first task is to formulate a theoretical simultaneous equation model for the study of production functions. Any such attempt must start with the pathbreaking paper by Marschak and Andrews [48]. The basic framework of the Marschak-Andrews model has provisions for both perfectly and imperfectly competitive markets for output and for labor and capital inputs. The differences in the efficiency of the various producing units are reflected in their model in the random disturbance terms in the functions.

[1]See n. 14, Chapter IV.
[2]Possible criticisms of our own estimates are discussed in Chapter IV, Section (5), after the findings are presented.

However, the meaning of the elasticity of demand for output in the Marschak-Andrews model requires clarification for application to imperfectly competitive industries. Beyond this, the specification of a perfectly elastic demand function for the output of a producing unit in a perfectly competitive industry, without bringing into the picture the demand elasticity for the output of the whole industry, falls short of the aim of a simultaneous equation construct. Finally, if, as in the Marschak-Andrews model, differences in efficiency are treated as random disturbances, one can measure such differences, but without explaining them.

Our purpose is to clarify and modify the Marschak-Andrews model in these respects, and to introduce the speed of adjustment as a dynamic element.

(1) The Demand Elasticity for Output of "Industry"

We shall first consider the difficult problem of the relationship between the demand elasticities for the outputs of the individual producing units and that for the "industry" as a whole. For this purpose, the exposition can be simplified by the assumption of perfectly competitive equilibrium in the labor market[3] with the amount of capital completely fixed. Fixed capital can be conveniently incorporated into the model by using a lagged capital variable. The Marschak-Andrews model would then appear as follows, the notations being our own.[4] Since our primary aim is to deal with cross-section data, the subscripts i and j refer to producing units during a given period of time. Only the capital variable is lagged.

[3]This assumption will be waived in later analysis.

[4]Equations (3.1)–(3.4) below correspond to the Marschak-Andrews equations (1.1)–(1.8), (1.11), (1.12), (1.13) and (1.14), after allowing for the simplifications given in the text above. See [48] pp. 151–154. The Marschak-Andrews notations correspond to ours as follows:

Marschak-Andrews	Ours
y_0	$Q_i P_i$
x_0	Q_i
y_1	$L_i W_i$
α_1	b
α_2	e
β_0	$1 - \dfrac{1}{h}$
β_1	1
w	$L_i W_i / Q_i P_i$

(continued)

45

$$V_i = P_i Q_i \tag{3.1}$$

$$Q_i = a L^b_i K^e_{i,-1} u_i \tag{3.2}$$

$$P_i = c Q_i^{-1/h} \tag{3.3}$$

$$\frac{\partial V_i}{\partial L_i} = \frac{\partial}{\partial L_i} P_i Q_i$$

$$= c \frac{\partial}{\partial L_i} Q_i^{1-1/h}$$

$$= \left(1 - \frac{1}{h}\right) P_i b \frac{Q_i}{L_i} = W_i \tag{3.4}$$

where V, P, Q, L, and K denote, as before, value of output, price, quantity of output, labor input, and capital input respectively. b and e are the labor-output and capital-output elasticities, while h is the elasticity of demand for output; W represents wage rate; u is a random disturbance term; a and c are constants.

For the perfectly competitive case, Marschak and Andrews let h approach infinity and obtain from (3.4) the familiar equality of labor-output elasticity and the share of wage bill in the total value of output:[5]

$$b = \frac{L_i W_i}{Q_i P_i}. \tag{3.5}$$

This, of course, is perfectly correct. However, it is desirable to bring into the picture the elasticity of demand for the output of the industry as a whole, which would not approach infinity in any

---

It is directly seen that our equation (3.4) is the same as (1.13) and (1.14) of [48] as follows:

$$\left(1 - \frac{1}{h}\right) P_i b \frac{Q_i}{L_i} = W_i,$$

$$\beta_0 \alpha_1 \frac{y_0}{y_1} = 1,$$

so that $\beta_0 y_0 \alpha_1 - y_1 = 0$, [(1.11′) and (1.12′) of [48], p. 154], with $\beta = 1$ in our model; and

$$\alpha_1 \frac{\beta_0}{\beta_1} = \frac{y_1}{y_0} = w \qquad [(1.13) \text{ and } (1.14) \text{ of } [48] \text{ . p. 154}].$$

See equations (1.15) and (1.16), [48], p. 154: $\alpha_1 = w_1$. Also see n. 4, above.

industry. In our study, we shall not be dealing empirically with the case of perfect competition. This point is discussed here only to supplement the formal analysis given in Marschak and Andrews [48], and then to extend the analysis to the case of imperfect competition. The easiest way to bring the industry elasticity of demand into the perfectly competitive model is to let h represent that elasticity in equation (3.3) and to assume that there are n firms of exactly the same size in the industry. The number of these firms is assumed to be very large but is not allowed to approach infinity. Accordingly, equation (3.3) becomes:

$$P = c \, (nQ_i)^{-1/h}. \tag{3.6}$$

Under the assumption of perfect competition, equation (3.4) should be written as:

$$P \frac{\partial Q_i}{\partial L_i} = P \, b \, \frac{Q_i}{L_i}$$

$$= \frac{c \, b \, n^{-1/h} \, a^{(1-1/h)} \, L_i^{\,b(1-1/h)} \, K_{i,-1}^{\,e(1-1/h)} \, u_i^{\,(1-1/h)}}{L_i} = W. \tag{3.7}$$

The demand elasticity for the output of the entire industry is thus an important factor determining the optimum quantity of labor input, a point that is important for the empirical studies presented later, even though perfect competition is not assumed there.

With h taking on finite values, equations (3.1) through (3.4) represent the model formulated by Marschak and Andrews for the case of imperfect competition. It requires no clarification for industries approaching monopoly, where the prices of the imperfect competitors can be ignored. For a study of manufacturing industries involving a relatively small number of producers (but significantly more than one) and product differentiation, the validity of equation (3.3) is not immediately clear. An appropriate form of the demand function for the output of producer i would be as follows:

$$Q_i = g_i \prod_j \left(\frac{P_j}{P_i}\right)^{h_{ji}} \left(\frac{P_o}{P_i}\right)^{h_i} \tag{3.8}$$

$$j = 1, 2, \ldots, i{-}1, i{+}1, \ldots, n$$

where n represents the number of producing units considered to be in the "industry"; h_{ji}, the cross elasticities of demand for the products within the "industry"; P_o, the general price level in the economy as a whole; and h_i, the cross elasticity of demand for the output of the producing unit i with respect to the ratio of the general price level to its own price.

Observations for P_i and P_j are lacking in the 1956–1957 census cross-section data used in this study, and equation (3.8) is impossible to estimate. Moreover, even if index numbers can be constructed to approximate P_i and P_j, the differentials between them would be small, as for the prices of a Ford, a Chevrolet, and a Plymouth in the same period of time. This is the well-known situation that cross price elasticities of competitive goods usually cannot be estimated with cross-section data for a given year. Moreover, the years 1956 and 1957 were still within the postwar price-wage spiral period, when the unit prices of different producers *in the same industry* moved more or less in unison with the movement of wage rates in that industry and with the effect of (generally upward) shifting demand for the output of the industry as a whole. Adjustments in prices were mostly in response to the cost-push and demand-pull influences on the industry, rather than to changes in intraindustry demand and cost elements.[6] Under the assumptions that all p_i (unit prices of the different establishments in the same industry) moved approximately proportionally during the year 1957 and that $h_{ji} = h_{ij}$, the term $\prod\limits_{j} \left(\dfrac{P_j}{P_i} \right)^{h_{ji}}$ would approximately be the same constant for all i.

Since P_o is the same for all i, the demand function for the output of producer i can then be reasonably written as:

$$Q_i = d_i P_i^{-h} \tag{3.9}$$

where h is the cross elasticity of demand for producer i's output with respect to the ratio of the general price level to P_i. (It appears to be a reasonable approximation to assume that h is the same for all i.) Equation (3.9) is in fact exactly the same as equation (3.3);

---

[6]The unit prices of *different* industries, however, changed sufficiently differently, partly in response to the different wage movements in the different industries and to the shifting importance of the different industries in the economy.

its use in this study appears to be justified by the preceding discussion. Owing to the absence of data on P_i and to the small differences between them even if they were available, equation (3.9) cannot be estimated empirically. It will be shown in Chapter IV, Sections (2) and (3), however, that the magnitudes of h can be approximately inferred from the estimates of some of the other parameters on the basis of the plausibility of these estimates as a group. Under the assumptions discussed above, h represents the elasticity of demand for the output of the industry.

(2) *The Treatment of Technological Change*

Technological change is a very complicated process. There is no simple way to measure either its occurrence or its effects. Certainly it is plausible to link differences in the efficiency of operating units to differences in levels of technology employed. But to assume that these are *random* variations, as Marschak and Andrews do, leaves much to be desired. Instead, we should aim at a *systematic* measurement of the effects of technology itself on efficiency and output, thus gaining more insight into the functional role it actually has played. This is a difficult problem. However, the essence of any fruitful approach to a difficult problem is to reduce complicated phenomena to relatively simple quantitative relationships of fairly general applicability. There is precedent for this in economics. For example, consumers spend money on a complicated and ever-changing product-mix. Yet it is known that income alone determines to a large extent all categories of consumption expenditure.

The task, then, is to devise some simple proxy or dummy variables that would reflect changing technology to a significant extent. We think it reasonable to assume that no important change in the level of technology employed in an establishment is possible without its being reflected in the following: (i) a change in the ratio of the value of equipment (machinery, tools, etc.) to the value of plant (structures, buildings, etc.), indicating the degree of elaborateness of the technical processes in use or "technology intensity"; (ii) a change in the "average age" of the capital assets as expressed in the ratio of the net value of assets (gross value minus accumulated depreciation) to the gross value, indicating

49

the "vintage" of technology;[7] and (iii) a change in the ratio of technical and professional personnel to production (manual) workers, again reflecting "technology intensity." We recognize that these measures may not fully or accurately reflect the levels of technology used in certain producing units in some industries. However, it is probable that for a majority of cases they would catch the major differences in technical processes utilized by the different establishments within a given industry.

These proxy variables would enable us to incorporate "technology" explicitly in the production functions. By contrast, in the Cobb-Douglas type of functions given as equation (3.2), the exponents b and e are the output-labor and output-capital elasticities, respectively. These exponents are assumed to be constant; thus the effects of technological change are assumed to be neutral. Clearly, it is more plausible to assume that the exponents vary with the level of technology. Let R represent the ratio of equipment to plant or, alternatively, the ratio of net value to gross value of capital assets; and r the ratio of technical personnel to production workers. These are the proxy variables just mentioned. A reasonable way to write the production function is then the following:

$$Q = aL^{b \log r} K^{e \log R} u. \qquad (3.10)$$

The labor and the capital exponents are therefore, respectively, b log r and e log R. Take the capital exponent as an example. The output-capital elasticity would increase with R but at a decreasing rate.[8] The rate of increase of the exponent with respect to R may decrease at a rapid or slow rate, depending upon the empirical evidence.

For a given level of technology, r and R are both constant, and therefore the exponents are also constant. In this case, changes

---

[7] For a more elaborate treatment of the different efficiency of capital installed in different periods of time, see Solow [68]. Solow's method, as has been explained in Chapter II, Section (2), cannot be applied to cross-section data.

[8]
$$\frac{d}{dR} (e \log R) = e/R > 0, \text{ if } e > 0.$$

$$\frac{d^2}{dR^2} (e \log R) = -e/R^2 < 0, \text{ if } e > 0.$$

in quantities of labor and capital inputs would result in changes in output *along a given production surface. Shifts* in a production function would take place as the exponents themselves change when the technological level itself undergoes change, modifying the original surface.

When the production function is formulated as in (3.10), the marginal productivity of an input can be separated into two component elements: a part due to the change in the physical quantity of input with technology remaining at a given level, and another part representing the marginal contribution of a change in the level of technology with the physical quantity of input remaining unchanged. Again take the capital variable as an example. Represent capital by the gross amount (K_g) and denote by R the ratio (in per cent) of net (K_n) to gross (K_g) capital as follows:

$$R = \frac{K_n}{K_g} \, 100.$$

Taking the differentials of the logarithmic form of (3.10) and leaving out the labor term, we have:

$$\frac{dQ}{Q} = e(\log R) \frac{dK_g}{K_g} + e(\log K_g) \frac{dR}{R} \qquad (3.11)$$

where

$$dR = \frac{K_g dK_n - K_n dK_g}{K^2_g} \, 100. \qquad (3.12)$$

At a given time, $dK_n = dK_g$ and it follows that:

$$\frac{dR}{R} = \frac{K_g - K_n}{K_n} \frac{dK_g}{K_g}$$

$$= \frac{100 - R}{R} \frac{dK_g}{K_g}. \qquad (3.13)$$

Substituting (3.13) into (3.11), the partial derivative of Q with respect to K_g can be easily derived as follows:

$$\frac{\partial Q}{\partial K} = (e \log R) \frac{Q}{K_g} + \left(e \, \frac{100 - R}{R} \log K_g \right) \frac{Q}{K_g}. \qquad (3.14)$$

51

The first term to the right of equation (3.14) represents the marginal productivity of capital under unchanged technology; the second, the marginal contribution of capital if it were possible to change the "vintage" of capital without changing its gross value. Thus, with the production function so formulated we can attempt to estimate separately the effects on output of changes in the physical quantity of capital and in technology. The "split" of the marginal product of capital into these two terms is analogous to the Hicksian "split" of the effect of a change in the price of a commodity on the quantity demanded into an income and a substitution effect. The latter represents the effect on quantity demanded if there were a change in income to "compensate" for the change in price. The first term to the right of equation (3.14) is the effect of a change in the quantity of capital, with technology remaining at the constant level R. If we assume that, when the different establishments expand their capital they would install the newest type, it would be impossible in fact for technology to remain at a constant level. Thus, the first term to the right of equation (3.14) is similar to the second term, that is, an abstract concept. The second term represents the effect of a change in technology, with a "compensated" change in the quantity of capital for the latter to remain constant.

The first term may be called the quantity component of the marginal product of capital, and the second, the technology component. For a given output-capital ratio, Q/K_g, the quantity component increases with R, the level of technology. Thus, the higher the level of technology on which an establishment is operating, the greater is the quantity component of the marginal product of capital. At a given ratio of Q to K_g, the technology component increases with K_g, the quantity of capital in existence, but decreases with R, the level of technology.

In the econometric studies presented in Chapter IV and Appendix III, we have not been able to construct the proxy variable r, the ratio of technical and professional employees to production workers, for use in estimating the production functions.[9] The other two proxy variables for technology, the ratio of net to gross

[9]For other modifications of labor inputs, see Section (4) of this chapter.

capital and the ratio of equipment to plant, play important roles in the empirical analyses in Chapter IV and Appendix III, respectively.

(3) *The Demand Function for Labor and the Speed of Adjustment*

Any production function implies a demand function for labor. In fact, this is the main reason for attempting a simultaneous equation model. With both the output and the labor variables included in equation (3.2), it is difficult to say whether a given statistical estimate of the equation is a production function, or a demand function for labor, or a "mongrel." The demand function for labor should be explicitly formulated and incorporated in the model, and simultaneous equation estimating procedures should be used to estimate all of the constituent equations. The problems of identification and of dynamic adjustments in making such estimates have been examined in a stimulating fashion by Nerlove [55].

In formulating the demand function for labor, we specifically avoid the assumption that the labor market was in equilibrium in 1957 in the sense that the quantity of labor employed was exactly at the profit-maximizing level. The steps in which the demand function for labor is derived from the production function are as follows.

Given the production function (3.2), the marginal revenue product of labor in the producing unit i is equal to the following:

$$\frac{\partial Q_i \, P_i}{\partial L_i} = \frac{b \, V_i \left(1 - \dfrac{1}{h}\right)}{L_i}$$

where h is the elasticity of demand for the output of the industry.[10]

The "equilibrium" demand for labor (L_i^*) is the amount of labor input the producing unit i would hire to maximize its profits. It is determined by the equality of the marginal revenue product of labor with the wage rate (W_i), with the latter assumed

[10]For a discussion of this elasticity, see Section (1) of this chapter.

to have been fixed through collective bargaining prior to the decision on employment:

$$\frac{bV_i\left(1 - \dfrac{1}{h}\right)}{L_i{}^*} = W_i.$$

The actual demand for labor is likely to be different from the equilibrium level for at least two reasons.

First, within the same industry, the different producing units may have unequal knowledge and unequal skill for achieving the profit-maximizing position. For example, none of the establishments is in a position to know precisely what its profit-maximizing output and price are, and the judgments of the different establishments on this matter will differ in degree of accuracy. This lack of perfect knowledge on the part of the establishments and the consequent deviations from equilibrium are likely to be more than merely a random phenomenon. It is, of course, very difficult to specify a function explaining this nonrandom source of market imperfection. In this study, we test the hypothesis that the degree of deviations from profit-maximizing equilibrium depends upon, first, the size of the producing unit (as measured by the value of output), and, second, the wage rate. The relevance of the size of the producing unit and the wage rate appears clear, even though it is difficult to say, a priori, whether the relationship is direct or inverse. The larger a producing unit is, the greater the likelihood that it would have a better knowledge of the input and output markets through its greater capability to invest in information-gathering and research activities. The larger unit may also be the older and more experienced one. The larger the organization, however, the more difficult it may be to communicate and coordinate information and decisions. Also, the larger and the older units may be the "tired" ones. One or the other consideration may be the determining influence, or they may cancel out.

Similar uncertainty exists with regard to the direction of the influence of wage rate on the degree of deviation from the profit-maximizing position. The producing units paying the higher wage rates may be the ones having better knowledge and information; they may obtain labor of superior quality by paying better rates; and they may also be the ones having greater incentive, urgency, and ability to achieve the optimum. As in all production function studies, the homogeneity of labor inputs in the different producing units in the same industry must be assumed, although this is contrary to fact.[11] Wage differences within the *same* industry across the states, however, are likely to reflect to a significant extent factors *other than differences in labor quality*—for example, differences in living costs and in strength of unions. The establishments in the high-wage regions would therefore be under greater compulsion to attain optimum, and as a result perhaps might be more skillful in doing so. Against this, it may be that the more skillful entrepreneurs would elect to operate where wage rates are low. These opposing influences may also cancel out, and leave the wage rate insignificant on balance as an explanatory variable for deviations from equilibrium.

We shall merely specify in equation (3.15) that the degree of deviation from the profit-maximizing position depends upon the size of the producing unit (as represented by V_i) and the wage rate, leaving the signs and the magnitude of the parameters g and m to be determined by empirical data.[12] In addition, a random disturbance term z_i is also included.[13]

$$\frac{b V_i \left(1 - \frac{1}{h}\right)}{L_i{}^*} = W_i f W_i{}^{-g} k V_i{}^m z_i \qquad (3.15)$$

$L_i{}^*$ now stands for establishment i's "equilibrium" demand for labor, modified by lack of complete knowledge and information and ability to achieve maximum profits, and by random variations.

[11] We have made an attempt to reduce the labor variable across the states to a more homogeneous basis, but, needless to say, it is doubtful that our attempt was a complete success.

[12] g and m now enter into the equation tentatively with a negative and a positive sign respectively. f is also a parameter such that the influence of W_i on the degree of deviation is $f W_i{}^{-g}$. k is similarly interpreted in connection with V_i.

[13] With mean equal to unity (and the mean of the logarithm of z_{it} equal to zero), and distributed independently among the establishments.

The second reason why the actual demand for labor L_i is different from the profit-maximizing level is that, for a host of considerations, the producing units would not and could not make the required adjustments instantaneously. Technological and institutional rigidities impose necessary lags upon any adaptive change. Psychological inertia, hesitations, and lack of complete confidence in one's constantly changing judgment all obstruct immediate responses to changing environments. Accordingly, a coefficient of the speed of adjustment of less than unity (i.e., $\lambda < 1$)[14] is introduced in the equation (3.16) to indicate explicitly this source of deviation from equilibrium.

$$\frac{L_i}{L_{i,-1}} = \left[\frac{L^*_i}{L_{i,-1}}\right]^\lambda \tag{3.16}$$

It appears from equations (3.15) and (3.16) that, in the determination of the demand for labor, we have used the actual, current values of Q_i, P_i, and W_i, instead of the expected magnitudes that are more relevant. However, as shown below, the complication occasioned by expectations is already taken into consideration in these equations.

Solving equations (3.15) and (3.16) for L_i, we obtain a solution for the current demand for labor as a function of $L_{i,-1}$ and the other explanatory variables V_i and W_i as follows:

$$L_i = (L_{i,-1})^{1-\lambda}\left[\frac{b}{fk}\left(1-\frac{1}{h}\right)W_i^{-(1-g)}V_i^{(1-m)}z_i^{-1}\right]^\lambda \tag{3.17}$$

or $\log L_i = \lambda \log C + (1-\lambda)\log L_{i,-1} + \lambda(1-m)\log V_i$
$\qquad\qquad\qquad - \lambda(1-g)\log W_i - \lambda \log z_i \tag{3.18}$

[14]In the equation (3.16), λ is actually the elasticity of adjustment. Taking the logarithm of equation (3.16), we have:

$$\log\frac{L_i}{L_{i,-1}} = \lambda \log\frac{L^*_i}{L_{i,-1}}$$

Taking differentials, we obtain:

$$\lambda = \frac{d\left(\dfrac{L_i}{L_{i,-1}}\right)}{\dfrac{L_i}{L_{i,-1}}}\bigg/\frac{d\left(\dfrac{L^*_i}{L_{i,-1}}\right)}{\dfrac{L^*_i}{L_{i,-1}}}$$

where $C = \dfrac{b}{fk}\left(1 - \dfrac{1}{h}\right)$.

Using a method formulated by Nerlove [56], it can be shown that equation (3.17) is identical in form with the result that would be obtained by following Nerlove's adaptive expectations approach, or by using Friedman's method for distinguishing permanent and transitory changes.[15]

(4) *The Complete Model Summarized*

Equations (3.21)–(3.27) constitute the theoretical model to be estimated statistically. They are constructed on the preceding analysis, with the following modifications. First, V_i now denotes value added, instead of the value of output. In making this modification, we give up the attempt to estimate the elasticity of output with respect to raw materials and fuels. Previous experience in production function studies indicates that collinearity between labor and capital inputs is sufficiently great to forestall any ambition to bring additional exploratory variables into the production function.

The second modification is that production and nonproduction workers (L_p and L_n) enter into the production function separately.

---

[15]To simplify the exposition, let us consider W_i, a predetermined variable in this analysis, to be free from expectations complications. Let $Q^*_i\, P^*_i$ be the expected normal (or in Friedman's terminology "permanent") magnitude of $Q_i\, P_i$. Denote what was previously the expected normal magnitude by $Q^*_{i,-1}\, P^*_{i,-1}$.
Let the expected normal magnitude be determined by the following expectations functions:

$$\log \frac{Q^*_i\, P^*_i}{Q^*_{i,-1}\, P^*_{i,-1}} = \lambda \log \frac{Q_i\, P_i}{Q^*_{i,-1}\, P^*_{i,-1}}. \qquad (3.19)$$

Then assume, as Friedman did in the case of his consumption study [23], that the current demand for labor L_i is determined by the "permanent" or expected normal magnitude of productivity. With proper changes in notation, we derive from equation (3.15) the following:

$$\frac{b\, Q^*_i\, P^*_i \left(1 - \dfrac{1}{h}\right)}{L_i} = W_i\, f\, W_i^{-g}\, k\, V^m_i\, z_i. \qquad (3.20)$$

As can be easily verified, equations (3.19) and (3.20) will yield a solution for $\log L_{it}$ identical in form with (3.18).

This disaggregation is one that we were unwilling to give up; we believe that sufficient variations in the ratios of these two categories of employees existed within most industries that would enable us to disaggregate the labor variable in this manner. However, we have not used the ratio of nonproduction employees to production workers as an index of the level of technology, as was suggested in Section (2) above. The data for nonproduction workers include many other kinds of employees besides professional and technical staff, and the ratio constructed with these data would not serve as a satisfactory proxy for the level of technology. An attempt has been made, however, to construct an index of the quality of production workers on the basis of the average number of years of education received (denoted by q_i). The exponent of production workers ($b \log q_i$) in the production function varies directly with this index.[16] In this way, differences in the quality of production workers across the states are taken into consideration in the estimated functions.[17]

The demand functions for output and for production workers have been discussed in the preceding sections. The "equilibrium" and actual demand functions for nonproduction employees are formulated in the same way as those for the production workers. The value added equation:

$$V_i = v \, P_i \, Q_i \tag{3.21}$$

The production function:

$$Q_i = a \, L_{pi}^{\,b \log q_i} \, L_{ni}^{\,c} \, K_{i,-1}^{\,e \log R_{i,-1}} \, u_i \tag{3.22}$$

The demand function for output:[18]

$$Q_i = d_i \, P_i^{-h} \tag{3.23}$$

[16]See equation (3.22) below. The exponent of L_p is now $b \log q_i$.

[17]When the difference in the quality of production worker is represented by q_i (see the preceding footnote), the equilibrium demand of labor, as given in equation (3.15), is also modified as in equation (3.24) below. The deviation from the profit-maximization position is assumed in equation (3.24) to be partially reflected in the term $r \, (\log q_i)^s$, r and s being constants, in addition to the terms fW_i^{-g}, kV_i^m and z_i included in (3.15).

[18]For the meaning of this particularly simple function, see the discussion in Section (1), of this chapter.

The "equilibrium" demand for production workers:[19]

$$b \log q_i \frac{V_i \left(1 - \frac{1}{h}\right)}{L_{pi}^*} = W_{pi} f_1 W_{pi}^{-g_1} k_1 V_i^{m_1} r(\log q_i)^s z_{pi} \quad (3.24)$$

The "equilibrium" demand for nonproduction employees:

$$c \frac{V_i \left(1 - \frac{1}{h}\right)}{L_{ni}^*} = W_{ni} f_2 W_{ni}^{-g_2} k_2 V_i^{m_2} z_{ni} \quad (3.25)$$

The actual demand for production workers:

$$\frac{L_{pi}}{L_{pi,-1}} = \left[\frac{L^*_{pi}}{L_{pi,-1}}\right]^{\lambda_p} \quad (3.26)$$

The actual demand for nonproduction employees:

$$\frac{L_{ni}}{L_{ni,-1}} = \left[\frac{L^*_{ni}}{L_{ni,-1}}\right]^{\lambda_n} \quad (3.27)$$

[19]See equation (3.15), and n. 16 and 17, above.

CHAPTER IV

Statistical Findings

ALTHOUGH the theoretical model formulated in equations (3.21)–(3.27) is the basis of our statistical estimation, it was anticipated that the data at our disposal would not in all instances yield plausible estimates for all the key parameters in which we are interested, even if our theoretical specification is essentially correct. The number of observations available is not large for all industries, and is very small for a number of them. A fairly strong tendency toward collinearity exists among most of the variables included in the model. Moreover, the labor quality index (q) we have used may not be appropriate or sufficiently good in certain instances. It was highly likely that, for some of the industries, the labor quality adjustment would not improve the results, and that even the attempt to disaggregate production and nonproduction workers would be a failure. It was to be expected that, given the data we have, the theoretical model (3.21)–(3.27) would not be applicable to all the industries, and in such cases alternative and simpler versions must be formulated. How, then, are we going to decide upon the proper version to use for each industry?

(1) *Decision among Alternative Specifications: The Conventional Practice and Statistical Decision Theory*

There are a number of alternative procedures to deal with this problem of decision among alternative specifications. We may follow what is perhaps still the conventional practice in econometric studies: making a series of "experimental" fittings to revised theoretical formulations after the regression results are observed for a given theoretical specification. In each round during the "experimental" fitting, the form of the functions and the variables entering into them would be modified in a way that would appear to remedy the unreasonable, implausible, or unsatisfactory results previously obtained. Very few econometricians, if any, have deviated from this procedure; and very often the result of only the most "successful" experiment is reported. When this method is used, the theoretical analysis made prior to the "experimental" fitting is, in view of the repeated revisions, rather unimportant; and since we have only one sample to work on, the conventional measurements of reliability become almost meaningless.

A better approach to this difficult problem is to apply statistical decision theory. It is indeed regrettable that the application of decision theory to econometric studies has barely made a start, especially for simultaneous equation models. Fisher [21] has shown that the appropriate estimating procedure differs according to the purpose of the model, which may be that of making predictions or that of formulating policy decisions in which some of the exogenous variables are under the control of the decision maker. In the former case, the optimum[1] estimates of the coefficients in the reduced form equations, under the assumption of equal prior probability of the unknown parameters and the usual assumptions about the disturbances including normality and independence, are equivalent to the classical least-squares estimates. In cases where the model is used for policy decisions involving the determination of the magnitudes of instrument variables, the optimum estimates of the reduced form coefficients would involve the parameters in the policy maker's welfare function. Fisher [21] has demonstrated for certain simple cases that the optimum estimates are adjusted least-squares estimates, the complexity of the adjustments being dependent upon the complexity of the model, and that the closeness of these estimates to the classical least-squares estimates depend upon the accuracy of the least-squares estimates. Suppose that the classical least-squares estimates have large standard errors relative to the coefficients themselves. Then it can be shown that in effect the optimum estimates would

[1]Optimum in the sense that the expected loss of welfare of the forecaster or the decision maker is minimized.

61

diminish the importance—in the decision—of the instrument variables to which these coefficients are attached in accordance with the relative inaccuracy, and, in extreme cases, this would amount to dropping these variables entirely. Thus, a formal decision rule is provided for "ranking" and dropping variables in a way rather similar to the evaluation of the estimates on the basis of the standard errors. How the evaluation should be transformed from the reduced form equations to the structural relationships (to which our production functions and demand functions for labor belong) has not yet been formulated.[2]

The assumption of equal probability of the unknown parameters is the prior-ignorance Bayes solution. The Bayesian statistician would go further and specify prior distributions other than the uniform distribution. Methods have been formulated to use prior distributions in regression analysis. (See Theil [74] and Raiffa and Schlaifer [60].) The difficulty in using the Bayesian approach in our study is that there are no existing estimates of the elasticities of output separately with respect to production workers, nonproduction workers, capital, and technology (as embodied in capital) in manufacturing industries to serve as a reference for the formulation of the prior distributions. To use the relative shares as the estimated central tendencies, with relatively small variances and covariances arbitrarily specified, would weaken the attempt to evaluate the closeness of the performance of manufacturing industries to equilibrium under perfectly competitive conditions. The specification of relatively large variances and covariances would not be very helpful, as the results so obtained would not really be very different from what would be obtained without imposing prior restrictions.

(2) Decision among Alternative Specifications: The Procedure Followed in This Study

The approach we have followed is based upon the criteria of plausibility and sharpness, as suggested by Theil ([72], pp. 204–208). These criteria are applied to four alternative specifications

---

[2]Theil's ingeneous application of decision theory to econometric model-building also deals with the reduced form equations only, with a brief reference to the bearing on structural coefficients. See [72], pp. 443–444.

for each of the two-digit industries. The difference between the conventional practice of successive "experimental" fittings and the procedure followed here is that in our approach the alternative specifications are not tailored to suit a specific industry after the regression results are observed, that they are the same for all industries, and that all results, whether plausible or not, are presented.

Before the procedure for deciding upon a particular specification is discussed, the four alternative specifications are presented here.

The first specification is the model formulated in Chapter III, consisting of the equations (3.21)–(3.27). This system of equations can be reduced to the following three equations, determining V_i (value added), L_{pi} (production workers), and L_{ni} (nonproduction workers) in logarithms:[3]

Version I

$$\log V_i = \log A_i + b \log q_i \log L_{pi} + c \log L_{ni}$$
$$+ e \log R_{i,-1} \log K_{i,-1} + \log u_i \qquad (4.1)$$

where $\quad A_i = v \, a \, P_i \qquad (4.1a)$

$$\log L_{pi} = \lambda_p \log B_1 + (1 - \lambda_p) \log L_{pi,-1} + (1 - m_1) \lambda_p \log V_i$$
$$- (1 - g_1) \lambda_p \log W_{pi} + (1 - s) \lambda_p \log (\log q_i) - \lambda_p \log z_{pi} \qquad (4.2)$$

where $\quad B_1 = \dfrac{b}{f_1 \, k_1 \, r} \left(1 - \dfrac{1}{h}\right) \qquad (4.2a)$

$$\log L_{ni} = \lambda_n \log C_1 + (1 - \lambda_n) \log L_{ni,-1} + (1 - m_2) \lambda_n \log V_i$$
$$- (1 - g_2) \lambda_n \log W_{ni} - \lambda_n \log z_{ni} \qquad (4.3)$$

where $\quad C_1 = \dfrac{c}{f_2 \, k_2} \left(1 - \dfrac{1}{h}\right) \qquad (4.3a)$

The jointly dependent variables in (4.1)–(4.3) are $\log V_i$, $\log L_{pi}$, and $\log L_{ni}$. The predetermined variables are $\log q_i$,[4] $\log R_{i,-1}$,

[3]Equation (4.1), (4.2), and (4.3) are obtained by substituting equations (3.22), (3.24), and (3.25) respectively into equations (3.21), (3.26), and (3.27) and then taking logarithms.

[4]Since $\log q_i$ is multiplied by $\log L_{p1}$ in equation (4.1), the system of equations (4.1)–(4.3) is no longer linear. However, Chernoff and Rubin [11] have shown that, under certain conditions, the estimates obtained by applying the limited information maximum likelihood procedure as though the equations were linear

$\log K_{i,-1}$, $\log L_{pi,-1}$, $\log W_{pi}$, $\log (\log q_i)$, $\log L_{ni,-1}$, and $\log W_{ni}$. u_i z_{pi} and z_{ni} in (4.1), (4.2), and (4.3), respectively, are random disturbances.[5] All three equations satisfy the condition of identification,[6] and can therefore be estimated by the simultaneous equation estimating procedures. Equations (4.1)–(4.3) are estimated by both the single-equation least-squares and the two-stage least-squares in Section (3) below.

It should be noted that the variable P_i is in equation (4.1) through the term $\log A_i$. Data on P_i, the unit prices of the representative establishments in the different states, are not available in the census reports. Moreover, as has been discussed, the differentials among P_i in cross-section data on a given manufacturing industry for the same year are small, especially in the postwar years 1956 and 1957, when prices charged by different producers in the same industry tended to respond more or less uniformly to the wage rates in the industry. The presence of the unobserved and undetermined P_i in equation (4.1) is therefore not a serious problem. For if P_i were exactly the same across the states, then the presence of P_i in (4.1) would only affect the intercept of the equation on the $\log V_i$ axis, without affecting the estimates of b, c, and e. They are, of course, not exactly the same. However, if price differences were only limited to transportation costs, price elasticities would come into the picture in a limited way, and would not affect the estimated values of b, c, and e significantly. If price differences occurred mainly through product differentiation, it may be assumed that they were distributed randomly and independently of the explanatory variables included in the right side of (4.1) so that they would increase the unexplained variance of V_i, again without causing biases to the estimates of b, c, and e.[7]

---

are consistent. Since the two-stage least-squares and the limited information maximum likelihood estimators have the same asymptotical properties, the former are also consistent estimates of parameters in nonlinear system (4.1)–(4.3) under the same conditions. The two-stage least-squares procedure is used in this study.

[5] It is assumed that $E(u_i) = 1$ (and hence $E(\log u_i) = 0$), $E(u^2_i) = \sigma^2_u$ (σ^2_u being constant and finite), and $E(u_i\ u_j) = 0$, $i \neq j$. A similar set of assumptions is made for z_{pi} and for z_{ni}. In addition, the disturbances in the different equations for different i must be independent. The covariance of the disturbances in the different equations for the same i must be finite and constant, but need not be zero.

[6] See, for instance, Koopmans and Hood [47], p. 138.

[7] When price differentials exist significantly—for instance, in time series studies

Three additional versions, successively simpler than (4.1)–(4.3), have been specified. Similar to those in Version I, the equations in the three additional versions satisfy the condition of identification, and are estimated by both the single-equation least-squares and the two-stage least-squares methods in Section (3) below. Each version, however, will give less of the information desired.

Version II

In this version, the quality index of the production worker, q, is omitted; but the other features of Version I are retained.

$$\log V_i = \log A_i + b \log L_{pi} + c \log L_{ni} + e \log R_{i,-1} \log K_{i,-1} + \log u_i \qquad (4.4)$$

where A_i is the same as in (4.1a).

$$\log L_{pi} = \lambda_p \log B_2 + (1 - \lambda_p) \log L_{pi,-1} + (1 - m_1) \lambda_p \log V_i - (1 - g_1) \lambda_p \log W_{pi} - \lambda_p \log z_{pi} \qquad (4.5)$$

where $B_2 = \dfrac{b}{f_1 k_1} \left(1 - \dfrac{1}{h} \right)$ (4.5a)

$$\log L_{ni} = \lambda_n \log C_2 + (1 - \lambda_n) \log L_{ni,-1} + (1 - m_2) \lambda_n \log V_i - (1 - g_2) \lambda_n \log W_{ni} - \lambda_n \log z_{ni} \qquad (4.6)$$

where $C_2 = \dfrac{c}{f_2 k_2} \left(1 - \dfrac{1}{h} \right)$ (4.6a)

Version III

Production workers and nonproduction employees are not segregated in this version. The labor variable is represented by L, the sum of production and nonproduction workers.

$$\log V_i = \log A_i + b \log L_i + e \log R_{i,-1} \log K_{i,-1} + \log u_i \quad (4.7)$$

where A_i is the same as in (4.1a)

$$\log L_i = \lambda \log B_3 + (1 - \lambda) \log L_{i,-1} + (1 - m) \lambda \log V_i - (1 - g) \lambda \log W_i - \lambda \log z_i \qquad (4.8)$$

where $B_3 = \dfrac{b}{f k} \left(1 - \dfrac{1}{h} \right)$ (4.8a)

---

or in the case of cross section data on public utilities (say, electricity) the output of which cannot be bought in one region and resold in another—the price variable cannot be dealt with in the manner explained above. Estimates of b, c, and e would then be affected by the price elasticities.

Version IV

This version, the simplest among the four, is the conventional Cobb-Douglas function as follows:

$$\log V_i = \log A_i + b \log L_i + e \log K_{k,-1} \qquad (4.9)$$

where A_i is the same as in (4.1a). The demand for labor function is the same as (4.8), and is therefore not reproduced.

All four versions have the following two varieties: (a) the capital variable is represented by K, the "owned" capital; and (b) it is represented by K', the sum of owned and an estimated rented capital. In addition, each type is estimated by both the single-equation and the two-stage least-squares methods, together with the corresponding demand functions for the type of workers involved.

All these functions are estimated for all the industries, and they are all presented below regardless of their plausibility and reliability.

The decision upon a particular version for a given industry is based upon the following procedure.[8] The analysis always starts with the two-stage least-squares estimate of the production function in Version I, with K' as the capital variable. The two-stage version is preferred to the single-equation estimate, other things being equal, because of the simultaneity nature of the model. K' is preferred to K, as it includes all capital stock, whether owned or rented, even though the rented element is our rough estimate. The plausibility of this equation is evaluated in the following manner. The marginal "physical" product (in terms of value added) of production workers per dollar of wage cost (MPP_p) is defined as the marginal output valued at the prevailing unit price:

$$MPP_p = \frac{b (\log q) V}{L_p W_p}. \qquad (4.10)$$

The marginal revenue product of production workers per dollar of wage cost (ϕ_p) is obtained by adjusting MPP_p by the elasticity of demand for the output of the industry (h)[9] as follows:

---

[8]The following discussion will be more easily understood if the reader would study the application of the procedure to the food products industry (see Section (3) (i) below) as a cross-reference while he is reading this section.

[9]For a discussion of this elasticity, see Chapter III, Section (1).

$$\phi_p = MPP_p \left(1 - \frac{1}{h} \right) \qquad (4.11)$$

or

$$h = \frac{MPP_p}{MPP_p - \phi_p}. \qquad (4.12)$$

For given values of MPP_p derived from the production function and the given wage rate, the magnitude of the demand elasticity for output depends upon that of ϕ_p. If the employment of production workers is adjusted to its equilibrium level (i.e., when profits are maximized with respect to variations in production workers), ϕ_p is equal to unity. Overemployment exists if ϕ_p is less than unity, and vice versa. The reasonableness of the combinations of the possible magnitudes of h and ϕ_p represents one important indication of the plausibility of the production function obtained. It will be shown in the analysis of the production functions for the different industries in Section (3) (i)–(xv) below that it is often not possible to get any plausible combinations of the values of h and ϕ_p from a given function, and this failure may constitute a sufficient ground for discarding the function.[10] In the cases where plausible combinations of magnitudes of h and ϕ_p exist, we can then proceed further to examine the acceptability of the function by estimating the extent of the adjustment required to achieve the profit-maximizing position under the conditions prevailing in 1957, and to compare this equilibrium adjustment with the estimated speed of adjustment from 1956 to 1957 given in the demand function for production workers and the actual changes in the employment of this category of workers during these years.

While throwing light on the plausibility of the equation concerned, nonetheless, this comparison involves much difficulty. By itself it cannot be considered as conclusive ground for accepting or rejecting the equation. The coefficient of the speed of adjustment is estimated on the 1956–1957 data, and thus indicates the rapidity of the process of adjustment from 1956 to 1957. On the other hand, the adjustment required to achieve the profit-maxi-

[10]In fact, for two industries, it has not been possible to obtain any plausible functions at all. See Section (3) of this chapter and Appendix IV.

mizing position is estimated under the conditions (wage rates, productivity, etc.) prevailing in 1957, and would be reflected more in the change from 1957 to 1958 than in that from 1956 to 1957. The estimated adjustment obtained by multiplying the 1956–1957 speed coefficient by the equilibrium adjustment required under conditions prevailing during 1957 is therefore a hybrid result. It cannot be expected to be very close either to the actual change during 1956–1957 or 1957–1958. In the following analysis, the estimated adjustment is compared with the actual change during 1956–1957. The year 1958 was one of recession. Much of the change during 1957–1958 took place on account of cyclical conditions in the economy as a whole and was not the result of the working of factors directly concerned with the respective industries considered. In view of the difficulties involved in the comparison of one-year changes, a longer term adjustment for 1956–1960 is also analyzed.[11] This longer term analysis was not relied upon, however, to decide upon the particular version of the production function accepted, except for the transportation equipment and instruments industries, where the short term comparison yields contradictory results despite the reasonableness of the magnitudes obtained for h and ϕ.[12]

The extent of the adjustment required to achieve the profit-maximizing position is derived as follows. From equation (4.11), (4.10), and (3.21)–(3.23), we have:

$$\phi_p = \left(1 - \frac{1}{h}\right) b \ (\log q) \ va^{(1-1/h)} d^{1/h} \ L_p^{b(\log q) \ (1-1/h) \ -1}$$
$$\cdot L_n^{c \ (1-1/h)} \ K^{e \ (\log R)(1-1/h)} \ W_p^{-1}.$$

Since we are now dealing with adjustments in L_p only, and since W_p is assumed as given, L_n, K, and W_p are considered as constants at this point. In logarithmic form, the above equation then becomes:

$$\left[b \left(\log q\right) \left(1 - \frac{1}{h}\right) - 1 \right] \log L_p + \text{constant} = \log \phi_p.$$

---

[11]See Section (4) (iv) of this chapter.

[12]It should be pointed out that the longer term analysis generally supports the plausibility of the production functions for the other industries also. See Section (4) (iv) of this chapter.

Differentiating, we have:

$$\frac{d\,L_p}{L_p} = \frac{d\,\phi_p}{\phi_p} \bigg/ b\left(\log q\right)\left(1 - \frac{1}{h}\right) - 1. \tag{4.13}$$

Thus, the proportional change in L_p required for a given proportional change in ϕ_p can be estimated approximately but conveniently from equation (4.13).

If the picture so obtained for the production workers appears plausible, we can then use the elasticity of demand for the output of the industry so determined to evaluate the marginal revenue product per dollar of salary cost (ϕ_n) of the nonproduction workers. It is easily seen that

$$\frac{\partial V}{\partial L_n} = \phi_n = \frac{c\left(1 - \dfrac{1}{h}\right)}{\dfrac{L_n\,W_n}{V}}. \tag{4.14}$$

From (4.11), we have:

$$\phi_n = \frac{c}{\dfrac{L_n\,W_n}{V}}\,\frac{\phi_p}{MPP_p}. \tag{4.15}$$

The adjustment required in the employment of overhead labor to attain the profit maximization position can then be evaluated in the same way as that for production workers. In other words,

$$\frac{dL_n}{L_n} = \frac{d\,\phi_n}{\phi_n} \bigg/ c\left(1 - \frac{1}{h}\right) - 1. \tag{4.16}$$

To examine the plausibility of the production function concerned with respect to nonproduction workers, the estimated ϕ_n and the adjustment required for achieving the profit-maximization position are then compared with the estimated speed of adjustment from 1956 to 1957 in the demand function for nonproduction workers and with the employment situation of this category of employees during these years.

Finally, the plausibility of the regression coefficient of the capital variable must be studied. It has been shown that the quantity component of the marginal productivity of capital is

$$e \, (\log R) \, \frac{V}{K} \text{ and the technology component is } e \, \frac{100 - R}{R} \, (\log K) \, \frac{V}{K}.\text{[13]}$$

The corresponding elasticities are therefore as follows:

$$\text{capital-output elasticity} = e \log R, \tag{4.17}$$

$$\text{technology-output elasticity} = e \, \frac{100 - R}{R} \log K. \tag{4.18}$$

Letting T denote property tax and D depreciation allowance, then the marginal revenue product of capital, including both the effects of a change in the physical quantity of capital and the concomitant change in technology as gross capital increases, is equal to

$$\phi_k = \left[e \log R + e \, \frac{100 - R}{R} \log K \right] \frac{V - T - D}{K} \left(1 - \frac{1}{h} \right). \tag{4.19}$$

The plausibility of these elasticity and productivity estimates for a given industry will be evaluated on the basis of the situation prevailing in 1957 and in relation to corresponding estimates for the other industries.

Similar analysis is also made for Versions II, III, and IV. Other things being equal, preference is given to the version yielding a greater amount of information about the various elasticities and productivities (i.e., Version I is preferred to II, II to III, and III to IV).

(3) Production Functions and Demand Functions for Labor for Individual Industries[14]

The procedure outlined in the preceding section is used to decide upon the particular version of production function and

[13]See Chapter III, equation (3.14). All terms in this equation are now multiplied by P so that Q is replaced by V in the above expression.

[14]Acceptable results have been obtained for the 15 industries presented in this section. All versions of the results for the textile mill products and the furniture and fixture industries are implausible. They are given in Appendix IV so that research workers in this field need not repeat this effort. The three industries for which production functions have not been estimated are "tobacco manufactures,"

demand functions for labor for each of the two-digit industries. The explanation of the application of the procedure and the considerations involved is given in greater detail for the first industry (food and kindred products in subsection (i) below), as the reasoning in the case of the other industries is quite similar.

Estimated production functions for all four versions are presented for all industries at the end of the subsections dealing with these industries, respectively. The production functions are numbered by version (roman numerals I, II, III, and IV), by the capital variable included (A for K and B for K'), and by the estimating procedure used (1 for single-equation least-squares and 2 for two-stage least-squares).[15] The demand functions for labor are given only for the version of the production function accepted.

The data for the variables included in the various versions of our model are computed from data given in census [6], [7], and [8] as follows:

V_i : Value added per establishment in state i in thousands of dollars in 1957.

L_{pi} and $L_{pi, -1}$: Employment of production workers per establishment in state i in thousands of man-hours in 1957 and 1956, respectively.

L_{ni} and $L_{ni, -1}$: Employment of nonproduction employees per establishment in state i in thousands of man-hours in 1957 and 1956, respectively.[16]

L_i and $L_{i, -1}$: Respectively equal to $L_{pi} + L_{ni}$, and $L_{pi, -1} + L_{ni, -1}$.

$K_{i, -1}$: Gross book value of plant and equipment per establishment in state i in thousand dollars at the beginning of 1957.[17]

"printing and publishing," and "miscellaneous". For the first and third industries, the number of states for which data on gross and net capital are available is too small to make the computation. Production functions have not been estimated for the second, because it is difficult to interpret the economic meaning of value added in publishing.

[15] The estimated constant terms in the functions obtained are omitted from the presentation.

[16] L_{ni} and $L_{ni, -1}$ are expressed in man-hours in order to combine them with L_{pi} and $L_{pi, -1}$ to get $L_{i, -1}$ (see below). It is assumed that a nonproduction employee worked 2,000 hours a year.

[17] For the use of book value to represent capital, see the discussion, p. 133.

$K'_{i, -1}$: $K_{i, -1}$ plus the corresponding data on rental payments for plant and equipment, after dividing the latter by 0.05 (i.e. an assumed discount rate of 5%).

$R_{i, -1}$: The ratio of net to gross book value of plant and equipment in state i in per cent at the beginning of 1957.

W_i, W_{pi}, W_{ni} : Average wage rate in state i in 1957 in dollars per hour respectively for L_i, L_{pi}, and L_{ni}.

q_i : Median school years completed by persons 25 years old and over in state i in 1960 in index numbers (the average of all states = 10).

(i) Food and Kindred Products

The numerical contents of all four equations in Version I are very close. Equation (I,B,2), the two-stage least-squares estimate of the production function with K'_g representing capital, is then selected as the first equation to be analyzed.

The marginal "physical" product (i.e., marginal product valued at the prevailing prices of output) of production workers per dollar of wage cost was $1.11.[18] If it is assumed that this industry had been able to adjust to the profit-maximizing position with respect to the employment of production workers in 1957 so that the marginal revenue product of production workers is $1.00 per dollar of wage cost (i.e., $\phi_p = 1$), the implied elasticity of demand for the output of the industry would be 9.9.[19] This appears to be too high. The demand elasticity for output is in the range of 4.8 to 3.6, if ϕ_p is specified within the range of 0.9 to 0.8.[20] The postwar development of packaged and precooked manufactured food has been phenomenal. In a generally "affluent" society in which the demand for food purely for the satisfaction of physical needs is no longer a problem for the great majority of people, the competitive efforts of the manufacturers of food products,

---

[18] On the basis of equation (4.10):
$$MPP_p = \frac{\dfrac{b \log q}{L_p \, W_p}}{V} = \frac{(0.315)(0.997)}{0.282} = 1.113.$$

[19] According to equation (4.12):
$$h = \frac{MPP_p}{MPP_p - \phi_p} = \frac{1.113}{0.113} = 9.85.$$

[20] Computed on the basis of equation (4.12) in a way similar to the preceding footnote.

even for staple products, are directed mainly toward the reduction of housewives' kitchen work and to the improvement of taste and appearance of food products. Soft drinks, wines, liquors, and candies are clearly in the classes of semi-luxury or luxury goods. Since the late 1950's, manufactured food products have been very much in competition with fashionable clothing, travel, entertainment, and housing comforts for the consumer's dollar. It does not appear implausible that a reduction of 1 per cent in the prices of manufactured food product would increase the quantities demanded in the neighborhood of 4 per cent. ϕ_p is therefore specified at 0.85, with the corresponding elasticity of demand for the output of the industry estimated at 4.2.[21]

With the marginal revenue product of production workers (ϕ_p) equal to 0.85, the employment of production workers must be reduced by approximately 23 per cent[22] for adjustment to the profit-maximizing position under the conditions prevailing during 1957. Such an adjustment would take time, even if the management were absolutely convinced of the feasibility and the profitability of this change. The management may not have been entirely convinced; in fact, it may not have been fully aware of the possibilities for greater profits. In addition, there are always inertia and the unwillingness to take the responsibility of making substantial changes. Finally, and certainly not least, there are the unions to be considered and dealt with. When the slow speed of adjustment is taken into consideration ($1 - 0.84 = 0.16$, see equation V_p below), the employment of production workers would decline only by about 3.7 per cent (i.e., 23×0.16). The employment of production workers (man-hours) actually fell by about 3.1 per cent from 1956 to 1957.

With the demand elasticity for output estimated at 4.2, the marginal revenue product of nonproduction workers was $1.55

[21] $h = \dfrac{1.113}{1.113 - 0.85} = 4.232$ (see n. 19, above.)

[22] According to equation (4.13):

$$\frac{\Delta L_p}{L_p} = \frac{(1 - \phi_p)/\phi_p}{b\,(\log q)\left(1 - \dfrac{1}{h}\right) - 1} = \frac{0.176}{-0.759} = -0.232.$$

73

per dollar of salary costs,[23] and an adjustment toward the equilibrium position would, under the conditions prevailing in 1957, call for an expansion of 51 per cent[24] of this category of employees. The estimated coefficient of the speed of adjustment in the demand function for nonproduction workers from 1956 to 1957 is very low (0.04) (see equation V_n, below). The actual increase would only be about 2 per cent (i.e., 51 $\times$ 0.04). The expansion that had actually taken place was in the neighborhood of 2.6 per cent.

The capital-output and the technology-output elasticities are respectively to 0.53[25] and 0.76[26] in 1957. The marginal revenue product of capital, including both the quantity and the technology components, is estimated at $1.02 per dollar invested before business income tax.[27] In an industry where the nature of output was undergoing changes almost revolutionary in nature, these figures do not appear to be unreasonable. While we have not made an estimate for the speed of adjustment in the demand function for

[23]According to equation (4.15):
$$\phi_n = \frac{c \quad \phi_p}{\dfrac{L_n W_n MPP_p}{V}} = \frac{(0.397) \quad (0.85)}{(0.196) \quad (1.113)} = 1.547.$$

[24]On the basis of equation (4.16):
$$\frac{\Delta L_n}{L_n} = \frac{(1 - \phi_n)/\phi_n}{c\left(1 - \dfrac{1}{h}\right) - 1} = \frac{-0.354}{-0.697} = 0.51.$$

One should not be surprised by this apparently large percentage adjustment. The optimum adjustment required for production workers was −23 per cent, but the number of production workers (1.2 million in 1957) was much greater than that of nonproduction workers (0.5 million 1957). Moreover, as explained below, the estimated speed of adjustment was very small.

[25]According to equation (4.17):
e log R = (0.309) (1.712) = 0.529.

[26]According to equation (4.18):
$$e \frac{100 - R}{R} \log K = (0.309) (2.445) = 0.756.$$

[27]According to equation (4.19):
$$\left[e \log R + \frac{100 - R}{R} \log K\right] \frac{V - T - D}{K} \left(1 - \frac{1}{h}\right)$$
$$= (0.309) (4.305) \frac{(0.85)}{1.113} = 1.02.$$

Production Functions

Version I.

(I,A,1) $\log V = 0.307 \log q \log L_p + 0.433 \log L_n + 0.302 \log R \log K_g$
          (0.086)   (0.070)   (0.048) $R^2 = 0.89$

(I,A,2)   0.299   +0.421   +0.307
          (0.096)   (0.077)   (0.053)   0.86

(I,B,1)   0.323   +0.408   +0.304 $\log R \log K'_g$
          (0.092)   (0.074)   (0.055)   0.87

(I,B,2)   0.315   +0.397   +0.309
          (0.100)   (0.081)   (0.059)   0.85

Version II.

(II,A,1) $\log V = 0.685 \log L_p + 0.274 \log L_n + 0.208 \log R \log K_g$
          (0.139)   (0.077)   (0.052) $R^2 = 0.91$

(II,A,2)   0.692   +0.256   +0.209   0.89
          (0.161)   (0.089)   (0.060)

(II,B,1)   0.733   +0.244   +0.195 $\log R \log K'_g$
          (0.147)   (0.080)   (0.059)   0.90

(II,B,2)   0.743   +0.228   +0.195
          (0.165)   (0.088)   (0.065)   0.88

Version III.

(III,A,1) $\log V = 0.916 \log L + 0.234 \log R \log K_g$
          (0.087)   (0.042) $R^2 = 0.91$

(III,A,2)   0.894   +0.241
          (0.100)   (0.048)   0.88

(III,B,1)   0.908   +0.237 $\log R \log K'_g$
          (0.095)   (0.048)   0.89

(III,B,2)   0.891   +0.242
          (0.106)   (0.053)   0.87

Version IV.

(IV,A,1) $\log V = 0.536 \log L + 0.618 \log K_g$
          (0.139)   (0.112) $R^2 = 0.90$

(IV,A,2)   0.467   +0.665
          (0.154)   (0.123)   0.89

(IV,B,1)   0.401   +0.724 $\log K'_g$
          (0.176)   (0.146)   0.89

(IV,B,2)   0.336   +0.773
          (0.190)   (0.156)   0.89

Demand Functions for Labor

(V_p): $\log L_p = 0.837 \log L_{p,-1} + 0.153 \log V - 0.210 \log W_p$
              (0.123)   (0.112)   (0.085)

          $+ 0.390 \log (\log q)$ $R^2 = 0.98$
              (0.239)

(V_n): $\log L_n = 0.963 \log L_{n,-1} + 0.103 \log V - 0.197 \log W_n$
              (0.047)   (0.057)   (0.107) $R^2 = 0.97$

capital, the experience we have gained with respect to the demand functions for labor would indicate that this coefficient was probably also very low during 1956 and 1957.

All four equations in Version II are close in their numerical contents, but they yield implausible estimates for the key parameters. With ϕ_p specified in the range of unity to 0.8, the marginal revenue product of nonproduction workers would be $0.44 per dollar of salary cost or lower.[28] This would indicate very great overemployment of nonproduction workers, a rather unlikely situation. Version II is therefore discarded.

The regression coefficients of the capital variables in the four equations in Version III are fairly close to those in Version I, and the labor coefficient is not greatly different from the sum of the two labor coefficients in the equations in Version I. Version III is disregarded because it yields no separate information on production and nonproduction workers.

A comparison of Versons I and IV indicate that the omission of the proxy variable for technology and the aggregation of L_p and L_n in Version IV have resulted in an overestimated capital-output elasticity. However, estimates of the labor-output elasticity in Version IV is smaller than the sum of the two labor-output elasticities in Version I.

(ii) *Apparel and Related Products*

In Version I, the two-stage least-squares equation (I,B,2) is selected as the basis of analysis first, because the regression coefficient for the capital variable (as represented by K') is substantially more significant than those in (I,A,1) or (I,A,2), where K is used as the capital variable. The implied demand elasticity for output falls within a reasonable range, if ϕ_p is within the range 0.85 to 0.95. ϕ_p is specified at 0.9, and the corresponding demand elasticity is 4.8. Similar to manufactured food products, the competitive efforts of the manufacturers of apparel in this country are directed toward style and comfort; and domestically produced apparel competes not only with other categories of consumption expenditures such as travel, entertainment, and fine food, but with im-

---

[28]The computations involved are similar to those explained in connection with the analysis of Version I.

ported apparel in the domestic market, and with foreign products abroad. A change in the neighborhood of 4.8 per cent in the quantities demanded in response to a 1 per cent change in prices is by no means implausible.

Under the conditions prevailing in 1957 and with the marginal revenue product of production workers specified at 0.9, an adjustment to the profit-maximizing level of employment for this category of production workers would require a 20 per cent reduction. The estimated coefficient of the speed of adjustment from 1956 to 1957 in the demand function for production workers is 0.25. (See equation V_p, below, $1 - 0.747 = 0.253$.) The estimated reduction that would have been carried out is 5 per cent (i.e., 20×0.25). The actual reduction of production workers, however, was only 2 per cent. While the difference between the estimated and the actual reductions is substantial, it must be emphasized that the estimated adjustment required to achieve the profit-maximizing position was made on the basis of the conditions prevailing during 1957, whereas the actual adjustment given above was what happened from 1956 to 1957.[29]

The estimated marginal revenue product of nonproduction workers corresponding to a demand elasticity for output of 4.8 is $1.68 per dollar of salary cost. An adjustment in the employment of this group of workers to the profit-maximizing position under the conditions prevailing in 1957 would call for an increase of 50 per cent. The estimated coefficient of the speed of adjustment from 1956 to 1957 in the demand function for nonproduction workers is only 0.1 (see equation V_n below). The estimated expansion of the employment of this category of workers is therefore 5 per cent. The actual expansion was about 3 per cent. The comment given for the difference between the estimated and the actual reduction in production workers is equally applicable here to the expansion of nonproduction workers.

Under the above assumptions, the capital-output and the technology-output elasticities are respectively 0.20 and 0.24. The marginal revenue product of capital, including both the quantity and the technology components, is estimated at $0.74 per dollar

[29]See the discussion on pp. 67–68, above.

Production Functions

Version I.

$(I,A,1)$ $\log V = 0.547 \log q \log L_p + 0.316 \log L_n + 0.064 \log R \log K_g$
$\quad\quad\quad\quad (0.130) \quad\quad\quad\quad\quad (0.114) \quad\quad\quad\quad (0.049) \quad R^2 = 0.94$

$(I,A,2)$ $\quad\quad\quad 0.581 \quad\quad\quad\quad\quad\quad +0.288 \quad\quad\quad\quad +0.065$
$\quad\quad\quad\quad (0.136) \quad\quad\quad\quad\quad (0.119) \quad\quad\quad\quad (0.050) \quad\quad\quad 0.94$

$(I,B,1)$ $\quad\quad\quad 0.557 \quad\quad\quad\quad\quad\quad +0.290 \quad\quad\quad\quad +0.110 \log R \log K'_g$
$\quad\quad\quad\quad (0.120) \quad\quad\quad\quad\quad (0.113) \quad\quad\quad\quad (0.066) \quad\quad\quad 0.94$

$(I,B,2)$ $\quad\quad\quad 0.591 \quad\quad\quad\quad\quad\quad +0.258 \quad\quad\quad\quad +0.114$
$\quad\quad\quad\quad (0.125) \quad\quad\quad\quad\quad (0.117) \quad\quad\quad\quad (0.068) \quad\quad\quad 0.94$

Version II.

$(II,A,1)$ $\log V = 0.372 \log L_p + 0.351 \log L_n + 0.079 \log K \log K_g$
$\quad\quad\quad\quad (0.089) \quad\quad\quad\quad (0.111) \quad\quad\quad\quad (0.048) \quad R^2 = -.94$

$(II,A,2)$ $\quad\quad\quad 0.385 \quad\quad\quad\quad +0.328 \quad\quad\quad\quad +0.083$
$\quad\quad\quad\quad (0.094) \quad\quad\quad\quad (0.118) \quad\quad\quad\quad (0.050) \quad\quad\quad 0.94$

$(II,B,1)$ $\quad\quad\quad 0.379 \quad\quad\quad\quad +0.357 \quad\quad\quad\quad +0.107 \log R \log K'_g$
$\quad\quad\quad\quad (0.089) \quad\quad\quad\quad (0.113) \quad\quad\quad\quad (0.070) \quad\quad\quad 0.94$

$(II,B,2)$ $\quad\quad\quad 0.393 \quad\quad\quad\quad +0.333 \quad\quad\quad\quad +0.113$
$\quad\quad\quad\quad (0.094) \quad\quad\quad\quad (0.120) \quad\quad\quad\quad (0.073) \quad\quad\quad 0.93$

Version III.

$(III,A,1)$ $\log V = 0.549 \log L + 0.141 \log R \log K_g$
$\quad\quad\quad\quad (0.103) \quad\quad\quad (0.045) \quad\quad\quad\quad\quad\quad\quad R^2 = 0.92$

$(III,A,2)$ $\quad\quad\quad 0.539 \quad\quad\quad +0.144$
$\quad\quad\quad\quad (0.109) \quad\quad\quad (0.047) \quad\quad\quad\quad\quad\quad\quad 0.91$

$(III,B,1)$ $\quad\quad\quad 0.562 \quad\quad\quad +0.200 \log R \log K'_g$
$\quad\quad\quad\quad (0.101) \quad\quad\quad (0.065) \quad\quad\quad\quad\quad\quad\quad 0.92$

$(III,B,2)$ $\quad\quad\quad 0.553 \quad\quad\quad +0.204$
$\quad\quad\quad\quad (0.107) \quad\quad\quad (0.068) \quad\quad\quad\quad\quad\quad\quad 0.91$

Version IV.

$(IV,A,1)$ $\log V = 0.501 \log L + 0.289 \log K_g$
$\quad\quad\quad\quad (0.102) \quad\quad\quad (0.080) \quad\quad\quad\quad\quad\quad\quad 0.93$

$(IV,A,2)$ $\quad\quad\quad 0.491 \quad\quad\quad +0.295$
$\quad\quad\quad\quad (0.108) \quad\quad\quad (0.084) \quad\quad\quad\quad\quad\quad\quad 0.92$

$(IV,B,1)$ $\quad\quad\quad 0.502 \quad\quad\quad +0.436 \log K'_g$
$\quad\quad\quad\quad (0.100) \quad\quad\quad (0.118) \quad\quad\quad\quad\quad\quad\quad 0.93$

$(IV,B,2)$ $\quad\quad\quad 0.493 \quad\quad\quad +0.445$
$\quad\quad\quad\quad (0.106) \quad\quad\quad (0.124) \quad\quad\quad\quad\quad\quad\quad 0.92$

Demand Functions for Labor

(V_p) $\log L_p = 0.747 \log L_{p,-1} + 0.175 \log V - 0.462 \log W_p$
$\quad\quad\quad\quad\quad (0.108) \quad\quad\quad\quad\quad (0.096) \quad\quad\quad\quad (0.195)$
$\quad\quad\quad\quad\quad\quad\quad\quad\quad\quad\quad\quad\quad\quad\quad\quad - 0.569 \log (\log q) \quad\quad R^2 = 0.99$
$\quad\quad\quad\quad\quad\quad\quad\quad\quad\quad\quad\quad\quad\quad\quad\quad\quad (0.627)$

(V_n) $\log L_n = 0.901 \log L_{n,-1} + 0.975 \log V - 0.051 \log W_n$
$\quad\quad\quad\quad\quad (0.093) \quad\quad\quad\quad\quad (0.105) \quad\quad\quad\quad (0.021) \quad\quad R^2 = 0.99$

invested before business income tax. These figures are all lower than the corresponding ones for the food product industries. While there has been substantial technological change in the replacement of natural fibers by synthetic products as the input of the apparel industry, the nature of the output of this industry perhaps did not undergo as radical a change as precooked and packaged food products.

All equations in Version II are discarded because the implied estimates for the elasticity of demand for the output of the industry are unreasonable. Take equation (II,B,2) as an example. The implied demand elasticity is negative if the market for production workers is assumed to be in equilibrium ($\phi_p = 1$); and it remains negative if ϕ_p is specified at 0.9.

Version III is rejected also because the implied estimates for the demand elasticity for output are implausible. In addition, Version I is superior to Version III in any case, because it disaggregates employment into production and nonproduction workers.

The capital-output elasticity in Version IV appears to be a gross overestimate because this equation omits technological effects and because of the aggregation of labor input.

(iii) *Lumber and Wood Products*

Version I and equations (II,B,1) and (II,B,2) of Version II are discarded because the coefficients of log L_N are negative. Equations (II,A,1) and (II,A,2) are also rejected because the implied estimates for the demand elasticity for output and the marginal revenue product for production workers are implausible. Take equation (II,A,2) as an illustration. The implied elasticity of demand for output is negative if the market for production workers is assumed to be in equilibrium. The implied elasticity is as large as 13 if ϕ_p is assumed at 0.9. It is rejected on the further ground that, with ϕ_p equal to 0.9, the corresponding implied marginal revenue product for the nonproduction worker is as small as 0.65. There is no reason to believe that there was overemployment of this category of workers, because the number of nonproduction workers increased between 1956 and 1957.

Version III gives plausible estimates for all the parameters. With ϕ specified at 0.8, the implied elasticity of demand for the

79

Production Functions

Version I.

$(I,A,1) \log V = 0.773 \log q \log L_p - 0.065 \log L_n + 0.133 \log R \log K_g$

	(0.269)	(0.251)	(0.075) $R^2 = 0.90$
(I,A,2)	0.829	−0.105	+0.124
	(0.275)	(0.269)	(0.074) 0.90
(I,B,1)	0.888	−0.105	+0.103 $\log R \log K'_g$
	(0.261)	(0.272)	(0.076) 0.89
(I,B,2)	0.941	−0.142	+0.095
	(0.262)	(0.287)	(0.075) 0.89

Version II.

$(II,A,1) \log V = 0.524 \log L_p + 0.068 \log L_N + 0.224 \log R \log K_g$

	(0.365)	(0.304)	(0.078) $R^2 = 0.84$
(II,A,2)	0.536	+0.107	+0.216
	(0.379)	(0.352)	(0.079) 0.85
(II,B,1)	0.724	−0.029	+0.198 $\log R \log K'_g$
	(0.352)	(0.337)	(0.080) 0.83
(II,B,2)	0.753	−0.020	+0.192
	(0.364)	(0.397)	(0.081) 0.83

Version III.

$(III,A,1) \log V = 0.588 \log L + 0.224 \log R \log K_g$

	(0.339)	(0.074)	$R^2 = 0.84$
(III,A,2)	0.630	+0.217	
	(0.343)	(0.074)	0.85
(III,B,1)	0.747	+0.191 $\log R \log K'_g$	
	(0.333)	(0.073)	0.82
(III,B,2)	0.792	+0.183	
	(0.336)	(0.073)	0.83

Version IV.

$(IV,A,1) \log V = 0.443 \log L + 0.462 \log K_g$

	(0.296)	(0.114)	0.89
(IV,A,2)	0.481	+0.451	
	(0.300)	(0.114)	0.89
(IV,B,1)	0.623	+0.398 $\log K'_g$	
	(0.301)	(0.117)	
(IV,B,2)	0.664	+0.386	
	(0.305)	(1.117)	0.86

Demand Function for Labor

$(V) \log L = 0.921 \log L_{-1} + 0.060 \log V - 0.072 \log W$

$$\quad\ (0.251) \qquad\quad (0.265) \qquad\quad (0.273) \qquad R^2 = 0.98$$

output of the industry is 3.1. An adjustment of employment to the profit-maximizing position under the condition prevailing during 1957 would require a reduction of employment by 54 per cent. The estimated coefficient of the speed of adjustment from 1956 to 1957 in the demand function for labor is 0.08. (See equation V below, $1 - 0.921 = 0.079$.) The reduction of employment is therefore estimated at 4.3 per cent (i.e., 54×0.08) under the condition prevailing during 1957. The actual decline, however, was as high as 7.4 per cent.

The capital-output and technology-output elasticities are both a little over 0.3, with the marginal revenue product of capital estimated at 0.42.

Similar to the preceding two industries, the capital-output elasticity is overestimated by the equations in Version IV.

(iv) *Pulp, Paper and Products*

The implausibly small regression coefficients of the log q log L_p variable in all the equations of Version I are such that the elasticity of the output of this industry would be negative for any reasonable magnitudes of ϕ_p. This version is therefore discarded.

Version II yields reasonable estimates. The demand elasticity for the output of the industry is within a plausible range, if ϕ_p is specified to be in the interval 0.85 to 0.95. This elasticity, not very sensitive to different values of ϕ_p in this range, is equal to 2.6, if ϕ_p is assumed to be 0.9. As of 1957, the adjustment required in the employment of production workers to achieve the profit-maximizing position is a reduction of 16.5 per cent. The estimated speed of adjustment in the demand function for production workers being 0.11, the estimated reduction is 1.8 per cent. The actual decline of production workers was 2.6 per cent from 1956 to 1957.

The marginal revenue product of nonproduction workers is estimated at $1.22 per dollar of salary cost. The required adjustment to the profit-maximization position is an expansion of 21.4 per cent for this category of workers. We have failed to get any reasonable estimate for the speed of adjustment for this group of workers. The actual expansion from 1956 to 1957 was 3.8 per cent. The coefficient of the speed of adjustment was therefore perhaps around 0.18.

The capital-output and technology-output elasticities are respectively 0.28 and 0.37. The estimated marginal revenue product of

81

Production Functions

Version I.

(I,A,1) $\log V = 0.074 \log q \log L_p + 0.597 \log L_N + 0.220 \log R \log K_g$
             (0.119)   (0.107)   (0.034) $R^2 = 0.97$

(I,A,2)   0.039   +0.646   0.217
             (0.111)   (0.101)   (0.131)   0.97

(I,B,1)   0.090   +0.600   0.229 $\log R \log K'_g$
             (0.128)   (0.116)   (0.039)   0.96

(I,B,2)   0.056   +0.65   +0.225
             (0.119)   (0.109)   (0.037)   0.97

Version II.

(II,A,1) $\log V = 0.540 \log L_p + 0.264 \log L_N + 0.152 \log R \log K_g$
               (0.115)   (0.101)   (0.027) $R^2 = 0.98$

(II,A,2)   0.484   +0.317   +0.155
              (0.122)   (0.108)   (0.028)   0.98

(II,B,1)   0.593   +0.222   +0.157 $\log R \log K'_g$
              (0.109)   (0.100)   (0.028)   0.98

(II,B,2)   0.547   +0.270   +0.159
              (0.115)   (0.107)   (0.028)   0.98

Version III.

(III,A,1) $\log V = 0.800 \log L + 0.145 \log R \log K_g$
                (0.070)   (0.026) $R^2 = 0.98$

(III,A,2)   0.795   +0.146
               (0.074)   (0.028)   0.98

(III,B,1)   0.808   +0.153 $\log R \log K'_g$
               (0.067)   (0.027)   0.98

(III,B,2)   0.805   +0.154
               (0.071)   (0.028)   0.98

Version IV.

(IV,A,1) $\log V = 0.669 \log L + 0.345 \log K_g$
               (0.085)   (0.057)   0.99

(IV,A,2)   0.656   +0.353
              (0.092)   (0.062)   0.98

(IV,B,1)   0.669   +0.374 $\log K'_g$
              (0.082)   (0.060)   0.99

(IV,B,2)   0.659   +0.381
              (0.088)   (0.064)   0.98

Demand Functions for Labor

(V_p) $\log L_p = 0.889 \log L_{p-1} + 0.089 \log V - 0.100 \log W_p$
             (0.056)   (0.054) $R^2 = 0.99$

(V_n) $\log L_n = 0.999 \log L_{n-1} + 0.045 \log V + 0.018 \log W_n$
                                    $R^2 = 0.99$

capital including both the quantity and the technology component, $0.30 per dollar invested before business income tax, is not large.

Version III yields estimates for the various elasticities and marginal products very close to Version II, except that it cannot give us separate information on production and nonproduction workers.

(v)   *Chemicals and Products*

On the basis of the two-stage least-squares equation (I,B,2) of Version I, the elasticity of demand for the output of the industry lies within a reasonable range and is not sensitive to small changes of ϕ_p, with the latter in the neighborhood of 0.7. With ϕ_p specified at 0.7, this elasticity is equal to 1.8; and the adjustment required in the employment of production workers to achieve the profit-maximizing position under the conditions prevailing in 1957, is a reduction of 51 per cent. While the required adjustment may appear to be large, the estimated coefficient of the speed of adjustment from 1956 to 1957 in the demand function for production workers is only 0.07. (See equation (V_p).) Thus, the estimated reduction is 3.4 per cent. This is greater than the actual reduction of 2 per cent in the employment of this category of workers from 1956 to 1957.

With the demand elasticity for output specified at 1.8, the estimated marginal revenue product of nonproduction workers is $1.70 per dollar of salary cost. Under the conditions prevailing in 1957, the employment of nonproduction workers would have to be expanded by 57 per cent if a complete adjustment to the profit-maximizing position were to be achieved. The estimated speed of adjustment from 1956 to 1957 is 0.15. At this speed, employment of this category of workers should increase by 8.4 per cent. Actually, the increase in the employment of nonproduction workers was only 5.3 per cent.

The capital-output and technology-output elasticities are respectively 0.27 and 0.48, the latter being fairly large relative to those of most of the other industries. The marginal revenue product is estimated at about $0.30 per dollar invested before business income tax.

Production Functions

Version I.

(I,A,1) $\log V = 0.376 \log q \log L_p + 0.539 \log L_n + 0.146 \log R \log K_g$
$\quad\quad\quad (0.205) \quad\quad\quad\quad (0.193) \quad\quad\quad (0.044) \quad R^2 = 0.88$

(I,A,2) $\quad\quad\quad 0.349 \quad\quad\quad\quad +0.564 \quad\quad\quad +0.146$
$\quad\quad\quad (0.216) \quad\quad\quad\quad (0.205) \quad\quad\quad (0.045) \quad\quad\quad 0.88$

(I,B,1) $\quad\quad\quad 0.375 \quad\quad\quad\quad +0.544 \quad\quad\quad +0.155 \log R \log K'_g$
$\quad\quad\quad (0.202) \quad\quad\quad\quad (0.191) \quad\quad\quad (0.045) \quad\quad\quad 0.89$

(I,B,2) $\quad\quad\quad 0.348 \quad\quad\quad\quad +0.570 \quad\quad\quad +0.156$
$\quad\quad\quad (0.213) \quad\quad\quad\quad (0.202) \quad\quad\quad (0.045)$

Version II.

(II,A,1) $\log V = 0.506 \log L_p + 0.442 \log L_n + 0.089 \log R \log K_g$
$\quad\quad\quad (0.199) \quad\quad\quad\quad (0.184) \quad\quad\quad (0.051) \quad R^2 = 0.90$

(II,A,2) $\quad\quad\quad 0.496 \quad\quad\quad\quad +0.455 \quad\quad\quad +0.089$
$\quad\quad\quad (0.209) \quad\quad\quad\quad (0.194) \quad\quad\quad (0.052) \quad\quad\quad 0.89$

(II,B,1) $\quad\quad\quad 0.491 \quad\quad\quad\quad +0.452 \quad\quad\quad +0.099 \log R \log K'_g$
$\quad\quad\quad (0.194) \quad\quad\quad\quad (0.182) \quad\quad\quad (0.051) \quad\quad\quad 0.90$

(II,B,2) $\quad\quad\quad 0.479 \quad\quad\quad\quad +0.467 \quad\quad\quad +0.100$
$\quad\quad\quad (0.204) \quad\quad\quad\quad (0.192) \quad\quad\quad (0.053) \quad\quad\quad 0.90$

Version III.

(III,A,1) $\log V = 0.949 \log L + 0.072 \log R \log K_g$
$\quad\quad\quad (0.181) \quad\quad\quad (0.048) \quad\quad\quad\quad\quad\quad R^2 = 0.89$

(III,A,2) $\quad\quad\quad 0.948 \quad\quad +0.072$
$\quad\quad\quad (0.111) \quad\quad (0.049) \quad\quad\quad\quad\quad\quad\quad 0.88$

(III,B,1) $\quad\quad\quad 0.943 \quad\quad +0.082 \log R \log K'_g$
$\quad\quad\quad (0.104) \quad\quad (0.048) \quad\quad\quad\quad\quad\quad\quad 0.89$

(III,B,2) $\quad\quad\quad 0.943 \quad\quad +0.082$
$\quad\quad\quad (0.107) \quad\quad (0.049) \quad\quad\quad\quad\quad\quad\quad 0.89$

Version IV.

(IV,A,1) $\log V = 0.801 \log L + 0.209 \log K_g$
$\quad\quad\quad (0.163) \quad\quad\quad (0.114) \quad\quad\quad\quad\quad 0.89$

(IV,A,2) $\quad\quad\quad 0.802 \quad\quad +0.209$
$\quad\quad\quad (0.168) \quad\quad (0.118) \quad\quad\quad\quad\quad\quad 0.89$

(IV,B,1) $\quad\quad\quad 0.762 \quad\quad +0.253 \log K'_g$
$\quad\quad\quad (0.160) \quad\quad (0.118) \quad\quad\quad\quad\quad\quad 0.90$

(IV,B,2) $\quad\quad\quad 0.762 \quad\quad +0.253$
$\quad\quad\quad (0.164) \quad\quad (0.121) \quad\quad\quad\quad\quad\quad 0.89$

Demand Functions for Labor

(V_p): $\log L_p = 0.935 \log L_{p-1} + 0.074 \log V - 0.141 \log W_p$
$\quad\quad\quad\quad\quad (0.073) \quad\quad\quad (0.080) \quad\quad\quad (0.118)$
$\quad\quad\quad\quad\quad\quad\quad\quad + 0.335 \log (\log q)$
$\quad\quad\quad\quad\quad\quad\quad\quad\quad (0.295) \quad\quad\quad\quad\quad\quad R^2 = 0.99$

(V_n): $\log L_n = 0.853 \log L_{n-1} + 0.113 \log V - 0.132 \log W_n$
$\quad\quad\quad\quad\quad (0.055) \quad\quad\quad (0.053) \quad\quad\quad (0.094) \quad\quad R^2 = 0.99$

The decisive reason for rejecting Version II is that the estimated technology-output elasticity and the marginal revenue product of capital are respectively only 0.31 and 0.15, much smaller than the more reasonable estimates yielded by Version I for this industry, where technological advances are by common knowledge very important.

Version III is discarded, not only because it does not differentiate production from nonproduction workers, but because it gives an even lower technology-output elasticity than Version II.

(vi) *Petroleum and Coal Products*

Version I is preferred to II, mainly because of the more plausible estimates it yields for the key parameters concerning nonproduction workers and capital.

With ϕ_p specified at 0.7, equation (I,B,2) of Version I yields a demand elasticity for the output of the industry equal to 3.3; and an adjustment to the profit-maximizing position with respect to variations of production workers would require a reduction of 53 per cent in this category of employees. The estimated speed of adjustment in the demand function for production workers is 0.08. The estimated reduction is therefore 4.2 per cent; the actual decline, however, was about 1.1 per cent. The corresponding estimate of the marginal revenue product of nonproduction workers is $2.70 per dollar of salary cost. Such a high marginal revenue product for nonproduction workers would, under the conditions prevailing during 1957, require a very large expansion, i.e., 97 per cent of this category of employees. The speed of adjustment in the demand function for nonproduction workers, however, is 0.14. The estimated expansion is about 13 per cent, but the actual increase of nonproduction employees from 1956 to 1957 was only 6.3 per cent. The capital-output and technology-output elasticities are respectively 0.23 and 0.51, with the marginal revenue product of capital estimated at $0.21 per dollar before business income tax.

For any plausible magnitudes of ϕ_p and the demand elasticity for the output of the industry, all equations in Version II would yield estimates for the marginal revenue product of nonpro-

Production Functions

Version I.

$(I,A,1)$ $\log V = 0.232 \log q \log L_p + 0.516 \log L_N + 0.148 \log R \log K_g$
          (0.210)   (0.233)   (0.134) $R^2 = 0.92$

$(I,A,2)$ 0.236   0.464   0.168
             (0.221)   (0.247)   (0.142)   0.91

$(I,B,1)$ 0.272   0.553   0.113 \log R \log K'_g
             (0.219)   (0.252)   (0.155)   0.91

$(I,B,2)$ 0.274   0.500   0.136
             (0.230)   (0.268)   (0.164)   0.91

Version II.

$(II,A,1)$ $\log V = 0.528 \log L_p + 0.358 \log L_N + 0.089 \log R \log K_g$
         (0.270)   (0.236)   (0.125) $R^2 = 0.93$

$(II,A,2)$ 0.555   0.286   0.108
          (0.286)   (0.253)   (0.133)   0.92

$(II,B,1)$ 0.581   0.380   0.054 \log R \log K'_g
          (0.271)   (0.248)   (0.139)   0.93

$(II,B,2)$ 0.605   0.306   0.076
          (0.287)   (0.266)   (0.148)   0.92

Version III.

$(III,A,1)$ $\log V = 0.864 \log L + 0.096 \log R \log K_g$
        (0.254)   (0.119)   0.93

$(III,A,2)$ 0.816   0.117
         (0.272)   (0.127)   0.92

$(III,B,1)$ 0.925   0.068 \log R \log K'_g
         (0.269)   (0.130)   0.93

$(III,B,2)$ 0.878   0.090
         (0.288)   (0.139)   0.92

Version IV.

$(IV,A,1)$ $\log V = 0.673 \log L + 0.291 \log K_g$
        (0.279)   (0.202)   0.94

$(IV,A,2)$ 0.615   0.331
         (0.297)   (0.215)   0.93

$(IV,B,1)$ 0.691   0.284 \log K'_g
         (0.310)   (0.232)   0.93

$(IV,B,2)$ 0.622   0.335
         (0.331)   (0.247)   0.93

Demand Functions for Labor

(V_p): $\log L_p = 0.921 \log L_{p-1} + 0.118 \log V - 0.112 \log W_p$
          (0.130)   (0.139)   (0.235)
                            $- 0.181 \log (\log q)$
                            (0.239) $R^2 = 0.99$

(V_n): $\log L_n = 0.864 \log L_{n-1} + 0.083 \log V - 0.286 \log W_n$
          (0.081)   (0.078)   (0.136) $R^2 = 0.99$

duction workers smaller than unity, indicating overemployment of this category of workers, a situation that apparently did not exist. The implausibility of Version II is further supported by the very small estimate for the marginal revenue product of capital (in the order of magnitude of six to eight cents per dollar invested before business income tax).

Version III yields similarly unreasonable estimates for the key parameters relating to capital.

(vii) *Rubber and Plastic Products*

Both Version I and Version II are rejected. The regression coefficients of log L_n are negative in equations (I,A,1)–(I,A,2), and in all equations in Version II. The exceedingly small and insignificant coefficients for log L_n in equations (I,B,1) and (I,B,2) would not yield any plausible estimates for the marginal product of nonproduction workers. It is therefore impossible to get separate estimates for the contributions of production and nonproduction workers in this industry.

By contrast, Version III provides us with a basis for making estimates. The elasticity of demand for the output of the industry is 2.8 if ϕ is specified at 0.95. The required adjustment in employment to achieve the profit-maximizing position is a reduction of about 10 per cent. The estimated speed of adjustment in the demand function for labor is 0.27, larger than in most industries. The estimated contraction is therefore 2.6 per cent, somewhat larger than the actual reduction of about 2 per cent during 1956–1957.

The capital-output and technology-output elasticities, respectively 0.23 and 0.49, are practically the same as the corresponding estimates for the chemicals and the petroleum and coal products industries. The estimated marginal revenue product of capital, estimated at $0.55 per capital invested, however, is considerably larger than those of the other two industries which also mainly utilize chemical processes.

Production Functions

Version I.

(I,A,1) $\log V = 0.838 \log q \log L_p - 0.129 \log L_N + 0.209 \log R \log K_g$
(0.281)   (0.275)   (0.072) $R^2 = 0.96$

(I,A,2)   0.813   −0.111   0.211
       (0.294)   (0.290)   (0.075)   0.96

(I,B,1)   0.710   0.015   0.221 $\log R \log K'_g$
       (0.290)   (0.263)   (0.075)   0.96

(I,B,2)   0.679   0.038   0.223
       (0.303)   (0.275)   (0.078)   0.96

Version II.

(II,A,1) $\log V = 1.082 \log L_p - 0.232 \log L_N + 0.123 \log R \log K_g$
(0.119)   (0.111)   (0.036) $R^2 = 0.99$

(II,A,2)   1.077   −0.234   0.126
       (0.140)   (0.132)   (0.042)   0.99

(II,B,1)   1.035   −0.174   0.131 $\log R \log K'_g$
       (0.124)   (0.108)   (0.038)   0.99

(II,B,2)   1.028   −0.172   0.134
       (0.145)   (0.127)   (0.044)   0.99

Version III.

(III,A,1) $\log V = 0.885 \log L + 0.109 \log R \log K_g$
(0.101)   (0.048)   0.98

(III,A,2)   0.870   0.116
       (0.115)   (0.055)   0.98

(III,B,1)   0.862   0.135 $\log R \log K'_g$
       (0.090)   (0.048) $R^2 = 0.98$

(III,B,2)   0.851   0.140
       (0.102)   (0.054)   0.98

Version IV.

(IV,A,1) $\log V = 0.716 \log L + 0.358 \log K_g$
(0.161)   (0.148)   0.98

(IV,A,2)   0.643   0.423
       (0.192)   (0.176)   0.98

(VI,B,1)   0.616   0.513 $\log K'_g$
       (0.130)   (0.135)   0.99

(IV,B,2)   0.557   0.572
       (0.156)   (0.162)   0.98

Demand Function for Labor

(V) $\log L = 0.728 \log L_{-1} + 0.273 \log V - 0.434 \log W$
     (0.148)   (0.138)   (0.195) $R^2 = 0.99$

(viii)   *Leather and Leather Products*

The attempt to disaggregate the contributions of production and nonproduction workers was disappointing. All four equations in Version I have negative coefficients for nonproduction workers.

Version II is also unsatisfactory. The marginal revenue product for nonproduction workers derived from equations (II,A,1) and (II,A,2) are smaller than unity, implying overemployment of this kind of employees, a situation that apparently did not exist in 1956 and 1957. Moreover, there is almost no decernible influence of the capital variable in equations (II,B,1) and (II,B,2). Versions I and II are therefore discarded.

The capital coefficients cannot be accurately estimated in Version III either, but the various elasticity and productivity measures obtained from equation (III,A,2) are not implausible. With ϕ specified at 0.95, the elasticity of demand for output is equal to 3.6. Under the conditions prevailing during 1957, an adjustment to the profit-maximizing position with respect to variations in employment would result in a reduction of 13.7 per cent. With an estimated speed of adjustment equal to 0.13 in the demand function for labor, the estimated reduction is 1.8 per cent. The actual decline from 1956 to 1957 was 1.4 per cent.

The capital-output and technology-output elasticities are among the smallest of all industries, respectively 0.07 and 0.13. The marginal revenue product per dollar invested (before business tax), however, is very large ($0.70), because of the large output-capital ratio.

Production Functions

Version I.
(I,A,1) log V = 0.994 log q log L_p − 0.072 log L_N + 0.030 log K log K_g
$$(0.338) \qquad (0.291) \qquad (0.065) \quad R^2 = 0.74$$

(I,A,2)	0.999	−0.074	0.029
	(0.348)	(0.306)	(0.065)	0.75
(I,B,1)	0.962	−0.044	0.039 log R log K'_g
	(0.351)	(0.279)	(0.076)	0.75
(I,B,2)	0.961	−0.040	0.039
	(0.360)	(0.292)	(0.076)	0.75

Version II.

(II,A,1) $\log V = 0.760 \log L_p + 0.112 \log L_n + 0.038 \log R \log K_g$
         (0.139) (0.158) (0.045) $R^2 = 0.88$

(II,A,2) 0.765 0.104 0.039
         (0.142) (0.115) (0.046) 0.87

(II,B,1) 0.756 0.164 $0.019 \log R \log K'_g$
         (0.150) (0.147) (0.055) $R^2 = 0.87$

(II,B,2) 0.758 0.161 0.019
         (0.153) (0.153) (0.055) 0.87

Version III.

(III,A,1) $\log V = 0.860 \log L + 0.039 \log R \log K_g$
          (0.115) (0.038) 0.88

(III,A,2) 0.849 0.041
          (0.124) (0.041) 0.86

(III,B,1) 0.890 $0.023 \log R \log K'_g$
          (0.125) (0.050) 0.87

(III,B,2) 0.877 0.026
          (0.135) (0.054) 0.85

Version IV.

(IV,A,1) $\log V = 0.824 \log L + 0.118 \log K_g$
         (0.115) (0.079) 0.89

(IV,A,2) 0.812 0.122
         (0.124) (0.085) 0.87

(IV,B,1) 0.752 $0.240 \log K'_g$
         (0.165) (0.189) 0.89

(IV,B,2) 0.725 0.266
         (0.178) (0.203) 0.87

Demand Function for Labor

(V): $\log L = 0.868 \log L_{-1} + 0.119 \log V - 0.297 \log W$
     (0.058) (0.056) (0.070) $R^2 = 0.99$

(ix) Stone, Clay, and Glass Products

The separate contributions to output by production and non-production workers can be fairly clearly seen from the equations in Version I. On the basis of equation (I,B,2), the elasticity of demand for the output of this industry is not sensitive to small changes in ϕ_p; it is equal to 1.9, if ϕ_p is assumed at 0.8. With an exceedingly small coefficient (0.05) of the speed of adjustment in the demand function for production workers, the correction that would have been carried out in the employment of production

90

workers is estimated at a reduction of 1.8 per cent, even though the reduction required to achieve maximum profits was a contraction of 36 per cent. However, the actual decline of 4.6 per cent between 1956 and 1957 was larger than the estimated magnitude under conditions prevailing in 1957.

The marginal revenue product of nonproduction employees is estimated at $1.10 per dollar of salary cost. The expansion required to attain maximum profits under the conditions prevailing in 1957 was 13 per cent. With a relatively large speed of adjustment (0.35) in the demand function for nonproduction workers, the estimated increase is 4.6 per cent. The actual expansion was 3.5 per cent.

The estimated capital-output elasticity (0.13), the technology-output elasticity (0.19), and the marginal revenue product per dollar invested before business tax (0.14) are among the smallest in all the industries.

Versions II and III yield results fairly close to Version I. Since Version I represents our complete model, the others are discarded.

Production Functions

Version I.

$(I,A,1)$ $\log V = 0.702 \log q \log L_p + 0.244 \log L_N + 0.080 \log R \log K_g$

	(0.160)	(0.155)	(0.067)	$R^2 = 0.92$
$(I,A,2)$	0.651	0.318	0.077	
	(0.178)	(0.180)	(0.036)	0.92
$(I,B,1)$	0.719	0.227	$0.081 \log R \log K'_g$	
	(0.157)	(0.155)	(0.038)	0.92
$(I,B,2)$	0.671	0.299	0.077	
	(0.175)	(0.180)	(0.037)	0.92

Version II.

$(II,A,1)$ $\log V = 0.626 \log L_p + 0.232 \log L_N + 0.111 \log R \log K_g$

	(0.109)	(0.126)	(0.030)	$R^2 = 0.94$
$(II,A,2)$	0.609	0.273	0.106	
	(0.119)	(0.142)	(0.029)	0.94
$(II,B,1)$	0.643	0.209	$0.115 \log R \log K'_g$	
	(0.109)	(0.127)	(0.031)	0.94
$(II,B,2)$	0.630	0.247	0.110	
	(0.118)	(0.143)	(0.030)	0.94

Version III.

(III,A,1) $\log V = 0.828 \log L + 0.116 \log R \log K_g$
         (0.068)   (0.029)   0.94

(III,A,2)   0.843   0.113
         (0.066)   (0.028)   0.94

(III,B,1)   0.828 $0.120 \log R \log K'_g$
         (0.068)   (0.030)   0.94

(III,B,2)   0.844   0.116
         (0.065)   (0.028)   0.94

Version IV.

(IV,A,1) $\log V = 0.699 \log L + 0.337 \log K_g$
         (0.085)   (0.079)   0.94

(IV,A,2)   0.717   0.325
         (0.085)   (0.078)   0.94

(IV,B,1)   0.675 $0.378 \log K'_g$
         (0.085)   (0.082) $R^2 = 0.94$

(IV,B,2)   0.695   0.362
         (0.084)   (0.080)   0.95

Demand Functions for Labor

(V_p): $\log L_p = 0.950 \log L_{p-1} + 0.001 \log V - 0.001 \log W_p$
        (0.201)   (0.239)   (0.247)

                    $+ 0.471 \log (\log q)$
                      (0.412) $R^2 = 0.98$

(V_n): $\log L_n = 0.651 \log L_{n-1} + 0.301 \log V - 0.246 \log W_n$
        (0.105)   (0.097)   (0.174) $R^2 = 0.93$

(x) *Primary Metals*

It was disappointing that the attempt to disaggregate production and nonproduction workers did not yield satisfactory estimates for the key parameters in this important industry.

Version I had to be discarded. The estimated elasticity of output with respect to production workers is so low in all equations of Version I that ϕ_p would have to be unacceptably small if any plausible estimate of the demand elasticity for the output of this industry is to be obtained. This unsatisfactory result is not surprising when we observe that the regression coefficients for the $\log L_p$ variable are among the statistically least significant ones in the accepted equations for the different industries.

On the basis of equation (II,B,2), the demand elasticity for output is as large as 11 for a ϕ_p as low as 0.7. The demand elasticity takes on plausible magnitudes only when ϕ_p is reduced to unreasonably small figures. While overemployment of production workers probably did exist significantly in this industry, it is extremely unlikely that ϕ_p would have been much lower than 0.7. We tentatively accept equation (III,B,2) of Version III as the production function for this industry. With ϕ specified at 0.8, the implied elasticity of demand for the output of this industry is 1.9. An adjustment in employment to achieve maximum profits would, under 1957 conditions, require a reduction of 47 per cent. The estimated coefficient of the speed of adjustment in the demand function for labor is as low as 0.03, most probably an underestimation. The estimated contraction is therefore only 1.5 per cent, much lower than the reduction (3.6 per cent) which actually occurred from 1956 to 1957.

The estimated capital-output elasticity (0.16) is small; but the technology-output elasticity (0.42) is much larger. The marginal revenue product per dollar invested (before business income tax) is \$0.24, a rather modest amount.

Production Functions

Version I.

(I,A,1) $\log V = 0.259 \log q \log L_p + 0.620 \log L_N + 0.113 \log R \log K_g$

	(0.221)	(0.192)	(0.041) $\quad R^2 = 0.91$
(I,A,2)	0.234	0.658	0.108
	(0.218)	(0.190)	(0.039) $\qquad$ 0.92
(I,B,1)	0.256	0.598	0.127 $\log R \log K'_g$
	(0.215)	(0.188)	(0.042) $\qquad$ 0.92
(I,B,2)	0.234	0.635	0.121
	(0.212)	(0.186)	(0.040) $\qquad$ 0.92

Version II.

(II,A,1) $\log V = 0.344 \log L_p + 0.578 \log L_N + 0.093 \log R \log K_g$

	(0.236)	(0.188)	(0.044) $\quad R^2 = 0.91$
(II,A,2)	0.335	0.604	0.088
	(0.232)	(0.184)	(0.042) $\qquad$ 0.92
(II,B,1)	0.350	0.546	0.109 $\log R \log K'_g$
	(0.223)	(0.181)	(0.044) $\qquad$ 0.92
(II,B,2)	0.343	0.571	0.103
	(0.219)	(0.178)	(0.042) $\qquad$ 0.92

Version III.

(III,A,1) $\log V = 0.988 \log L + 0.079 \log R \log K_g$

	(0.118)	(0.046) $\qquad$ 0.90
(III,A,2)	1.000	0.075
	(0.117)	(0.046) $\qquad$ 0.90
(III,B,1)	0.945	0.103 $\log R \log K'_g$
	(0.115)	(0.046) $\qquad$ 0.90
(III,B,2)	0.958	0.099
	(0.114)	(0.045) $\qquad$ 0.91

Version IV.

(IV,A,1) $\log V = 0.764 \log L + 0.303 \log K_g$
          (0.186)   (0.137) $R^2 = 0.90$

(IV,A,2)   0.791   0.285
                  (0.188)   (0.138)   0.91

(IV,B,1)   0.594   0.445 $\log K'_g$
                  (0.171)   (0.128)   0.92

(IV,B,2)   0.620   0.427
                  (0.172)   (0.129)   0.92

Demand Function for Labor

(V): $\log L = 0.969 \log L_{-1} + 0.053 \log V - 0.218 \log W$
          (0.115)   (0.099)   (0.164) $R^2 = 0.99$

(xi) *Fabricated Metal Products*

Version I is discarded in favor of Version II. It has therefore been possible to disaggregate the contribution of production workers from that of the nonproduction employees, even though the different levels of education received by the labor force in the different states apparently did not have appreciable effects.

On the basis of equation (I,B,2), the demand elasticity for the output of the industry is negative, if ϕ_p is specified at 0.9, and for $\phi_p = 0.8$, it is as large as 11. The implied elasticity is obviously too large for any plausible magnitudes of ϕ_p; moreover, this version is rejected also because the estimated underemployment of nonproduction workers is much too large to be consistent with the observed change of employment in this category.

With ϕ_p specified at 0.9, the demand elasticity for output derived from equation (II,B,2) is 3.5. The adjustment required in the employment of production workers for profit maximization is a reduction of 18 per cent. The estimated coefficient of the speed of adjustment (0.28) in the demand function for production workers is large relative to other industries. It implies a reduction of 4.9 per cent, higher than the 1.3 per cent contraction which actually occurred from 1956 to 1957.

The corresponding marginal revenue for nonproduction employees is $1.37 per dollar of salary cost, and the adjustment required for profit maximization for this group of workers is an expansion of 36 per cent. The estimated speed of adjustment (0.4) is again more rapid than in other industries and is perhaps an overestimate. The estimated expansion of 14.3 per cent is much larger than the actual one of 6 per cent from 1956 to 1957.

94

The estimated capital-output elasticity (0.15), technology-output elasticity (0.19), and the marginal revenue product of capital before business income tax ($0.33) are all very modest.

Version III yields results rather close to those of Version II, except that the separate contributions of production and nonproduction workers cannot be identified. Accordingly, Version II is preferred.

Production Functions

Version I.

(I,A,1) $\log V = 0.403 \log q \log L_p + 0.456 \log L_N + 0.099 \log R \log K_g$
  (0.130)   (0.105)   (0.032) $R^2 = 0.93$

(I,A,2)   0.402   0.434   0.106
  (0.162)   (0.133)   (0.039)   0.90

(I,B,1)   0.377   0.495   0.108 $\log R \log K'_g$
  (0.133)   (0.102)   (0.035)   0.92

(I,B,2)   0.374   0.478   0.114
  (0.168)   (0.130)   (0.042)   0.89

Version II.

(II,A,1) $\log V = 0.523 \log L_p + 0.362 \log L_N + 0.067 \log R \log K_g$
  (0.106)   (0.091)   (0.029) $R^2 = 0.95$

(II,A,2)   0.539   0.322   0.074
  (0.142)   (0.123)   (0.037)   0.92

(II,B,1)   0.512   0.376   0.079 $\log R \log K'_g$
  (0.103)   (0.088)   (0.030)   0.95

(II,B,2)   0.529   0.337   0.086
  (0.143)   (0.123)   (0.039)   0.92

Version III.

(III,A,1) $\log V = 0.876 \log L + 0.071 \log R \log K_g$
  (0.079)   (0.030)
        $R^2 = 0.94$

(III,A,2)   0.832   0.084
  (0.105)   (0.040)   0.90

(III,B,1)   0.886   0.079 $\log R \log K'_g$
  (0.073)   (0.032)   0.94

(III,B,2)   0.847   0.092
  (0.098)   (0.042)   0.90

Version IV.

(IV,A,1) $\log V = 0.649 \log L + 0.276 \log K_g$
  (0.116)   (0.079)   0.95

(IV,A,2)   0.522   0.356
  (0.154)   (0.103)   0.92

(IV,B,1)   0.668   0.305 $\log K'_g$
  (0.106)   (0.083)   0.95

(IV,B,2)   0.543   0.394
  (0.145)   (0.112)   0.92

Demand Functions for Labor

(V_p): log L_p = 0.725 log L_{p-1} + 0.217 log V − 0.306 log W_p
$\quad\quad\quad$ (0.087) $\quad\quad\quad$ (0.094) $\quad\quad\quad$ (0.121) $\quad\quad$ R^2 = 0.98

(V_n): log L_n = 0.599 log L_{n-1} + 0.376 log V − 0.580 log W_n
$\quad\quad\quad$ (0.143) $\quad\quad\quad$ (0.163) $\quad\quad\quad$ (0.173) $\quad\quad\quad\quad$ 0.96

(xii) *Machinery, except Electrical*

Version I yields plausible estimates for the key parameters, except that the estimated adjustment in the employment of non-production workers required to attain profit-maximization is probably unsatisfactory.

On the basis of equation (I,A,2) and with ϕ_p specified at 0.9, the demand elasticity for output is estimated at 4.4. To achieve maximum profits, employment of production workers should be reduced by 17 per cent. The estimated speed of adjustment being 0.19, the estimated contraction is 3.3 per cent. The actual decline between 1956 and 1957 was 5.3 per cent. The corresponding estimate of the marginal revenue product of nonproduction employees is $1.04 per dollar of salary cost. Since this is only very slightly above one dollar and since the estimated speed of adjustment is 0.15, the implied adjustment toward the profit-maximizing position is practically zero. The actual expansion of nonproduction workers, however, was 7.8 per cent from 1956 to 1957. As has been explained, this discrepancy is not a sufficient ground for rejecting this equation.[30]

The capital-output and technology-output elasticities are respectively 0.33 and 0.45, relatively high compared to those of some of the other industries. The marginal revenue product of capital, estimated at $1.10 per dollar invested before business income tax, is also relatively large.

All equations in Version II indicate that there was overemployment of nonproduction workers in this industry, a situation contrary to fact. The estimates of the various parameters with respect to the capital variable are unreasonably low. This version is therefore rejected.

Version III must also be discarded. The contributions of production and nonproduction workers cannot be separated with

[30]See the discussion on pp. 67–68, above.

this formulation, which also yields estimates of the parameters relating to capital as low and unsatisfactory as those obtained from Version II.

Production Functions

Version I

$(I,A,1) \log V = 0.473 \log q \log L_p + 0.289 \log L_N + 0.182 \log R \log K_g$

	(0.098)	(0.111)	(0.028)	$R^2 = 0.97$
(I,A,2)	0.467	0.272	0.190	
	(0.125)	(0.143)	(0.035)	0.96
(I,B,1)	0.519	0.273	0.187 $\log R \log K'_g$	
	(0.100)	(0.114)	(0.030)	0.97
(I,B,2)	0.516	0.258	0.193	
	(0.125)	(0.144)	(0.036)	0.96

Version II.

$(II,A,1) \log V = 0.786 \log L_p + 0.101 \log L_N + 0.092 \log R \log K_g$

	(0.119)	(0.108)	(0.027)	$R^2 = 0.98$
(II,A,2)	0.788	0.076	0.100	
	(0.170)	(0.156)	(0.037)	0.97
(II,B,1)	0.820	0.084	0.092 $\log R \log K'_g$	
	(0.114)	(0.108)	(0.027)	0.98
(II,B,2)	0.829	0.058	0.098	
	(0.159)	(0.151)	(0.036)	0.97

Version III.

$(III,A,1) \log V = 0.884 \log L + 0.099 \log R \log K_g$

	(0.059)	(0.026)	$R^2 = 0.98$
(III,A,2)	0.863	0.106	
	(0.079)	(0.035)	0.97
(III,B,1)	0.904	0.098 $\log R \log K_g'$	
	(0.055)	(0.027)	0.98
(III,B,2)	0.891	0.104	
	(0.072)	(0.035)	0.97

Version IV.

$(IV,A,1) \log V = 0.763 \log L + 0.269 \log K_g$

	(0.112)	(0.095)	
			0.98
(IV,A,2)	0.680	0.336	
	(0.148)	(0.124)	0.96
(IV,B,1)	0.715	0.347 $\log K'_g$	
	(0.114)	(0.108)	0.98
(IV,B,2)	0.648	0.407	
	(0.145)	(0.136)	0.97

Demand Functions for Labor

(V_p): $\log L_p = 0.811 \log L_{p-1} + 0.160 \log V - 0.184 \log W_p$
$\quad\quad\quad\quad\ \ (0.178) \quad\quad\quad\ \ (0.182) \quad\quad\ (0.151)$
$\quad\quad\quad\quad\quad\quad + 0.274 \log (\log q)$
$\quad\quad\quad\quad\quad\quad\quad\ (0.400) \quad\quad\quad\quad\quad\quad\quad R^2 = 0.99$

(V_n): $\log L_n = 0.854 \log L_{n-1} + 0.118 \log V - 0.195 \log W_n$
$\quad\quad\quad\quad\ \ (0.093) \quad\quad\quad\ \ (0.087) \quad\quad\ (0.139) \quad\quad R^2 = 0.98$

(xiii) *Electrical Machinery*

Version I is unsatisfactory because the coefficients of the $\log L_n$ variables are either negative or implausibly low, the latter indicating very severe overemployment of nonproduction workers, a situation which apparently did not exist.

On the basis of equation (II,A,2), the elasticity of demand for the output of the industry is 4.9 if ϕ_p is specified at 0.9. The reduction required to achieve the profit-maximization position and the speed of adjustment are estimated at 16 per cent and 0.19, respectively. The estimated reduction required under the conditions prevailing during 1957 is 3.1 per cent. The actual decline from 1956 to 1957 was 3.3 per cent. The corresponding estimate of the marginal revenue product of nonproduction employees is $0.97 or practically one dollar per dollar of salary cost. This would indicate that the employment of nonproduction employees is at the profit-maximizing position. However, although actual employment of this category of workers increased by 9.5 per cent from 1956 to 1957, this discrepancy is not a sufficient basis for rejecting this equation.[31]

The capital-output and technology-output elasticities are respectively 0.30 and 0.39, with a very high estimated value of the marginal revenue product of capital at $1.40 per dollar invested before business income tax.

Version III is discarded because it cannot throw any light on the situation of production workers, whereas Version II does. The estimates of the parameters relating to capital derived from this version are similar to those obtained from Version II.

[31]See the discussion on pp. 67–68, above.

Production Functions

Version I.

(I,A,1) $\log V = 0.366 \log q \log L_p + 0.164 \log L_N + 0.240 \log R \log K_g$
　　　　　　(0.098)　　　　　　　(0.084)　　　　　(0.027)　$R^2 = 0.97$
(I,A,2)　　　0.365　　　　　　　0.159　　　　　0.241
　　　　　　(0.105)　　　　　　　(0.089)　　　　　(0.029)　　　　0.97
(I,B,1)　　　0.508　　　　　　　−0.011　　　　0.318 $\log R \log K'_g$
　　　　　　(0.132)　　　　　　　(0.130)　　　　　(0.057)　　　　0.94
(I,B,2)　　　0.509　　　　　　　−0.025　　　　0.325
　　　　　　(0.138)　　　　　　　(0.136)　　　　　(0.059)　　　　0.94

Version II.

(II,A,1) $\log V = 0.413 \log L_p + 0.247 \log L_N + 0.169 \log R \log K_g$
　　　　　　(0.123)　　　　　(0.073)　　　　　(0.040)　$R^2 = 0.97$
(II,A,2)　　0.410　　　　　0.244　　　　　0.171
　　　　　　(0.133)　　　　　(0.078)　　　　　(0.043)　　　　0.96
(II,B,1)　　0.594　　　　　0.145　　　　　0.168 $\log R \log K'_g$
　　　　　　(0.125)　　　　　(0.093)　　　　　(0.063)　　　　0.95
(II,B,2)　　0.590　　　　　0.138　　　　　0.173
　　　　　　(0.135)　　　　　(0.099)　　　　　(0.068)　　　　0.95

Version III.

(III,A,1) $\log V = 0.697 \log L + 0.153 \log R \log K_g$
　　　　　　(0.096)　　　　(0.040)
　　　　　　　　　　　　　　　　　　　　$R^2 = 0.96$
(III,A,2)　　0.704　　　　0.151
　　　　　　(0.098)　　　　(0.041)　　　　0.96
(III,B,1)　　0.738　　　　0.166 $\log R \log K'_g$
　　　　　　(0.118)　　　　(0.062)　　　　0.95
(III,B,2)　　0.751　　　　0.160
　　　　　　(0.120)　　　　(0.063)　　　　0.95

Version IV.

(IV,A,1) $\log V = 0.584 \log L + 0.337 \log K_g$
　　　　　　(0.111)　　　　(0.079)　　　　0.96
(IV,A,2)　　0.574　　　　0.344
　　　　　　(0.120)　　　　(0.085)　　　　0.96
(IV,B,1)　　0.588　　　　0.404 $\log K'_g$
　　　　　　(0.158)　　　　(0.140)　　　　0.95
(IV,B,2)　　0.580　　　　0.411
　　　　　　(0.169)　　　　(0.149)　　　　0.95

Demand Functions for Labor

(V_p): $\log L_p = 0.807 \log L_{p-1} + 0.166 \log V - 0.091 \log W_p$
　　　　　(0.093)　　　　　(0.097)　　　　(0.127)　$R^2 = 0.99$
(V_n): $\log L_n = 0.897 \log L_{n-1} + 0.066 \log V - 0.112 \log W_n$
　　　　　(0.038)　　　　　(0.044)　　　　(0.103)　　　　0.99

99

(xiv) *Transportation Equipment*

On the basis of equation (I,A,2), the demand elasticity of output is about 5 if ϕ_p is specified at 0.7. In the late 1950's, the growth of suburban communities was in full bloom, and the number of households in the middle-income brackets which were (or were considering) buying a second car must have been increasingly significant. Competition with imported cars became intense. Accordingly, an estimated demand elasticity of 5 does not appear implausible. While a magnitude of ϕ_p equal to 0.7 implies a 64 per cent reduction of production workers if the profit-maximizing position were to be achieved, the coefficient of the speed of adjustment is only 0.12, implying a contraction of only 7.8 per cent. Actually, employment of production workers increased slightly by 2 per cent from 1956 to 1957. While this contrast is not a sufficient reason for rejecting the equation,[32] it is accepted only because the longer-term analysis, appearing in the next section,[33] tends to support its validity rather strongly.

The corresponding estimate ϕ_n for the marginal revenue product of nonproduction employees is \$1.27. An adjustment to the profit-maximizing position would require an expansion of 27 per cent of this category of workers. Unfortunately, we have failed to get any plausible estimates of the speed of adjustment for this labor group. The actual increase from 1956 to 1957 was about 15 per cent. This would imply a much more rapid speed of adjustment than in other industries.

The capital-output and technology-output elasticities are respectively 0.32 and 0.52. These are among the largest relative to the estimates for the other industries. The marginal revenue product of capital per dollar invested before business tax is \$2.40, the largest of all the estimates.

All equations in Version II must be rejected because the coefficients for the log L_n variable are extremely small and insignificant. They would indicate very great overemployment of this category of employees, a rather implausible situation.

[32]See the discussion on pp. 67–68, above.
[33]See the figure given for this industry in Columns (3) and (8) of Table 7 below and the discussion of that table, pp. 115–116.

100

Version III would yield plausible estimates for the key parameters, but is inferior to Version I because it precludes separation of the contributions of production and nonproduction workers.

Production Functions

Version I.

(I,A,1) $\log V = 0.485 \log q \log L_p + 0.244 \log L_N + 0.183 \log R \log K_g$
$\quad\quad\quad$ (0.207) $\quad\quad\quad\quad$ (0.150) $\quad\quad\quad\quad$ (0.039) $\quad R^2 = 0.92$

(I,A,2) $\quad\quad\quad$ 0.415 $\quad\quad\quad\quad\quad$ 0.284 $\quad\quad\quad\quad\quad$ 0.187
$\quad\quad\quad$ (0.243) $\quad\quad\quad\quad$ (0.174) $\quad\quad\quad\quad$ (0.043) $\quad\quad\quad$ 0.90

(I,B,1) $\quad\quad\quad$ 0.449 $\quad\quad\quad\quad\quad$ 0.196 $\quad\quad\quad\quad\quad$ 0.243 $\log R \log K'_g$
$\quad\quad\quad$ (0.211) $\quad\quad\quad\quad$ (0.154) $\quad\quad\quad\quad$ (0.053) $\quad\quad\quad$ 0.91

(I,B,2) $\quad\quad\quad$ 0.387 $\quad\quad\quad\quad\quad$ 0.228 $\quad\quad\quad\quad\quad$ 0.250
$\quad\quad\quad$ (0.241) $\quad\quad\quad\quad$ (0.174) $\quad\quad\quad\quad$ (0.057) $\quad\quad\quad$ 0.90

Version II.

(II,A,1) $\log V = 0.878 \log L_p + 0.074 \log L_N + 0.135 \log R \log K_g$
$\quad\quad\quad$ (0.148) $\quad\quad\quad\quad$ (0.094) $\quad\quad\quad\quad$ (0.029) $\quad R^2 = 0.96$

(II,A,2) $\quad\quad\quad$ 0.832 $\quad\quad\quad\quad\quad$ 0.092 $\quad\quad\quad\quad\quad$ 0.141
$\quad\quad\quad$ (0.194) $\quad\quad\quad\quad$ (0.122) $\quad\quad\quad\quad$ (0.036) $\quad\quad\quad$ 0.94

(II,B,1) $\quad\quad\quad$ 0.872 $\quad\quad\quad\quad\quad$ 0.023 $\quad\quad\quad\quad\quad$ 0.181 $\log R \log K'_g$
$\quad\quad\quad$ (0.149) $\quad\quad\quad\quad$ (0.094) $\quad\quad\quad\quad$ (0.038) $\quad\quad\quad$ 0.96

(II,B,2) $\quad\quad\quad$ 0.836 $\quad\quad\quad\quad\quad$ 0.034 $\quad\quad\quad\quad\quad$ 0.188
$\quad\quad\quad$ (0.187) $\quad\quad\quad\quad$ (0.118) $\quad\quad\quad\quad$ (0.046) $\quad\quad\quad$ 0.94

Version III.

(III,A,1) $\log V = 0.913 \log L + 0.138 \log R \log K_g$
$\quad\quad\quad$ (0.066) $\quad\quad\quad\quad$ (0.027) $\quad\quad\quad\quad\quad\quad R^2 = 0.96$

(III,A,2) $\quad\quad\quad$ 0.904 $\quad\quad\quad\quad\quad$ 0.140
$\quad\quad\quad$ (0.081) $\quad\quad\quad\quad$ (0.033) $\quad\quad\quad\quad\quad\quad$ 0.94

(III,B,1) $\quad\quad\quad$ 0.845 $\quad\quad\quad\quad\quad$ 0.181 $\log R \log K'_g$
$\quad\quad\quad$ (0.080) $\quad\quad\quad\quad$ (0.038) $\quad\quad\quad\quad\quad\quad$ 0.96

(III,B,2) $\quad\quad\quad$ 0.842 $\quad\quad\quad\quad\quad$ 0.182
$\quad\quad\quad$ (0.092) $\quad\quad\quad\quad$ (0.043) $\quad\quad\quad\quad\quad\quad$ 0.95

Version IV.

(IV,A,1) $\log V = 0.887 \log L + 0.252 \log K_g$
$\quad\quad\quad$ (0.076) $\quad\quad\quad\quad$ (0.056) $\quad\quad\quad\quad\quad\quad$ 0.96

(IV,A,2) $\quad\quad\quad$ 0.871 $\quad\quad\quad\quad\quad$ 0.260
$\quad\quad\quad$ (0.094) $\quad\quad\quad\quad$ (0.069) $\quad\quad\quad\quad\quad\quad$ 0.94

(IV,B,1) $\quad\quad\quad$ 0.766 $\quad\quad\quad\quad\quad$ 0.373 $\log K'_g$
$\quad\quad\quad$ (0.102) $\quad\quad\quad\quad$ (0.088) $\quad\quad\quad\quad\quad\quad$ 0.95

(IV,B,2) $\quad\quad\quad$ 0.749 $\quad\quad\quad\quad\quad$ 0.386
$\quad\quad\quad$ (0.120) $\quad\quad\quad\quad$ (0.102) $\quad\quad\quad\quad\quad\quad$ 0.94

Demand Functions for Labor

$$(V_p): \log L_p = \underset{(0.132)}{0.878} \log L_{p-1} + \underset{(0.108)}{0.134} \log V - \underset{(0.344)}{0.879} \log W_p$$
$$+ \underset{(0.559)}{0.140} \log (\log q)$$
$$R^2 = 0.98$$

$$(V_n): \log L_n = \underset{(0.063)}{1.033} \log L_{n-1} - \underset{(0.073)}{0.031} \log V - \underset{(0.119)}{0.345} \log W_n$$
$$0.99$$

(xv) *Instruments and Related Products*

For whatever plausible magnitudes of the elasticity of demand for the output of the industry and for the marginal revenue product of production workers, all the equations in Versions I and II would yield estimates for the marginal revenue product of nonproduction employees equal to $0.54 per dollar of salary cost or lower. This would indicate severe overemployment of this class of workers, a situation that apparently did not exist. This is not surprising because of the statistical insignificance of the log L_n variable in these equations. Other equations in Version I are worse in this respect. Versions I and II are therefore discarded.

Version III yields plausible estimates for the key parameters. On the basis of equation (III,B,2), the elasticity of demand for the output of the industry is about 5 if the marginal revenue product of labor (ϕ) is specified at 0.85. The estimated adjustment in employment required to maximize profits under the conditions prevailing during 1957 is a reduction of about 38 per cent. With the speed of adjustment in the demand function of labor estimated at 0.19, the estimated contraction is 7.4 per cent. Actually, employment in this industry increased by 3.4 per cent from 1956 to 1957. Although this apparent discrepancy is not a sufficient basis for discarding this equation,[34] it is accepted only because the analysis of the longer-term changes (presented in the next section) indicates that this equation is satisfactory.[35]

The capital-output and technology-output elasticities, respectively 0.44 and 0.56, are high relative to other industries. The marginal revenue product of capital per dollar invested is $1.49 before business tax, the second highest among all industries.

[34]See the discussion on pp. 67–68, above.
[35]See the figures given for this industry in columns (3) and (8) of Table 7, below, and the discussion of that table, pp. 115–116.

Production Functions

Version I.

(I,A,1) $\log V = 0.725 \log q \log L_p + 0.024 \log L_N + 0.242 \log R \log K_g$
        (0.222)   (0.207)   (0.073) $R^2 = 0.97$

(I,A,2)   0.671   0.071   0.238
        (0.261)   (0.256)   (0.082)   0.96

(I,B,1)   0.608   0.073   0.278 $\log R \log K'_g$
        (0.211)   (0.188)   (0.077)   0.97

(I,B,2)   0.550   0.132   0.270
        (0.231)   (0.217)   (0.080)   0.97

Version II.

(II,A,1) $\log V = 0.653 \log L_p + 0.055 \log L_N + 0.237 \log R \log K_g$
        (0.195)   (0.195)   (0.072) $R^2 = 0.97$

(II,A,2)   0.593   0.115   0.231
        (0.238)   (0.247)   (0.084)   0.96

(II,B,1)   0.538   0.112   0.270 $\log R \log K'_g$
        (0.191)   (0.181)   (0.078)   0.97

(II,B,2)   0.473   0.177   0.263
        (0.221)   (0.217)   (0.087)   0.96

Version III.

(III,A,1) $\log V = 0.715 \log L + 0.218 \log R \log K_g$
        (0.111)   (0.065) $R^2 = 0.96$

(III,A,2)   0.728   0.212
        (0.117)   (0.068)   0.96

(III,B,1)   0.649   0.264 $\log R \log K'_g$
        (0.117)   (0.072)   0.97

(III,B,2)   0.668   0.254
        (0.119)   (0.072)   0.97

Version IV.

(IV,A,1) $\log V = 0.666 \log L + 0.362 \log K_g$
        (0.126)   (0.111)   0.96

(IV,A,2)   0.675   0.356
        (0.136)   (0.119)   0.96

(IV,B,1)   0.567   0.457 $\log K'_g$
        (0.135)   (0.122) $R^2 = 0.97$

(IV,B,2)   0.579   0.448
        (0.145)   (0.130)   0.97

Demand Functions for Labor

(V): $\log L = 0.805 \log L_{-1} + 0.197 \log V - 0.347 \log W$
        (0.218)   (0.216)   (0.242) $R^2 = 0.99$

(4) *Industrial Production Functions: Summary and Analysis of Findings*

Production functions have been estimated with varying degrees of elaborateness for 15 two-digit industries mainly from census data for 1957 across the states. These functions are summarized in Table 2. As shown in the following analysis, they throw considerable light on the roles played by technological change and the scale of operation in manufacturing industries, on the relationships between the input-output elasticities and income shares received by different inputs, and on the pattern of resource allocation from the points of view of profit-maximization and of social welfare.

Table 2. Production Functions for 15 Two-Digit Manufacturing Industries, 1957.[a]

Dependent Variable: V

Industry	log L	log q log L_p	log L_p	log L_n	log R_{-1}	log K_{-1}	R^2
Food products		0.315 (0.100)		0.397 (0.081)	0.309 (0.059)		0.85
Apparel		0.591 (0.125)		0.258 (0.117)	0.114 (0.068)		0.94
Lumber products	0.792 (0.336)				0.183 (0.073)		0.83
Paper products			0.547 (0.115)	0.270 (0.107)	0.159 (0.028)		0.98
Chemicals		0.348 (0.213)		0.570 (0.202)	0.156 (0.045)		0.89
Petroleum and coal products		0.274 (0.230)		0.500 (0.268)	0.136 (0.164)		0.91
Rubber products	0.851 (0.102)				0.140 (0.054)		0.98
Leather products	0.849 (0.124)				0.041 (0.041)		0.86
Stone, clay, and glass products		0.671 (0.175)		0.299 (0.180)	0.077 (0.037)		0.92

104

Table 2. (continued)

Industry	log L	log q	log L_p	log L_p	log L_n	log R log K	R^2
Primary metals	0.958 (0.114)					0.099 (0.045)	0.91
Fabricated metal products			0.529 (0.143)		0.337 (0.123)	0.086 (0.039)	0.92
Machinery		0.467 (0.125)			0.272 (0.143)	0.190 (0.035)	0.96
Electrical machinery			0.410 (0.133)		0.244 (0.078)	0.171 (0.043)	0.96
Transportation equipment		0.415 (0.243)			0.284 (0.174)	0.187 (0.043)	0.90
Instruments	0.668 (0.019)					0.254 (0.072)	0.97

[a]These functions are taken from Section (3) of this chapter. Definitions and sources of data for the variables are given on pp. 71–72. Also see n. 14, above.

(i) *The Importance of Technological Change for Production*

The bearing of the level of technology on production is truly impressive. It may be measured by the technology-output elasticities we have estimated for the different industries.[36] This elasticity varies from 0.76 for the food products industry to 0.13 for the leather industry. The magnitudes and the ranking of this important parameter for the different industries are given in Table 3. That this elasticity is very high for such industries as food products,[37] instruments, transportation equipment, and the three industries utilizing chemical processes (petroleum and coal products, rubber products, and chemicals) is not surprising. While they rank lower, the magnitudes of this elasticity for the machinery (nonelectrical), primary metals and electric machinery industries are not much smaller than those for the three chemical industries. Among the low ranking industries, only the small magnitude of the technology-output elasticity for the fabricated metal products industry is rather unexpected.

[36]See pp. 49–53 and p. 70.
[37]See discussion on pp. 72–76.

By assumption, the technology effects are embodied in capital. It is of interest to observe that the technology-output elasticities account for the greater portion of the sum of capital-output and technology-output elasticities in all industries. We shall call the ratio of the technology-output elasticity to the sum of the two elasticities, presented in the last column of Table 3 in percentage form, the technology-capital intensity. The higher this ratio, the greater is the portion of the increase in input due to the change in technology accompanying a "compensated" change in capital.[38] The ranking of the different industries with respect to the technology-capital intensity is different from that on the basis of the magnitude of the technology-output elasticity. Although the former is interesting, the latter bears directly on output.

The most striking feature of the data in Table 3, however, is the rather large magnitudes of the sum of the capital-output and technology-output elasticities in most of the industries. These figures measure the percentage increase in output in response to a 1 per cent increase in capital, with both the quantity effect and the technological influence included. For 11 of the 15 industries, this sum exceeds 0.5, and it is as high as 1.3 for food products and unity for instruments. This contrasts sharply with the generally small output-capital elasticity found in other studies.[39]

(ii) *The Scale and the Technology Effects*

The earlier estimates of production functions of the Douglas type were made on the assumption that there were constant returns to scale. The "weighted-input approach" of more recent years [1], [14], [40], and [62], and Solow's 1957 estimate [67] of the aggregate production function, were made on the same assumption. However, the evidence we have found tends to corroborate the findings of the more recent studies of agricultural production functions (see Griliches [26]) that there were substantial increasing returns to scale. As shown in Table 4, the sum of the labor-output and the capital-output elasticities is greater than unity in 12 of the 15 industries, the lowest being 0.92. Factors of general importance, such as entrepreneurship and land, have not been included in

[38]See Chapter III, pp. 51–52.
[39]See, for instance, Bronfenbrenner and Douglas [4] and Douglas [16].

our functions. It is clear, then, that when all factors (including the
missing ones) are increased proportionally, the actual returns to

Table 3. Technology-Output and Capital-Output Elasticities.

Industry	Rank according to the technology-output elasticity	Technology-output elasticity	Capital-output elasticity	Sum of technology-output and capital-output elasticities	Percentage of technology-output elasticity in the sum %
Food products	1	0.76	0.53	1.29	59
Instruments	2	0.56	0.44	1.00	56
Transportation equipment	3	0.52	0.32	0.84	62
Petroleum and coal products	4	0.51	0.23	0.74	69
Rubber products	5	0.49	0.23	0.72	68
Chemicals	6	0.48	0.27	0.75	64
Machinery	7	0.45	0.33	0.78	58
Primary metals	8	0.42	0.16	0.58	72
Electrical machinery	9	0.39	0.30	0.69	57
Paper products	10	0.37	0.28	0.65	57
Lumber products	11	0.32	0.31	0.63	50
Apparels	12	0.24	0.20	0.44	55
Fabricated metal products	13	0.19	0.15	0.34	56
Stone, clay, and glass products	14	0.19	0.13	0.32	59
Leather products	15	0.13	0.07	0.20	65

Source: Tabulated and computed from data presented in Section (3) of this
chapter.

scale would be even greater than the estimated figures given in Table 4. Thus the latter figures may be considered the lower bound of the true values. In other words, it is likely that increasing returns existed in all industries, including the three with estimated returns ranging from 0.92 to unity. It should be noted that the measure of increasing returns given in Table 4 refers to the scale effects under *constant technology.*

It is useful to know the comparative importance of the technology effects relative to all other factors. This can be measured by the ratio of the technology-output elasticity to the sum of this elasticity and the scale returns. The industries are ranked by this ratio in Table 5. Column (2) gives the *returns to scale including technological effects;* column (3) represents the estimated contributions, in percentage terms, of technological change to the increase in output, when labor and capital factors are all increased proportionally. The industries are ranked by the magnitude of this ratio; the ranking here is very close to that in Table 3. The percentage contribution of technology to output under the condition of an equal proportional increase in capital and labor ranged from 38 to about 30 per cent in food products, transportation equipment, petroleum and coal products, instruments, rubber products, machinery (both electrical and nonelectrical), chemicals, and primary metal products. It is lower in other industries, the lowest being about 12 per cent in the leather and leather products industry.

The ratios given in column (3) of Table 5 may be considered as a measurement of technological intensity in the different industries. Their ranking on this basis is quite close to that according to technology-output elasticity.

The figures on the sum of returns to scale and the technology-output elasticities given in column (2) of Table 5 strongly show that the well-known historical tendency for output to increase at a faster rate than the rates of increase of inputs was in operation in 1957. This historical finding is the main conclusion of the analysis of the "weighted-input" approach and Solow's study [67]. The indicated persistence of this tendency is obtained in the present investigation without making the assumptions of competitive equilibrium and constant returns to scale. Instead, we have assumed that technological changes are embodied in capital and that equilibrium did not necessarily prevail.

Table 4. Measurement of Returns to Scale under Constant Technology.

Industry	Rank according to returns to scale	Labor-output elasticity	Production worker-output elasticity	Nonproduction employee-output elasticity	Capital-output elasticity	Returns to scale
	(1)	(2)	(3)	(4)	(5)	(6)
Food products	1		0.31	0.40	0.53	1.24
Chemicals	2		0.34	0.57	0.27	1.18
Primary metals	3	0.96			0.16	1.12
Instruments	4	0.67			0.44	1.11
Lumber products	5	0.79			0.31	1.10
Paper products	6		0.55	0.27	0.28	1.10
Stone, clay, and glass products	7		0.66	0.30	0.13	1.09
Rubber products	8	0.85			0.23	1.08
Machinery	9		0.47	0.27	0.33	1.07
Apparel	10		0.58	0.26	0.20	1.04
Fabricated metal products	11		0.53	0.34	0.15	1.02
Transportation equipment	12		0.41	0.28	0.32	1.01
Petroleum and coal products	13		0.27	0.50	0.23	1.00
Electric machinery	14		0.41	0.24	0.30	0.95
Leather products	15	0.85			0.07	0.92

Source: Tabulated from data presented in Tables 2 and 3 of this chapter.

Table 5. Returns to Scale and Technology Effect.

Industry	Rank according to data in column (3)	Sum of returns to scale and technology-output elasticity	Ratio of technology-output elasticity to the sum given in column (2) %
	(1)	(2)	(3)
Food products	1	2.00	38.0
Transportation equipment	2	1.53	34.0
Petroleum and coal products	3	1.51	33.8
Instruments	4	1.67	33.5
Rubber products	5	1.57	31.2
Machinery	6	1.52	29.6
Electric machinery	7	1.34	29.1
Chemicals	8	1.66	28.9
Primary metal products	9	1.54	27.3
Paper products	10	1.47	25.2
Lumber products	11	1.42	22.5
Apparel	12	1.28	18.8
Fabricated metal products	13	1.21	15.7
Stone, clay, and glass products	14	1.28	14.8
Leather products	15	1.05	12.4

Source: Tabulated and computed from data presented in Tables 3 and 4 of this chapter.

(iii) *Income Shares and Input-Output Elasticities*

The "weighted input" approach uses the shares received by factors as estimates of the respective input-output elasticities. Solow's 1957 paper [67] and the recent study of Arrow, Chenery, Minhas, and Solow [2] also rely on some variations of this method. Our findings indicate that this approach is unsatisfactory. The income-share method would underestimate the respective labor-output elasticities in all industries except two.[40] As shown in Table 6, the degrees of underestimation vary among the groups. In all

Table 6. Input-Output Elasticities and Income Shares.
(A) Production Workers

Industry	Production worker-output elasticity	Wage bill in value added %	Ratio of column (2) to column (1) %
	(1)	(2)	(3)
Food products	0.31	0.28	90
Apparel	0.58	0.51	88
Paper products	0.55	0.37	67
Chemicals	0.34	0.22	65
Petroleum and coal products	0.27	0.27	100
Stone, clay, and glass products	0.66	0.39	59
Fabricated metal products	0.53	0.42	79
Machinery	0.47	0.40	85
Electric machinery	0.41	0.36	88
Transportation equipment	0.41	0.47	115

[40]These exceptions are production workers in the transportation equipment industry and the petroleum and coal products industries. See Table 6, (A).

(B) Nonproduction Employees

Industry	Nonproduction employee-output elasticity	Salary bill in value added %	Ratio of column (2) to column (1) %
	(1)	(2)	(3)
Food products	0.40	0.20	50
Apparel	0.26	0.12	46
Paper products	0.27	0.14	52
Chemicals	0.57	0.15	26
Petroleum and coal products	0.50	0.13	26
Stone, clay, and glass products	0.30	0.12	40
Fabricated metal products	0.34	0.18	53
Machinery	0.27	0.20	74
Electric machinery	0.24	0.20	83
Transportation equipment	0.28	0.18	64

(C) All Employees

Industry	Labor-output elasticity	Wage and salary paid in value added %	Ratio of column (2) to column (1) %
	(1)	(2)	(3)
Lumber products	0.79	0.67	85
Rubber products	0.85	0.57	67
Leather products	0.85	0.65	76
Primary metals	0.96	0.58	60
Instruments	0.67	0.63	94

(D)   Capital

Industry	Sum of capital-output and technology-output elasticities	Returns to capital in value added	Ratio of column (2) to column (1) %
	(1)	(2)	(3)
Food products	1.29	0.52	40
Apparel	0.44	0.37	84
Lumber products	0.64	0.33	52
Paper products	0.65	0.49	75
Chemicals	0.75	0.63	84
Petroleum and coal products	0.74	0.60	81
Rubber products	0.72	0.43	60
Leather products	0.20	0.35	175
Stone, clay, and glass products	0.32	0.49	153
Primary metals	0.58	0.42	72
Fabricated metal products	0.34	0.40	118
Machinery	0.78	0.40	51
Electric machinery	0.69	0.44	64
Transportation equipment	0.84	0.35	42
Instruments	1.00	0.37	37

industries, the income-share method would underestimate the elasticity of output for nonproduction employees a great deal more than that for production workers.

Similarly, our findings show that use of the income share net of payments to labor as the capital-output elasticity[41] leads to under-

[41]In our approach, the sum of the capital-output and technology-output elasticities is relevant here.

estimation of these elasticities in 12 of the 15 industries. The reverse is true only for leather products; stone, clay, and glass products; and fabricated metal products. The degrees of underestimation and the extent of overestimation in the three exceptional cases are given in Table 6, (D). The fact that both the labor-output and the capital-output elasticities are in the great majority of cases underestimated by the respective income shares implies increasing returns to scale, as indicated in the preceding section.

(iv) *Deviations of the Allocation of Resources from the Profit-Maximizing Position*

In Section (3) of this chapter, the adjustments in the employment of workers that would have been required to achieve the profit-maximizing position under the conditions prevailing during 1957 have been estimated. The nature of these estimates should be clearly understood. For production workers, the adjustments required are reductions of rather substantial magnitudes. However, these estimates are made with the 1957 wage rates assumed given and fixed. If the required adjustments had actually been carried out within a short period of time on the assumption that such actions were not precluded by union resistance, labor unrest, and the consideration of other consequences, wage rates would have fallen substantially. As a result, the required adjustments would have been smaller. Nevertheless, the relative magnitudes of the estimated adjustments required in the different industries indicate the comparative degrees of deviation from the profit-maximizing position. After allowing for different speeds of adjustment in the various industries, these figures should bear some relationship to the changing employment patterns in the ensuing years. In Section (3) we have compared the estimated changes required in 1957 with the actual changes from 1956 to 1957. The adjustments toward the profit-maximizing position, however, probably would not have been made smoothly and by just the right amounts in each year. A comparison of the degrees of deviation from the profit-maximizing position and the changes in employment over a longer period would be more meaningful.

Many difficulties exist that preclude a conclusive comparison of the estimated adjustments required for profit-maximization with the actual changes, either during 1956–1957 and 1957–1958, or for a longer period. The difficulties in making the one-year comparison have been discussed.[42] Those involved in the longer-term comparison will be made clear in the process of explaining the rough comparison presented below.

The longer-term comparison is made for the changes during a four-year span from 1956 to 1960. A four-year span is probably long enough for the different year-to-year changes to smooth out. At the same time, it is probably not so lengthy that the production functions estimated on the 1957 data would cease to be realistic for comparative purposes, granting that technological changes flowing from capital outlays during 1958–1960 would make these functions somewhat less exact. The estimated adjustments in production workers or in total employees, as the case may be,[43] required for achieving the profit-maximizing position for the different industries, are presented in column (1) of Table 7.[44] On the assumption that the speed of adjustment over the four-year span 1956–1960 is equal to four times the speed during 1956–1957,[45] the total adjustment that would have been completed by 1960 can then be easily computed in column (3). The integers given in column (4) are the ranks assigned the various industries on the basis of the magnitudes of the adjustments given in column (3).

The actual changes in production workers or in total employees, as the case may be,[46] are given in column (5). In the meantime, however, outputs have also changed (see column (6)). Part of the changes in employment were in response to these output changes, and this must be allowed for in order to trace the efforts gradually developing to remedy the rather substantial deviations from the

[42]See pp. 67–68, above.

[43]For lumber products, rubber products, leather products, primary metal products, and instruments, the comparison is made for total employees. For the other industries, changes in the employment of production workers are compared. This difference is necessitated by the different types of production function obtained for the different industries (see Table 2, this chapter).

[44]For the derivation of these estimates, see Section (3) of this chapter.

[45]The estimated speeds of adjustment given in column (2) are equal to four times the respective coefficients of the speed of adjustment given for the different industries in Section (3) of this chapter.

[46]See n. 43, above.

profit-maximizing position in 1956–1957. The percentage changes in output in the different industries divided by their respective labor-output elasticities represent, other things being equal,[47] the changes in employment in response to the changes in output; these are given in column (7). The changes in employment given in column (8), obtained by subtracting the figures in column (7) from those in column (5), are the adjustments that may be attributed to the efforts, gradually developing from 1956, to remedy the substantial deviations from the profit-maximization position. The integers in column (9) rank the magnitudes of the adjustment given in column (8).

In 11 of the 15 cases, the estimated adjustments given in column (3) are substantially lower than the corresponding figures in column (8). This is expected because both nonproduction workers[48] and capital have increased in most industries during 1956–1960, and part of the change in output should have been attributed to these factors. The figures in column (8) are therefore the upper bound of the absolute values of the changes in production workers of total employees, as the case may be,[49] as a result of the effort to adjust to the profit-maximizing position.[50]

If the estimated adjustments required for achieving the profit-maximizing position in the different industries are indicative of the relative magnitudes of the pressure on the different industries to make changes in employment, the figures in columns (4) and (9) should have a significant rank correlation. This coefficient is equal to 0.68.[51] There is a less than 1 per cent chance for these two series to have a rank correlation as high as 0.66 if they are in fact independent.[52] This significant rank correlation lends support to our estimates of the relative degrees of deviation from the profit-

[47]See the discussion in the next paragraph about the changes in other factors.

[48]In the case of the ten industries for which production workers and nonproduction employees have been segregated in the production functions. See n. 43, above.

[49]See n. 43 above.

[50]For reasons to be explained presently, we have not tried to estimate the portion of the changes in output attributable to nonproduction workers and to capital. The comparison attempted in Table 7, however, is meaningful due to the fact that the figures in column (8) are the upper bound of the figures in column (3).

[51]Computed on the basis of the formula given in Ferber [20], p. 341.

[52]See Ferber [20], pp. 386–387.

Table 7. Analysis of Change in Employment, 1956 to 1960.[a]

Industry	Required change to achieve profit maximization as estimated from the 1957 production functions, in per cent of 1956 employment[b]	Estimated speed of adjustment during 1956–1960[c]	Estimated change to remedy deviation from position of maximum profits [col. (1) x col. (2)] in per cent of 1956 employment[b]	Industries ranked by data in col. (3)
	(1)	(2)	(3)	(4)
Food products	−23.2	0.64	−14.8	7
Apparel	−20.4	1.00	−20.4	3
Lumber products	−54.0	0.32	−17.3	5
Paper products	−16.5	0.44	− 7.3	12
Chemicals	−50.8	0.28	−14.2	8
Petroleum and coal products	−53.0	0.32	−17.0	6
Rubber products	− 9.7	1.08	−10.5	11
Leather products	−13.7	0.52	− 7.1	14
Stone, clay, and glass products	−36.2	0.20	− 7.2	13
Primary metals	−46.8	0.12	− 5.6	15
Fabricated metal products	−17.7	1.12	−19.8	4
Machinery	−17.2	0.76	−13.1	9
Electrical machinery	−16.3	0.76	−12.4	10
Transportation equipment	−64.0	0.48	−30.7	1
Instruments	−37.9	0.76	−28.8	2

[a]See n. 43, above.

[b]For the meaning of these estimates, see the discussion on p. 114.

[c]Four times the speeds of adjustment during 1956–1957. The estimated speeds of adjustment are derived from the demand functions for labor, and are presented in Section (3) of this chapter.

Table 7. (continued)

Industry	Change in employment in per cent of 1956 employment[d]	Change in output in per cent of 1956 output[e]	Change in employment attributable to change in output in per cent of 1956 employment	Upper limits of change in employment attributable to attempt to remedy deviations from position of maximum profits, in per cent of 1956 employment [col. (5)–col. (7)]	Industries ranked by data in col. (8)
	(5)	(6)	(7)	(8)	(9)
Food products	− 7.3	+ 9.0	+29.0	−36.3	5
Apparel	+ 0.5	+26.3	+45.3	−44.8	2
Lumber products	−14.0	− 2.7	− 3.4	−10.6	12
Paper products	− 3.5	+10.9	+19.8	−23.3	10
Chemicals	− 2.5	+26.0	+76.4	−78.9	1
Petroleum and coal products	−11.6	+ 8.0	+29.6	−41.2	3
Rubber products	0	+19.8	+23.3	−23.3	9
Leather products	− 5.3	0	0	− 5.3	14
Stone, clay, and glass products	− 5.7	+ 7.8	11.8	−17.5	11
Primary metals	−14.0	−12.5	−13.0	− 1.0	15
Fabricated metal products	− 6.4	+ 9.3	+17.5	−23.9	8
Machinery	−11.1	− 1.0	− 2.1	− 9.0	13
Electrical machinery	− 0.7	+ 9.8	+23.9	−24.6	7
Transportation equipment	−14.5	+10.9	+26.6	−41.1	4
Instruments	+ 1.5	+22.7	+33.9	−32.4	6

[d]For the ten industries for which employment of production workers is computed (see n. 43, above), the source of data is "production and related workers," *Business Statistics*, 1961, pp. 65–67. For the five industries for which all employees are computed, the source of data is "number of full-time equivalent employees," *Survey of Current Business*, July 1962, p. 29.

[e]Computed on the indexes of industrial production for the respective industries given in *Business Statistics*, 1961, pp. 14–16.

maximizing position in the different industries, and also indicates that the particular versions of the production function we have selected for the different industries are on the whole not unsatisfactory.

The extent of the desired reductions in production workers from the point of view of profit-maximization may serve as an indication of the pressure on employment from the strong tendency toward automation of the production processes in the different industries. On the basis of the ranking presented in column (4), the intensity of this pressure decreases in the following order: transportation equipment; instruments; apparel; fabricated metal products; lumber products; petroleum and coal products; food products; chemicals; machinery; electric machinery; rubber products; paper products; stone, clay, and glass products; leather products; and primary metal products.

Although we have also estimated the adjustments required in the employment of nonproduction workers to achieve the profit-maximization position in the different industries, we have not made a longer-term comparison between these adjustments and the actual changes in the employment of this category of workers for the following reasons. First, a consistent series of nonproduction workers during 1956–1960 is not available for the different industries because of the extensive change in the standard industrial classification used by the Census Bureau after the 1958 census. Second, in sharp contrast with production workers, changes in professional and technical staff depend much more closely upon the availability of people with these special skills, both locally and nationally. In consequence, interstate migrations of such persons are critically important, and it is likely that these movements varied radically in speed among different years, influenced by forces we cannot consider here.

For the six industries for which we have obtained plausible estimates for both the required adjustment in nonproduction employees in 1957 and the coefficient of the speed of adjustment during 1956–1957, the ranking of the magnitudes of the estimated changes, required for profit-maximization and adjusted by the speed of adjustment, and that of the actual changes during

1956–1957 are very close, as shown in Table 8. The rank correlation coefficient between the required and the actual changes is 0.91, which is significant at the 5 per cent level.[53]

Since we have not made estimates for the demand functions for capital and, hence, we have no information on the speed of adjustment of capital to the profit-maximization position in the different industries, a comparison between required changes of capital, after allowance for the speed of adjustment, and the actual changes cannot be made for the capital variable. However, the estimates of the marginal revenue products, per dollar invested before business income tax, for the different industries may be taken as a first approximation to the relative profitability of these alternative outlets for investment. These estimates are given in Table 9.

The variations are very large indeed. Nonetheless, this could

Table 8. Change in Employment of Nonproduction Employees.

Industry	Estimated increase "required" for profit maximization and adjusted by the speed of adjustment, 1957		Actual increase from 1956 to 1957	
	In % of 1956 employment	Rank	In % of 1956 employment	Rank
Food products	2.0	6	2.6	6
Apparel	5.0	4	2.9	5
Chemicals	8.4	3	5.3	3
Petroleum and coal products	13.2	2	6.3	1
Stone, clay, and glass products	4.6	5	3.5	4
Fabricated metal products	14.3	1	5.9	2

[53]See Ferber [20], p. 523.

Table 9. Marginal Revenue Product of Capital, 1957.
(In dollar per dollar invested before business income tax)

Industry	Rank	Marginal revenue product
Transportation equipment	1	2.44
Instruments	2	1.49
Electric machinery	3	1.44
Machinery	4	1.10
Food products	5	1.02
Apparel	6	0.74
Leather products	7	0.70
Rubber products	8	0.55
Lumber products	9	0.42
Fabricated metal products	10	0.33
Paper products	11	0.30
Chemicals	12	0.29
Primary metals	13	0.24
Petroleum and coal products	14	0.21
Stone, clay, and glass products	15	0.14

Source: Tabulated and ranked from data presented in Section (3) of this chapter.

be expected. Commitments to capital investment, unlike those to production workers or even nonproduction employees, are of a long-run nature. Once made, it is difficult for business to change them. It is therefore natural that the leveling of profitability in different industries through transfer of capital resources will be an extremely slow process. This is especially so during a period of rapid technological change. What is new and up to date at a given time may become obsolete in a year or two; and the risk of making prompt changes may be very large and very different in different industries. The tendency to postpone decisions will therefore be very great. Thus, in most industries, the marginal revenue products greatly exceed the relevant long-term rates of interest and by very different amounts. Significantly different cyclical patterns of operations in the various industries further increase the probability of large differences of profitability in any given year.

(v) Deviations of the Allocation of Resources from the Pareto Optimum

The allocation of labor resources is at the Pareto optimum if the marginal "physical" product (i.e., marginal product valued at the unit price of output) of labor per dollar of labor cost is unity in every industry. On the basis of this criterion, there was underemployment of production workers in 1957 in all industries for which production workers and nonproduction employees have been segregated in our production functions, the only exception being the transportation equipment industry. As shown in Table 10, the estimated marginal "physical" products are all greater than unity, except in the transportation equipment industry. This is, of course, not inconsistent with the previous finding that reduction of production workers was required in all industries to achieve the profit-maximizing position. For allocation of labor resources to be optimal in the Pareto sense, the wage rate must be equal to the marginal "physical" product, whereas, in profit-maximization, it must be equated to marginal revenue product.

The degree of underemployment was the greatest in the three industries producing stone, clay, and glass products; chemicals; and paper products; the marginal physical product per dollar of wage cost being $1.71, $1.55, and $1.48, respectively. There was also very substantial underemployment in the fabricated metals product industry, where the marginal physical product was $1.26. In all other industries, the marginal physical products per dollar of wage cost were less than 20 per cent from one dollar. The required adjustments to achieve optimum may be computed readily by an approximate formula[54] and are presented in column (2) of Table 10.[55]

[54]This formula, derived in a way similar to equation (4.13), is as follows:

$$\frac{dL}{L} = \frac{d(MPP)}{MPP} \bigg/ [b\ (\log q) \left(1 - \frac{1}{h}\right) - 1].$$

[55]Similar to the interpretation of the estimated changes required to achieve profit-maximization, the magnitudes of the estimated adjustments to achieve

The estimated marginal "physical" products per dollar of salary cost of nonproduction employees are, without exception, very substantially above unity. These data are shown in column (3) of Table 10. As shown in column (4), in order to achieve the Pareto optimum, very great expansion must take place in the employment of this category of employees in all industries, the expansions in percentage terms being much larger than the corresponding expansions required for production workers.[56] However, since the number of people in the category of nonproduction employees is much less than that of productive workers in all industries, the expansions of the former were generally smaller than those of the production workers in numbers of people involved.

For the five industries for which we have not been able to disaggregate employment into production and nonproduction workers, the estimated marginal "physical" products of employment as a whole and the required adjustments[57] to achieve the Pareto optimum are presented in columns (5) and (6) of Table 10.

The marginal "physical" products of capital of the different industries are ranked in Table 11. The data indicate that, for a more optimal allocation of capital resources, capital expenditure should be expanded relatively more in the four industries producing capital equipment: transportation equipment, instruments, electrical machinery, and machinery other than electrical, in the order given.[58] Next come the consumer's goods industries: food products, leather goods, rubber goods, and apparel. The marginal "physical" products of capital in chemicals, lumber products, primary metals, paper products, and fabricated metal products were lower, but they were still in the range of about 45 cents to 65 cents per dollar invested before business tax. At the bottom of the list are found the petroleum and coal products and the stone, clay, and glass products industries, where a dollar invested would

---

optimum should be considered as an indication of the *relative* degree of deviation from the optimum prevailing in 1957 rather than a measurement of the changes that should be carried out. These estimates were made on the assumption that the wage rates in 1957 are fixed and given. If the substantial expansions required were actually carried out in all industries, wage rates would rise and the required adjustments to optimum would then be much less than the magnitudes given here.

[56]See n. 55, above.

[57]*Ibid.*

[58]Consumers' durable equipment figures very importantly, of course, in the output of the transportation equipment and the electrical machinery industries.

Table 10. Deviations from the Optimum in the Allocation of Labor Resources, 1957.[a]

Industry	Production Labor		Nonproduction labor		All labor	
	Marginal "physical" product (dollars)	Required change in employment (%)	Marginal "physical" product (dollars)	Required change in employment (%)	Marginal "physical" product (dollars)	Required change in employment (%)
	(1)	(2)	(3)	(4)	(5)	(6)
Food products	1.11	+13	2.03	+67		
Apparel	1.14	+23	2.12	+98		
Lumber products					1.18	+33
Paper products	1.48	+49	2.00	+75		
Chemicals	1.55	+42	3.85	+88		
Petroleum and coal products	1.00	0	3.88	+92		
Rubber products					1.49	+72
Leather products					1.32	+63
Stone, clay, and glass products	1.71	+60	2.41	+85		
Primary metals					1.64	+73
Fabricated metal products	1.26	+33	1.92	+77		
Machinery	1.17	+23	1.35	+41		
Electrical machinery	1.13	+17	1.22	+27		
Transportation equipment	0.87	−22	1.58	+55		
Instruments					1.06	+12

Source: Tabulated from material presented in Section (3) of this chapter.
[a]Marginal "physical" products are in dollars per dollar of labor compensation. For interpretation of required adjustments in employment, see n. 55, p. 122.

Table 11. Marginal "Physical" Product of Capital, 1957.
(In dollars per dollar invested before business tax)

Industry	Marginal "physical" product
Transportation equipment	3.04
Instruments	1.86
Electrical machinery	1.81
Machinery	1.43
Food products	1.33
Apparel	0.94
Leather products	0.93
Rubber products	0.86
Chemicals	0.65
Lumber products	0.62
Primary metals	0.49
Paper products	0.48
Fabricated metal products	0.46
Petroleum and coal products	0.31
Stone, clay, and glass products	0.29

Source: Tabulated from material presented in Section (3) of this chapter.

produce a marginal return, valued at the respective unit prices, of about 30 cents before business tax. The wide variations of the marginal "physical" products in the different industries are not unexpected, and are accountable by the considerations discussed previously in connection with the similarly great variations in the marginal revenue products of capital in the different industries.[59]

(vi) *Analysis of the 15 Manufacturing Industries as a Whole*

In the absence of disaggregated functions, more aggregated ones have to be relied upon to throw light on many questions that can be answered meaningfully only through the disaggregated functions. For instance, a production function for manufacturing industries as a whole might have been fitted, from which marginal "physical' and revenue products would be estimated as shown in the preceding analysis. At any given moment, however, the margin-

[59]See pp. 120–122, above.

125

al products are substantially different in different industries. Even if the criteria of aggregation developed by Klein [44], Nataf [54], or Theil [71] are all satisfied, and the marginal product estimated from the aggregate function is "correct," one would not know from which industry this estimated marginal product is obtained, and to which industry an additional application of certain available input would lead to a more optimal allocation of resources. By contrast, if separate functions can be estimated for each of the 15 industries, one would be able to say, for instance, that if the assumption underlying the estimates are essentially correct, additional capital should, from the point of view of optimal allocation of resources, flow first to the transportation equipment industry, next to the instruments industry, and so on in the order given in Table 10. Nevertheless, one might suppose that a more aggregated function would be more useful for comparison of the manufacturing group with other sectors, e.g., agriculture. But this would be incorrect. More information can be obtained by ranking the marginal product of agriculture (or rather those of different segments of agriculture) together with the different manufacturing industries, because a pattern of optimal allocation would then be discerned that would indicate the desirable directions resource flows, not from manufacturing to agriculture or vice versa, but among all groups in manufacturing and agriculture together.

Nonetheless, it is still convenient to have an idea of the "average" or "over-all" state of affairs. Such a picture for the 15 industries as a whole is presented in this section by providing answers to the question: What would be the percentage increase in value added in the 15 industries if production workers in all these industries are increased by 1 per cent at the same time, or if all factors of production are increased by 1 per cent at the same time? These percentage increases may be defined as the output-production worker elasticities and the scale returns for the 15 industries as a whole. Parameters relating to nonproduction employees, capital, and technology are similarly defined.

These aggregate elasticities can be obtained by computing the averages of the elasticities of the individual industries, weighted by their respective outputs, here value added. Take the scale returns as an example. Given the following production functions:

$$V_i = a_i L_{pi}^{b_i \log q_i} \ L_{ni}^{c_i} \ K_i^{e_i \log R_i}$$

where i indicates a given industry. Differentiating and summing up with respect to i, we have:

$$\Sigma_i dV_i = \Sigma_i b_i \log q_i \frac{dL_{pi}}{L_{pi}} V_i + \Sigma_i c_i \frac{dL_{ni}}{L_{ni}} V_i$$

$$+ \Sigma_i \left(e_i \log R_i + e_i \frac{100-R_i}{R_i} \log K_i \right) \frac{dK_i}{K_i} V_i.$$

Since, by the nature of the question posed, $\dfrac{dL_{pi}}{L_{pi}} = \dfrac{dL_{ni}}{L_{ni}} = \dfrac{dK_i}{K_i} = 1$ per cent for all i, we obtain,

$$\frac{\Sigma dV_i}{\Sigma V_i} = \frac{\Sigma b_i (\log q_i) V_i}{\Sigma V_i} + \frac{\Sigma c_i V_i}{\Sigma V_i} + \frac{\Sigma e_i (\log R_i) V_i}{\Sigma V_i}$$

$$+ \frac{\Sigma e_i \dfrac{100-R_i}{R_i} (\log K_i) V_i}{\Sigma V_i}.$$

The partial (aggregate) elasticities can be obtained from the above by dropping the unwanted terms.

This system of weighting by output (value added) is in fact the same as that suggested by Klein [44], even though he derived the result with much more ambitious criteria.[60]

We shall first compare the over-all elasticities of output with respect to production and nonproduction workers in the ten industries for which we have been able to disaggregate these two types of workers. The two elasticities are, respectively, 0.43 and 0.34 (see Table 12). The value added by these ten industries amounted to \$102.2 billion in 1957. The respective wage and salary bills for these two categories of workers are \$34.4 billion and \$16.8 billion. On the assumption that all relevant prices and salary and wage rates do not change for small changes in employment,

---

[60]The two criteria at which Klein aimed are discussed in Chapter II, Section (1), (ii), above.

Table 12. Elasticities of Output with Respect to Production and
Nonproduction Employees in Ten Industries as a Whole.[a]

Industry	Value added, 1957 ($ million)	Weights	Production worker-output elasticity	Wage bill, 1957 ($ million)	Nonproduction labor-output elasticity	Salary bill, 1957 ($ million)
Food products	16,349	0.160	0.050	4,244	0.064	2,898
Apparel	6,066	0.059	0.034	2,867	0.015	796
Paper products	5,724	0.056	0.031	2,010	0.015	723
Chemicals	12,474	0.122	0.042	2,337	0.070	1,743
Petroleum and coal products	3,249	0.032	0.009	771	0.016	378
Stone, clay, and glass products	4,980	0.049	0.032	1,802	0.015	552
Fabricated metal products	9,543	0.093	0.049	3,802	0.031	1,581
Machinery	15,977	0.156	0.073	6,060	0.042	2,989
Electrical machinery	9,620	0.094	0.039	3,292	0.023	1,841
Transportation equipment	18,235	0.178	0.073	7,174	0.051	3,312
Over-all total	102,217	1.000	0.432	34,359	0.342	16,813

Source: Computed from data presented in this chapter and from Census of Manufactures, 1957.

[a]Figures for production-worker output elasticities obtained by multiplying values in column (1) of Table 6, Section (A), by weights shown here. Nonproduction labor-output elasticities computed by multiplying values in column (1) of Table 6, Section (B), by weights shown here.

then a 1 per cent change in production workers would imply an increase of $0.34 billion in wage bill and an increase of $0.44 billion in value added. On the other hand, a similar change in nonproduction workers would result in an increase of only $0.17

billion in salary bill for an increase of $0.35 billion in value added. The tendency toward expansion of nonproduction employees at the expense of production workers analyzed above for the individual industries is again clear in the over-all picture presented here. The above analysis may be taken as an indication of the pressure toward automation in the ten industries as a whole.

Total labor-output elasticities for each of these ten industries can be obtained simply by summing up the respective elasticities for production workers and nonproduction employees.[61] Those for the other five industries have been estimated directly. The aggregate elasticities of output, capital, and technology for the 15 industries as a whole are computed in Table 13, and are equal to 0.80, 0.29, and 0.45, respectively.

Similar to the conclusion we have reached for the individual industries (see Table 4, above), increasing returns to scale under constant technology exist in the 15 industries as a whole, with the sum of the labor-output and capital-output elasticities at 1.1. The aggregate technology-capital intensity (see p. 106) and the aggregate technology intensity (see p. 108) are 60 and 29 per cent, respectively. The aggregate scale returns including technological effect (see p. 108 and Table 5) are 1.55, greatly exceeding unity. This again clearly indicates that the underlying production processes in the 15 manufacturing industries were such that, if all inputs increase, output would increase much faster than any of the inputs.

As has been explained, Nataf [54] has developed a scheme of aggregation which has a great deal of merit. The weighting system implied is different from the Klein approach, the one used in the preceding analysis. For our type of functions, the Nataf weights for deriving the various aggregate input-output elasticities should be computed from the logarithms of the magnitudes of the inputs. We have used the Nataf method to recompute the data given in Table 13. The results are shown in Table 14. As can be seen, they are very close to those shown in Table 13: for labor, the weighted aggregate output elasticity in 0.802, as against 0.794; for capital, 0.267 as against 0.290; for technology, 0.415 as against 0.446.

[61]It should be noted that we aim at calculating the elasticities for a 1 per cent change in one or all factors, as the case may be. (See p. 126).

Table 13. First Computation of Aggregate Input-Output Elasticities.

Industry	Weights	Labor		Capital		Technology	
		Output elasticity	Weighted output elasticity	Output elasticity	Weighted output elasticity	Output elasticity	Weighted output elasticity
	(1)	(2)	(3)	(4)	(5)	(6)	(7)
Food products.....	0.129	0.711	0.092	0.529	0.068	0.756	0.098
Apparel...........	0.048	0.841	0.040	0.195	0.009	0.238	0.011
Lumber products...	0.026	0.792	0.021	0.314	0.008	0.321	0.008
Paper products....	0.045	0.817	0.037	0.281	0.013	0.373	0.017
Chemicals.........	0.099	0.912	0.090	0.267	0.026	0.480	0.048
Petroleum and coal products......	0.026	0.772	0.020	0.231	0.006	0.508	0.013
Rubber products...	0.021	0.851	0.018	0.232	0.005	0.486	0.010
Leather products...	0.015	0.849	0.013	0.067	0.001	0.127	0.002
Stone, clay, and glass products......	0.039	0.962	0.038	0.132	0.005	0.186	0.007
Primary metals....	0.105	0.958	0.101	0.164	0.017	0.423	0.044
Fabricated metal products..........	0.075	0.866	0.065	0.149	0.011	0.189	0.014
Machinery........	0.126	0.739	0.093	0.325	0.041	0.448	0.056
Electrical machinery........	0.076	0.654	0.050	0.297	0.023	0.385	0.029
Transportation equipment........	0.146	0.695	0.101	0.319	0.047	0.518	0.076
Instruments.......	0.023	0.668	0.015	0.440	0.010	0.558	0.013
Over-all values....	1.000		0.794		0.290		0.446

Source: **Data** previously presented in this chapter.

(5) *Criticisms of Our Approach*

A number of weaknesses exist in our study, and they should be candidly faced. Some of them perhaps are unavoidable because of limitations in the data. Others can be remedied by refinements that we have decided not to attempt here. In some cases, the possible criticisms lose validity upon further examination. Beyond this, a few of the criticisms raised with regard to previous studies can be charged against our own, and we do not have satisfactory answers to all of them.

(i) The first objection that could be raised is that these two-digit industries are aggregates of sub-industries of rather diverse

Table 14. Second Computation of Aggregate Input-Output Elasticities.[a]

Industry	Labor		Capital		Technology
	Weights	Weighted labor-output elasticities	Weights	Weighted capital-output elasticities	Weighted output elasticities
	(1)	(2)	(3)	(4)	(5)
Food products...........	0.075	0.053	0.075	0.039	0.570
Apparel.................	0.072	0.061	0.055	0.011	0.013
Lumber products.........	0.065	0.051	0.064	0.020	0.021
Paper products..........	0.064	0.052	0.070	0.020	0.026
Chemicals...............	0.067	0.061	0.075	0.020	0.036
Petroleum and coal products...............	0.053	0.041	0.071	0.016	0.036
Rubber products.........	0.056	0.048	0.060	0.014	0.029
Leather products.........	0.060	0.051	0.049	0.003	0.006
Stone, clay, and glass products............	0.063	0.061	0.068	0.009	0.013
Primary metals..........	0.072	0.069	0.077	0.013	0.033
Fabricated metal products.	0.071	0.061	0.069	0.010	0.018
Machinery..............	0.075	0.055	0.073	0.024	0.033
Electrical machinery......	0.071	0.046	0.066	0.020	0.025
Transportation equipment.	0.076	0.053	0.072	0.023	0.037
Instruments.............	0.058	0.039	0.057	0.025	0.032
Over-all values..........		0.802		0.267	0.415

Source: Computed from data previously presented in this chapter.
[a]Using Nataf weights computed on logarithms of inputs. For labor, log L used; for capital, log K.

types, hence are not sufficiently homogeneous to be meaningfully represented by a single production function for each group.

We are, of course, painfully aware of this criticism.[62] Data on capital and supplementary wage costs, however, are available across the states only for two-digit industries. It is therefore impossible to estimate production functions for more narrowly defined industries, with capital appearing as a separate variable, using the published census data. Moreover, disaggregation loses a great deal of its merit in the present instance, as compared to studies of other

[62]In [28], Grunfeld and Griliches put forth certain interesting merits of aggregated studies, but they agree that aggregate functions cannot throw any light on the components from which the aggregates are constructed.

131

topics, such as estimates of consumption functions. In the latter case, disaggregated studies of the demand for automobiles and that for household appliances, for instance, yield more useful information on the income and price elasticities of demand for these two types of goods than could be learned from an aggregate demand function for the two goods; and the disaggregation does not result in any deterioration in the quality of the basic data used. By contrast, for estimating production functions, the basic data would, in many important cases, suffer severe loss of quality because of the multiple-product nature of the output of most of the important manufacturing establishments in this country. In the census reports, the data of a given establishment are assigned exclusively to the group to which their principal product belongs. When one reaches for a narrowly defined industry, two consequences follow. First, the data for output, labor, and capital for a given establishment in this case contain components involving other products. Second, and perhaps even more important, some of the largest producers in a narrowly defined industry in fact are classified in other industries because they produce even greater amounts of other products; hence data on their operations are missing from this particular industry. For these compelling reasons, production functions estimated at the four-digit level would be quite unsatisfactory. For the three-digit and two-digit levels, the weight of the argument probably would be in favor of estimating the former rather than the latter. But this is not necessarily so in all cases. Take the electric machinery industry (a two-digit group) as an example. It is unlikely that many major establishments are not producing significant amounts of both "electrical industrial apparatus" and "communication equipment," the classifications under quotations being three-digit ones.

It may also be pointed out that not many production functions exist for manufacturing industries even at the two-digit level. Our own estimates, it is hoped, represent a step forward in filling this gap.

(ii) A second objection would be that the data for output and input are not aggregated in the most desirable theoretical way.

The basic data on outputs and inputs for the "representative firms" of the different states are computed from the census data, and are arithmetic averages of the corresponding data of the individual establishments. According to the criteria developed by Klein [44] and Nataf [54], however, geometric averages of the establishment data should be used to estimate functions of the type we have used. Since we have no access to the census establishment data, there is no way to remedy this defect. Neither can an analysis of the aggregation bias in the production functions of the different two-digit industries along the Theil approach [71] be attempted, because knowledge is lacking of certain important parameters. There is no satisfactory remedy for this weakness of our study.

(iii) The next objection concerns the measures of capital we have used. The basic data on capital are book values of historical cumulations of purchases of assets at original cost. They do not represent "quantities" of capital in existence, even less capital actually in use.

Looking at the latter part of the criticism, although capital in existence is admittedly not the same thing as capital in use, this argument loses force for cross-section data of a single year. It is much more valid to assume that the rates of capacity utilization are more or less the same across the states in the same year than to make the same assumption for time series analysis. If the degree of capacity utilization is the same across the states, the use of data on capital in existence would yield the same estimate for the capital exponents as those obtained by using data on capital in use, the only difference being in the constant terms in the functions.[63] Even if the rates of utilization are significantly different (though these differences could not possibly be as serious as for time series analysis covering any reasonable length of time), this complication would reduce the variance explained by the estimated function without affecting the capital exponent if the different rates of utilization are not significantly correlated with the capital vari-

---

[63]Assume that output is a function of capital only and that the rate of capacity utilization is r for all producing units i, $i = 1, \ldots\ldots, I$, as follows:
$$V_i = a \ (rK_i)^e u_i$$
$$\log V_i = (\log a + e \log r) + e \log K_i + \log u_i$$
where u_i is the disturbance term. Thus, r affects the constant term only.

133

able.[64] There is no reason to believe that the larger establishments either underutilized or overutilized their capacities proportionally in larger degree than the smaller ones, so that the different rates of utilization would be correlated with the capital variable.[65]

Solow [67] has attempted to adjust the rate of capacity utilization by the ratio of current man-hours to the preceding peak. This adjustment, however, would impart a fixed proportion tendency to the estimated functions, and would defeat to some extent the purpose of estimating substitutability. Accordingly, we conclude that differences in the rate of capacity utilization are unlikely to be serious in our cross-section study. Whatever differences did exist may not affect the estimated exponents significantly.

The use of book values as measurements of quantity of capital in existence grossly neglects the different vintages of assets bought in different years and the various prices at which these assets were acquired. However, the deflation of book values to a constant or current cost basis poses extremely difficult problems. Deflated values obtained by using the currently available price indices for capital goods quite seriously understate the quantity of assets bought in more recent years, because improvements in efficiency have not been adequately taken into consideration in the construction of these indices. Questions also have been raised about the reliability of the substantially different movements in the price indices for structure and for equipment.[66]

Moreover, some of the defects of using historical book values in a regression analysis of production function on cross-section data have been exaggerated, while others can at least partially be remedied. First, consider the different rates of historical purchases at varying prices in the various establishments. If the available price deflators were satisfactory,[67] it would naturally be better to

[64]The equation in the preceding footnote becomes:

$$\log V_1 = \log a + e \log K_1 + (\log u_1 + e \log r_1).$$

The existence of the $e \log r_1$ term would not cause biases in the estimated e if it is not correlated with $\log K_1$. Similarly, if a labor variable is present in the equation, both the labor and the capital exponents would not be affected by $e \log r_1$ if the latter is independent of both $\log K_1$ and $\log L_1$.

[65]Or the labor variable. See *ibid.*

[66]See Gordon [25].

[67]As we have explained, they are not.

deflate the historical purchases by the appropriate prices, and then sum the results after proper allowances for depreciation. The omission of this step because satisfactory price data and other information are lacking, however, is far less serious than might be thought for cross-sectional regression analysis of single year data. Needless to say, if the purchases by the different establishments in a past period were all of the same proportion to their book values in 1957, and if this were true with regard to purchases in all past periods, the use of book values as the capital variable would affect only the constant term of the function, without causing biases in the estimated exponents. The reason is exactly the same as that given for effects of underutilization of capacity.[68] The historical purchases by different establishments in a given past period were not, of course, of the same proportion with their book values in 1957. Insofar as these different proportions are independent of the total book values of capital or labor employed in 1957, however, this complication only would increase the unexplained variance of the function, without causing biases to the estimated exponents.[69] But there is no reason to believe that either the sizes of the book values or the amounts of labor employed by the different establishments in 1957 would be systematically related to the distributions of the proportions of capital purchases in different past years.

This argument provides no answer to the criticism that the book values do not take into consideration the differences in efficiency of the old and the new capital. Our device of using the ratio of net to gross capital as a proxy variable for technology is a method, admittedly very rough, to incorporate in the production function the differences in efficiency of capital of different age structures.

[68]See n. 64, above.

[69]For simplicity of exposition, assume there are only two past periods with respective prices for capital goods at p_1 and p_2. Let r_{11} and r_{12} be the proportions of capital purchases of establishment i in the two periods. The production function to be estimated would appear as follows if the capital assets are deflated:

$$\log V_i = a + b \log L_i + c \log \left(\frac{r_{i1}}{P_1} + \frac{r_{i2}}{P_2} \right) K_i + \log u_i$$

$$= a + b \log L_i + c \log K_i + c \log \left(\frac{r_{i1}}{P_1} + \frac{r_{i2}}{P_2} \right) + \log u_i.$$

135

(iv) Next, it could be objected that important variables are missing from our production functions. Of special importance is entrepreneurship.

Admittedly, we have failed to construct a proxy variable for entrepreneurship and top management, but we have a fair idea as to what the effects of this omission are. In the postwar years of rapid technological change, the quality of entrepreneurship in manufacturing industries can best be judged by its knowledge of up-to-date technology, its ability to utilize technological advances, and its willingness to take calculated risks in improving production processes. In other words, it is reasonable to believe that the missing variable of entrepreneurship is more highly correlated with the log R log K variable than with that for labor. Under such conditions, it can be shown that the capital exponent will necessarily be overestimated in our findings. By contrast, the biases of the estimated labor exponents are smaller and their signs uncertain; they could be positive, zero, or negative.[70]

Our inability to separate the capital variable, adjusted for efficiency, from entrepreneurship is a fact with which we shall have to live. We may even go so far as to say that this lack of identification would cause little harm if we recognize that the estimated returns to capital include a part of the returns to entrepreneurship, and that investment in fixed capital is the leading element of business decisions that involve confronting uncertainty and assuming risks.

(v) Another possible objection would be that industry elasticities of demand and the production functions in our study are determined in an arbitrary manner.

Our answer to this criticism is that to take the elasticities of

---

[70]Using the same notations given in n. 11, Chapter II, but with K now representing log K log R, we have:

$$b - \hat{b} = - \frac{(r_{ML} - r_{MK}\, r_{KL})\, S_M}{(1 - r^2_{KL})\, S_L}$$

$$c - \hat{c} = - \frac{(r_{MK} - r_{ML}\, r_{KL})\, S_M}{(1 - r^2_{KL})\, S_K}.$$

If, by hypothesis, r_{MK}, or $r_{LM} > 0$ and $r_{MK} > r_{LM}$, and since $r_{KL} < 1$, then:
$$\hat{c} > c;$$
but the sign of $b - \hat{b}$ is uncertain.

demand explicitly into consideration, as we did, in studying production functions that are closely related to demand factors is much
less arbitrary than to neglect the demand elasticities, as is almost
universally done in existing studies. We wish that there were
available estimates of industrial elasticities of demand for cross-
checking. Unfortunately there are none. Moreover, cross-sectional
data for a single year would not enable us to estimate the demand
elasticities in the conventional manner. The criterion we have
used—plausibility of all the related key parameters—in fact was
an attempt to reduce arbitrariness to a minimum. Our success in
obtaining plausible estimates for all the key parameters in several
instances shows that the criterion we have used can screen out
those cases in which the available data and methods of estimation
cannot yield meaningful findings.

(vi) It might also be objected that we have not considered the
supply elasticities of capital and labor.

The capital variable reasonably can be assumed to be predetermined, since data on capital at the beginning of the year are used.
Investment during the year admittedly would have some influence
over current output, but the effects in most manufacturing industries are probably small.

Wage rates for production workers are taken as given in this
study. Implicit in this are the assumptions that wage rates are
determined by collective bargaining over discrete intervals, and
that normally the supply elasticity of production workers is nearly
infinite at given wage rates. While 1957 was not a recession year,
employment was not nearly full. Indeed, in some of these industries, workers were on layoff. Accordingly, the assumptions made
do not appear to be excessively unrealistic.

An apology is probably needed for making the assumption that
the salary rates for nonproduction employees are also given. However, the model would have to be expanded substantially to take
into consideration such factors as interstate movements of nonproduction employees in response to differential salary rates in
different regions. The decisive consideration for not expanding
the model in this respect was lack of readily available data about

fringe benefits in the different industries in the different states, except for the year 1957. Lagged salary rates, including fringe benefits, must be included in the model if supply functions of nonproduction employees are to be estimated. Moreover, the response of supply would not merely be interstate for the same industry. For a large portion of employees, there was probably substantial interindustry and interstate mobility. Time and resources were not available for us to attempt estimating a model of general equilibrium on an interstate and interindustry level. We are satisfied for the moment with a preliminary estimate of the structure of interindustry and interstate differences in productivities on the assumption that candidates for vacancies were available in 1957 at the going salary rates. This assumption perhaps was not satisfied for all types of employees in all industries everywhere.

(vii) Last, it could be argued that our adjustment for differences in the quality of labor falls short of the purpose.

This is probably correct. Plausible estimates of production functions were obtained on the basis of the adjusted data on production workers for only seven out of the 15 industries. For the other eight, the unadjusted data have yielded more meaningful results, but there are no apparent reasons why differences in the quality of labor were less important in the latter eight industries than in the first seven. In any case, it is fortunate that the adjustment made has resulted at least in more plausible estimates for seven industries.

(6) *Variations of Labor and Capital Productivities by States*

The analysis in Section (4) is based on the estimated productivities of labor and capital obtained from production functions for the respective industries taken as a whole. These estimates may be called industry averages. For a given industry, however, the marginal productivities of labor and capital differ from state to state. In Appendix II, the estimated marginal physical and revenue products of labor and capital are given for each industry and each state in which the industry was of significance in 1957.

138

A description of the data in Appendix II would add little to what they themselves reveal. For an allocation of resources closer to the Pareto optima, labor and capital should flow from industries and locations where their marginal physical products are low to where they are high. For greater profit realization, the figures for marginal revenue products provide similar guidance. Needless to say, these estimates cannot be better than the assumptions and data from which they are derived, and we have made many reservations about both.[71] These results should be regarded as a basis for further studies rather than as definitive in themselves.

In this section, the estimates of marginal physical and revenue products of production workers and nonproduction employees are examined to see whether the estimated industry averages conceal, as any aggregative estimates always to some extent would, important variations among the states. Finally, a rather compact analysis of the relative efficiency of labor and capital in different industries in various states and regions is made to provide a summary picture of the large mass of data presented in Appendix II.

(*i*) Industry-wide averages of the marginal physical products of production workers per dollar of wage cost in 1957 have been estimated for ten of the 15 groups.[72] They were larger than one dollar in nine, indicating expansion of employment of this category of employees if the Pareto optimum is to be achieved. Only in the transportation equipment industry was the marginal physical product of production workers less than unity.

Although the estimates for the different states vary substantially, relatively few contradict the general picture represented by the industry averages. The states in which the marginal physical products of production workers were smaller than unity or were not substantially different from unity are given below.

[71]See Section (5) of this chapter.
[72]See Table 10 in Section (4) (v) of this chapter.

Industry	Total number of states in which the industry significantly existed in 1957	States in which the marginal physical products of production workers per dollar of wage cost were substantially less than unity[73] (contrary to the industry averages which are greater then unity)	States in which the marginal physical products of production workers were not substantially different from unity[74]
Food and kindred products	35	West North Central: South Dakota, Iowa	East North Central: Wisconsin West North Central: Kansas, Minnesota, Nebraska Mountain: Montana, Utah Pacific: Washington South Atlantic: Delaware, Maryland East South Central: Alabama New England: Vermont East North Central: Indiana
Apparel and related products	18	East South Central: Mississippi South Atlantic: Virginia	South Atlantic: South Carolina, North Carolina, Georgia East North Central: Michigan West North Central: Missouri Middle Atlantic: New Jersey East South Central: Alabama
Pulp, paper, and products	28	none	none
Chemicals and products	31	Mountain: Montana	none
Petroleum and coal products	18	East North Central: Indiana West South Central: Arkansas Middle Atlantic: Pennsylvania, New Jersey Mountain: Wyoming	East South Central: Alabama West South Central: Texas West North Central: Missouri, Minnesota New England:Massachusetts East North Central: Illinois Middle Atlantic: New York
Stone, clay, and glass products	25	none	South Atlantic: West Virginia

Industry	Total number of states in which the industry significantly existed in 1957	States in which the marginal physical products of production workers per dollar of wage cost were substantially less than unity[73] (contrary to the industry averages which are greater than unity)	States in which the marginal physical products of production workers were not substantially different from unity[74]
Fabricated metal products	32	Mountain: Arizona	East South Central: Kentucky
Machinery, except electrical	25	none	East North Central: Michigan, Ohio New England: Rhode Island, Vermont, Connecticut East South Central: Alabama Pacific: Washington Middle Atlantic: Pennsylvania
Electrical machinery	22	none	East South Central: Alabama West North Central: Missouri, Iowa East North Central: Indiana, Wisconsin, Ohio, Illinois Middle Atlantic: New Jersey New England: Massachusetts, New Hampshire West South Central: Texas South Atlantic: Florida Pacific: California
Transportation equipment	26	This industry is unique. See text	Middle Atlantic: Pennsylvania New England: Connecticut, Massachusetts East North Central: Ohio, Indiana, Michigan, Wisconsin South Atlantic: Maryland, Georgia West North Central: Kansas

[73]I.e., smaller than $0.90.
[74]I.e., within the range $0.90 to $1.10.

Some interesting features stand out in the above analysis. First, a large number of states had marginal physical products not substantially different from unity in the food products, apparel, petroleum and coal products, machinery, electrical machinery, and transportation equipment industries. These states account for from one-third to slightly under one-half of all the states in which these six industries were of significant size. In this large number of cases, no substantial adjustment was required to reach the Pareto equilibrium. Second, the two states in which the marginal physical products were substantially below one dollar in the food products industry are both in the West North Central region. Third, with the exception of Indiana, Pennsylvania, New Jersey, and the two states in the West North Central region mentioned above, all the other states in which the marginal physical products were below unity in the various industries are either in the South or in the Mountain region.

For the unique case of the transportation equipment industry, those states in which the marginal physical products of production workers were above one dollar per dollar of wage costs are: Kentucky, Illinois, Washington, Montana, New Jersey, and California.

(ii) It has been shown that employment of production workers would have to be reduced to achieve the profit-maximizing position in all the ten industries for which production and nonproduction employees have been segregated in the production functions.[75] This is true because the marginal revenue products of production workers per dollar of wage cost are estimated to be smaller than unity.[76] The majority of the estimates of the marginal revenue products of production workers by states do not contradict this picture. The exceptions are shown below:

[75]See Table 7 in Section (4) (iv) of this chapter.
[76]See Section (3) of this chapter.

Industry	Total number of states in which the industry significantly existed in 1957	States in which the marginal revenue products of production workers per dollar of wage cost were substantially greater than unity[77] (contrary to the industry averages which are smaller than unity)	States in which the marginal revenue products of production workers were not substantially different from unity[78]
Food and kindred products	35	East South Central: Kentucky	West South Central: Oklahoma, Louisiana, Texas East South Central: Tennessee Mountain: Colorado South Atlantic: District of Columbia, South Carolina, North Carolina, Georgia, Florida New England: Maine
Apparel and related products	18	Pacific: California Mountain: Colorado South Atlantic: Delaware	New England: Massachusetts, Maine, Connecticut East North Central: Wisconsin, Indiana Middle Atlantic: New York
Pulp, paper and products	28	Pacific: Washington West North Central: Minnesota South Atlantic: Georgia	Pacific: California East South Central: Mississippi, Tennessee West South Central: Arkansas, Texas West North Central: Missouri South Atlantic: Virginia, South Carolina, Florida Mountain: Colorado
Chemicals and products	31	none	East North Central: Indiana West North Central: Minnesota West South Central: Texas
Petroleum and coal products	18	Mountain: Utah	East South Central: Kentucky

[77]I.e., larger than $1.10.
[78]I.e., within the range $0.90 to $1.10.

143

Industry	Total number of states in which the industry significantly existed in 1957	States in which the marginal revenue products of production workers per dollar of wage cost were substantially greater than unity[77] (contrary to the industry averages which are smaller than unity)	States in which the marginal revenue products of production workers were not substantially different from unity[78]
Stone, clay, and glass products	25	Mountain: Utah, Nevada	Mountain: Colorado East North Central: Wisconsin South Atlantic: Florida, Virginia
Fabricated metal products	32	South Atlantic: Florida East South Central: Mississippi	Middle Atlantic: New Jersey East North Central: Illinois, Wisconsin West North Central: Missouri, Minnesota, Nebraska, Kansas, Iowa New England: Massachusetts South Atlantic: Virginia, Delaware, North Carolina Pacific: Washington, California East South Central: Alabama West South Central: Louisiana, Oklahoma
Machinery, except electrical	25	East South Central: Kentucky West South Central: Texas	West North Central: Iowa, Minnesota East North Central: Indiana, Wisconsin Mountain: Colorado Pacific: California Middle Atlantic: New York West South Central: Oklahoma South Atlantic: Virginia, Maryland New England: New Hampshire

[77]I.e., larger than $1.10.
[78]I.e., within the range $0.90 to $1.10.

Industry	Total number of states in which the industry significantly existed in 1957	States in which the marginal revenue products of production workers per dollar of wage cost were substantially greater than unity[77] (contrary to the industry averages which are smaller than unity)	States in which the marginal revenue products of production workers were not substantially different from unity[78]
Electrical machinery	22	South Atlantic: Georgia, North Carolina West South Central: Oklahoma	East South Central: Kentucky South Atlantic: Maryland Middle Atlantic: Pennsylvania New England: Connecticut
Transportation equipment	26	East South Central: Kentucky	Pacific: California, Washington Middle Atlantic: New Jersey West North Central: Missouri East North Central: Illinois

There are 18 exceptional cases where the marginal revenue products of production workers were substantially larger than unity, hence where greater employment of production workers would have increased profits. With one single exception (Minnesota), all these states are in the South, or the Mountain, or Pacific Coast region. A fairly large proportion of states had marginal revenue products not substantially different from unity in the food products, pulp and paper products, fabricated metal products, and machinery industries. Here there was not much incentive for adjusting employment of production workers for profit maximization.

(iii) The industry-wide averages of the marginal physical products of nonproduction employees per dollar of salary cost all greatly exceed unity in all ten industries for which estimates have been made.[79] On a state-by-state basis, the findings conform to those on an industry-wide basis, except in three states for the

[79]See Table 10 in Section (4) (v) of this chapter.

Industry	Total number of states in which the industry significantly existed in 1957	States in which the marginal physical products of nonproduction employees per dollar of salary cost were substantially less than unity[80] (contrary to the industry averages which are greater than unity)	States in which the marginal physical products of nonproduction employees were not substantially different from unity[81]
Food and kindred products	35	none	South Atlantic: District of Columbia
Apparel and related products	18	none	none
Pulp, paper and products	28	none	none
Chemicals and products	31	none	none
Petroleum and coal products	18	none	none
Stone, clay, and glass products	25	none	none
Fabricated metal products	32	none	none
Machinery, except electrical	25	none	South Atlantic: Maryland
Electrical machinery	22	South Atlantic: Maryland, Florida West South Central: Texas	West South Central: Iowa Middle Atlantic: New Jersey, New York South Atlantic: South Carolina West North Central: Missouri East North Central: Illinois
Transportation equipment	26	West South Central: Oklahoma	Pacific: Washington, California South Atlantic: Maryland

[80]I.e., smaller than $0.90.

[81]I.e., within the range $0.90 to $1.10.

electrical machinery industry, and in one for transportation equipment. These data are tabulated above. All four exceptional states are in the South. For all ten industries, there are 11 states in which the marginal revenue products were not substantially different from unity. Except for these 15 states, employment of nonproduction employees should have been expanded in all industries and in all states to reach the Pareto optimum.

(iv) For the nonproduction employees, the industry averages of the marginal revenue products of the ten industries are all similar to the corresponding marginal physical products; that is, larger than one dollar per dollar of salary cost.[82] However, the number of states in which the marginal revenue products were smaller than unity is greater than for marginal physical product. There are 26 such exceptional states, and there is no clear regional pattern among them. In these states, the employment of nonproduction employees would have to be reduced to yield greater profits. There is a fairly large number of states in the pulp and paper products, machinery, electrical machinery, and the transportation equipment industry in which the marginal revenue products of nonproduction employees were not substantially different from unity. In this instance, there would have been no strong incentive for these establishments to adjust employment of this category of workers.

(v) There are five industries for which we have not been able to disaggregate production workers and nonproduction employees in the production functions obtained. The industry averages of the marginal physical products per dollar of salary and wage cost for employment as a whole are above unity in all five, except that the estimated marginal physical product in the instruments industry was not significantly different from unity.[83] As shown in the table given below, the estimates for the different states do not at all contradict this general picture. In none of the states in which these industries were significant was the marginal physical product substantially below unity. Except in the instruments industry,

[82]See Section (3) of this chapter.
[83]See Table 10 in Section (4) (v) of this chapter.

Industry	Total number of states in which the industry significantly existed in 1957	States in which the marginal revenue products of nonproduction employees per dollar of salary cost were substantially less than unity[84] (contrary to the industry averages which are greater than unity)	States in which the marginal revenue products of nonproduction employees were not substantially different from unity[85]
Food and kindred products	35	South Atlantic: District of Columbia	South Atlantic: South Carolina
Apparel and related products	18	none	none
Pulp, paper and products	28	West North Central: Minnesota East South Central: Kentucky East North Central: Illinois New England: Massachusetts	New England: Connecticut East North Central: Indiana, Michigan, Ohio Middle Atlantic: New Jersey, Pennsylvania, New York Mountain: Colorado
Chemicals and products	31	none	Pacific: Washington
Petroleum and coal products	18	none	none
Stone, clay, and glass products	25	New England: Massachusetts Middle Atlantic: New York East South Central: Tennessee West North Central: Minnesota East North Central: Wisconsin	New England: Connecticut, New Hampshire East North Central: Michigan South Atlantic: Florida
Fabricated metal products	32	none	West South Central: Oklahoma

Industry	Total number of states in which the industry significantly existed in 1957	States in which the marginal revenue products of nonproduction employees per dollar of salary cost were substantially less than unity[84] (contrary to the industry averages which are greater than unity)	States in which the marginal revenue products of nonproduction employees were not substantially different from unity[85]
Machinery, except electrical	25	South Atlantic: Maryland West South Central: Oklahoma West North Central: Minnesota	New England: Rhode Island, Massachusetts, Vermont Middle Atlantic: New York, New Jersey, Pennsylvania Pacific: California, Washington East North Central: Wisconsin, Illinois, Michigan, Indiana West North Central: Iowa, Missouri East South Central: Alabama West South Central: Texas
Electrical machinery	22	South Atlantic: Maryland, Florida, North Carolina West South Central: Texas West North Central: Iowa, Missouri Middle Atlantic: New York, New Jersey East North Central: Illinois	Pacific: California East North Central: Wisconsin, Ohio New England: Maine, Connecticut, New Hampshire Middle Atlantic: Pennsylvania
Transportation equipment	26	West South Central: Oklahoma Pacific: Washington, California South Atlantic: Maryland	West South Central: Texas New England: Massachusetts, Connecticut Middle Atlantic: New York West North Central: Iowa East North Central: Ohio South Atlantic: Georgia

[84]I.e., smaller than $0.90.
[85]I.e., within the range $0.90 to $1.10.

the number of states in which the marginal physical product was not substantially different from unity is also very small. The estimates for the different states support the conclusion reached earlier that employment in these industries generally should have expanded for attaining the Pareto optimum.

(vi) Our analysis has shown that employment would have to be reduced for attaining the profit maximizing position in the five industries discussed in (v) above.[86] The exceptions in the estimates for the different states are given in the following tabulation. The number of states in which the marginal revenue products of

Industry	Total number of states in which the industry significantly existed in 1957	States in which the marginal physical products of employment per dollar of salary and wage cost were substantially less than unity[87] (contrary to the industry averages which are greater than unity)	States in which the marginal physical products of employment were not substantially different from unity[88]
Lumber and wood products	14	none	West South Central: Oklahoma Pacific: Washington South Atlantic: North Carolina
Rubber products	16	none	none
Leather and leather goods	15	none	South Atlantic: Virginia
Primary metal industries	28	none	South Atlantic: Delaware
Instruments and related products	12	none	South Atlantic: Maryland, North Carolina Middle Atlantic: New Jersey, Pennsylvania West North Central: Iowa East North Central: Ohio, Michigan

[86]See Table 7 in Section (4) (iv) of this chapter.
[87]I.e., smaller than $0.90.
[88]I.e., within the range $0.90 to $1.10.

Industry	Total number of states in which the industry significantly existed in 1957	States in which the marginal revenue products of employment per dollar of salary and wage cost were substantially larger than unity[89] (contrary to the industry averages which are less than unity)	States in which the marginal revenue products of employment were not substantially different from unity[90]
Lumber and wood products	14	none	none
Rubber products	16	West North Central: Iowa East South Central: Tennessee, Alabama	New England: Connecticut East North Central: Wisconsin Pacific: California South Atlantic: Maryland, North Carolina West North Central: Minnesota
Leather and leather goods	15	South Atlantic: Georgia West South Central: Arkansas East South Central: Tennessee	South Atlantic: Maryland, Delaware Middle Atlantic: New York East North Central: Wisconsin, Michigan, Illinois West North Central: Missouri
Primary metal industries	28	Pacific: Washington West South Central: Louisiana Mountain: Nevada	East South Central: Tennessee East North Central: Indiana Middle Atlantic: New York New England: Massachusetts Mountain: Colorado
Instruments	12	none	New England: Massachusetts Middle Atlantic: New York East North Central: Indiana East South Central: Tennessee Mountain: Colorado

[89] I.e., those larger than $1.10.
[90] I.e., within the range $0.90 to $1.10.

employment per dollar of salary and wage cost were substantially larger than unity is very small. Six of the nine exceptional states are in the South. In a somewhat larger number of states, the estimated marginal revenue products were not much different from unity. There is no clear regional pattern in the distribution of these states.

(vii) In order to obtain a bird's-eye view of the relative efficiency of the different industries across the states and regions, we have listed the states in a given industry according to whether marginal physical product per dollar of wage cost of the industry is in the upper third of the estimated marginal physical products of this industry in all the states in which it was significant, or whether it belongs to the middle third, or the lower third. These groupings appear in Table 15. This classification can be done, of course, only for the ten industries for which we have estimates for the productivities of production workers and nonproduction employees separately. The states are grouped by the nine census regions.

The states are also classified on the basis of their marginal physical products of capital in the different industries in Table 16 in the same way as in Table 15. However, Table 16 includes all the 15 industries for which we have obtained estimates of production functions.

Although the number of industries covered in Tables 15 and 16 are different, some interesting features are readily observable by a comparison of the two tables. It is seen from Table 15 that about half of the marginal physical products of production workers in the states where industrial development took place earlier (i.e., the New England, the Middle Atlantic, and the East North Central Regions) are in the middle third.[91] Only about 17 per cent are in the upper third,[92] and about 34 per cent in the lower third.[93] However, as shown in Table 16, in the case of the distribution of

[91]For these three regions, the total number of entries in Table 15 is equal to $(5+5+7) + (14+14+22) + (11+9+15) = 102$. There are 50 entries in the middle third.

[92]$(5+5+7)/102$, or 17 per cent.

[93]$(11+9+15)/102$, or 34 per cent.

marginal physical products of capital in the same regions,[94] about 36 per cent of the entries are in the upper third,[95] and only 28 per cent in the lower third.[96]

In the South Atlantic, the West South Central, the Mountain, and the Pacific Coast regions, the situation stands in sharp contrast to that for the North East and East North Central regions. A much greater percentage (45 per cent[97]) of marginal physical products of production workers lies in the upper third than in the lower third (29 per cent[98]). However, a larger proportion (43 per cent[99]) of marginal physical products of capital falls in the lower third than in the upper third (30 per cent[100]).

These two comparisons suggest that the marginal physical product of capital tended to be higher in the regions where the marginal physical products of production workers were lower, and vice versa.

A similar but weaker contrast also can be observed for the industrially less advanced East South Central region, as against the East and East North Central regions.

In the West North Central region, the percentages in the upper third and in the lower third are about equal in the distribution of the marginal products of production workers and of capital, and the contrast observed for the other regions is absent.

[94] For these three regions, the total number of entries in Table 16 is equal to $(18+12+20) + (12+16+22) + (9+10+19) = 138$.

[95] $(18+12+20)/138$, or 36 per cent.

[96] $(9+10+19)/138$, or 28 per cent.

[97] The total number of entries in Table 15 for these four regions is $(22+13+7+8) + (10+5+1+5) + (14+7+4+3) = 99$. Those in the upper third account for $(22+13+7+8)/99$, or 45 per cent.

[98] $(14+7+4+3)/99$, or 28 per cent.

[99] From Table 16, those in the lower third accounted for $(25+13+11+9)/(23+8+2+6) + (14+11+3+7) + (25+13+11+9)$, or 43 per cent.

[100] $(23+8+2+6)/132$, or 30 per cent.

153

Table 15. Comparative Efficiencies of Production Workers by State and Region.[a]

State and region	Marginal physical products by industry and state					
	Upper third for industry	No. of cases	Middle third for industry	No. of cases	Lower third for industry	No. of cases
Maine..............	FD	1	AP, TE	2	PP	1
New Hampshire.....	MA	1	PP, EM	2	ST	1
Vermont...........			FD	1	MA	1
Massachusetts......	ST, TE	2	FD, AP, PC, MA, FM	5	CH, PP, EM	3
Rhode Island......					MA, FM	2
Connecticut........	EM	1	AP, CH, ST, TE	4	MA, PP, FM	3
New England........		5		14		11
New York..........	AP, CH	2	FD, PC, ST, MA, EM	5	TE, PP, FM	3
New Jersey.........	CH, TE	2	FD, AP, MA, PP, FM	5	PC, EM	2
Pennsylvania.......	EM	1	FD, CH, TE, PP	4	PC, ST, MA, FM	4
Middle Atlantic......		5		14		9
Ohio..............			FD, CH, TE, EM	4	ST, MA, PP, FM	4
Indiana............	AP, CH	2	FD, MA, TE, FM	4	PC, ST, PP, EM	4
Illinois............	CH, TE	2	FD, PC, ST, MA, EM, FM	6	PP	1
Michigan...........			FD, CH, ST, TE	4	AP, MA, PP, FM	4
Wisconsin..........	AP, ST, TE	3	CH, MA, PP, FM	4	FD, EM	2
East North Central....		7		22		15

State	No.	Industries	No.	Industries	No.	Industries
Minnesota	4	CH, MA, PP, FM	1	PC	2	FD, ST,
Iowa	3	CH, MA, FM	1	TE	2	FD, EM
Missouri	2	CH, TE	3	PC, PP, FM	5	FD, AP, ST, MA, EM
North Dakota					1	FD
South Dakota	1	FM			1	FD
Nebraska		FM			1	FD
Kansas	2	PC, FM	2	CH, TE		FD
West North Central.....	12		7		12	
Delaware	3	AP, CH, FM	5	FD, CH, ST, TE, FM	1	FD
Maryland	2	MA, EM				
D. C.	1	FD				
Virginia	3	ST, MA, PP	1	FM	3	AP, CH, TE
West Virginia					4	CH, ST, TE, FM
North Carolina	3	FD, EM, FM			3	AP, CH, PP
South Carolina	2	FD, PP			1	AP
Georgia	4	FD, TE, PP, EM	2	AP, ST	1	CH
Florida	4	FD, ST, PP, FM	2	CH, EM	1	TE
South Atlantic.........	22		10		14	
Kentucky	4	FD, PC, MA, TE	2	CH, EM	3	ST, PP, FM
Tennessee	1	PP	1	FD	3	CH, ST, FM
Alabama			4	AP, CH, ST, FM	5	FD, PC, MA, TE, EM
Mississippi	2	EM, FM	1	PP	2	AP, CH
East South Central.....	7		8		13	

[a] The industry symbols are as follows: (FD), Food and kindred products; (AP), Apparel and related products; (LM), Lumber and wood products; (CH), Chemicals and products; (PC), Petroleum and coal products; (RU), Rubber and plastic products; (LT), Leather and leather products; (ST), Stone, clay, and glass products; (PM), primary metals; (FM), Fabricated metal products; (MA), Machinery, except electrical; (EM), Electrical machinery; (TE), Transportation equipment; and (IN), Instruments and related products.

Table 15. (continued)

State and region	Upper third for industry	No. of cases	Middle third for industry	No. of cases	Lower third for industry	No. of cases
Arkansas			PP	1	CH, PC	2
Louisiana	FD, PC, ST	3	PP, FM	2	CH, TE	2
Oklahoma	FD, PC, MA, EM, FM	5	ST	1	TE	1
Texas	FD, CH, MA, PP, FM	5	PC	1	TE, EM	2
West South Central		13		5		7
Montana					CH	1
Idaho						
Wyoming					PC	1
Colorado	FD, AP, ST, PP	4	MA	1		
New Mexico						
Arizona					FM	1
Utah	PC, ST	2			FD	1
Nevada	ST	1				
Mountain		7		1		4
Washington	TE, PP	2	FM	1	FD, CH, MA	3
Oregon			FD	1		
California	FD, AP, CH, PC, TE, FM	6	MA, PP, EM	3		
Pacific		8		5		3

Source: Appendix II.

156

Table 16. Comparative Efficiencies of Capital by State and Region.[a]

State and region	Marginal physical products by industry and state					
	Upper third for industry	No. of cases	Middle third for industry	No. of cases	Lower third for industry	No. of cases
Maine................			FD	1	AP, TE, PP	3
New Hampshire......	ST, MA, PP	3	LT	1	EM	1
Vermont............	MA	1			FD	1
Massachusetts........	ST, PM, IN, PP, EM, FM	6	FD, RU, LT, MA, TE	5	AP, CH, PC	3
Rhode Island........	RU, PM	2	FM	1	MA	1
Connecticut.........	AP, CH, PM, TE, PP, EM	6	RU, ST, MA, FM	4		
New England.........		18		12		9
New York...........	FD, CH, PC, PM, PP	5	LT, ST, TE, IN, EM, FM	6	AP, RU, MA	3
New Jersey.........	FD, CH, PM	3	TE, FM	2	AP, PC, MA, IN, PP, EM	6
Pennsylvania........	FD, CH, MA, FM	4	LM, LT, ST, PM, TE, IN, PP, EM	8	PC	1
Middle Atlantic.......		12		16		10
Ohio...............	FD, RU, ST, MA, PP, EM	6	PM	1	CH, LT, TE, IN, FM	5
Indiana.............	CH	1	FD, AP, RU, ST, PM, MA, IN, PP, EM, FM	10	PC, TE	2
Illinois.............	FD, PC, LT, ST, PP	5	CH, PM, MA, EM, FM	5	RU, TE	2

Table 16. (continued)

State and region	Upper third for industry	No. of cases	Middle third for industry	No. of cases	Lower third for industry	No. of cases
Michigan..........	FD, IN	2	CH, ST, PP	3	AP, RU, LT, PM, MA, TE, FM	7
Wisconsin..........	AP, CH, RU, ST, PM, MA	6	TE, PP, EM	3	FD, LT, FM	3
East North Central...		20		22		19
Minnesota..........	PC, PM, MA	3	FD, CH, PP	3	RU, ST, FM	3
Iowa............	CH, MA, IN, EM	4	TE, EM	2	FD, RU, PM	3
Missouri..........	LM, LT, PP	3	FD, AP, CH, ST, PM, MA, TE, EM	8	PC, EM	2
North Dakota..........						
South Dakota.........	FD	1				
Nebraska.........	FD	1			FM	1
Kansas.........	FM	1	PC	1	FD, CH, TE	3
West North Central....		13		14		12
Delaware..........	AP, CH, FM	3	PM	1	FD, LT	2
Maryland..........	RD, RU, TE, EM	4	CH	1	LT, ST, PM, MA, IN, FM	6
D. C............	FD	1				
Virginia..........	AP, LM, CH, TE, FM	5	LT, PP	2	ST, PM, MA	3
West Virginia.........	ST, FM	2	CH, PM	2	TE	1
North Carolina......	LM, IN	2	AP, CH, RU, FM	4	FD, PP, EM	3
South Carolina......	PP	1	AP	1	FD, LM	2
Georgia............	LT, ST, TE	3	FD, AP, CH	3	PP, EM	2
Florida..........	LM, EM	2			FD, CH, ST, TE, PP, FM	6
South Atlantic.........		23		14		25

Kentucky	2	FD, PC	6	CH, ST, TE, PP, EM, FM	2	PM, MA
Tennessee	4	LM, RU, LT, PM	5	FD, CH, IN, PP, FM	1	ST
Alabama	4	ST, PM, TE, FM	4	FD, AP, PC, RU	3	CH, MA, EM
Mississippi	2	AP, PP			3	CH, EM, FM
East South Central	12		15		9	
Arkansas	1	LT	1	PC	2	CH, PP
Louisiana	1	FM	5	FD, LM, PC, TE, PP	3	CH, ST, PM
Oklahoma	3	PC, TE, FM	2	ST, MA	4	FD, LM, PM, EM
Texas	3	PC, MA, TE	3	FD, LM, EM	4	CH, PM, PP, FM
West South Central	8		11		13	
Montana					2	LM, CH
Idaho						
Wyoming					1	PC
Colorado	1	AP	1	MA	4	FD, ST, IN, PP
New Mexico						
Arizona	1	FM	1	PM		
Utah			1	PC	2	FD, ST
Nevada					2	ST, PM
Mountain	2		3		11	
Washington	3	CH, TE, FM	4	FD, LM, PM, MA	1	PP
Oregon	1	FD			1	LM
California	2	TE, EM	3	FD, LM, PC	7	AP, CH, RU, PM, MA, PP, FM
Pacific	6		7		9	

Source: Appendix II.

[a]See footnote to Table 15 for meaning of industry symbols.

APPENDIX I

Output-Labor, Capital-Labor, and Certain Other Important Data on 17 Manufacturing Industries in 1957.

In computing the production functions presented in this study, we have processed certain data which are of general interest and which, in our knowledge, are not now completely available. These statistics, computed from census reports [7] and [8], are presented in this Appendix. They cover various output-labor and capital-labor ratios for 17 two-digit industries and for all the states in which these industries existed significantly.

V/L: Ratio of value added (V) to employment (L, production workers and nonproduction employees[1]) in dollars per man-hour in 1957.

V/L_p: Ratio of value added to employment of production workers (L_p) in dollars per man-hour in 1957.

W_L: Average wage and salary rate for production workers and nonproduction employees[1] in dollars per man-hour.

W_p: Average wage rate for production workers in dollars per man-hour.

K_g/L: Ratio of gross book value (owned) of plant and equipment at the beginning of 1957 (K_g) to employment in 1957 in dollar per man-hour.

K_g'/L: Ratio of gross book value (owned plus rented[2]) of plant and equipment at the beginning of 1957 (K_g') to employment in 1957 in dollar per man-hour.

K_n/L: Same as K_g/L, except K_n, gross book value minus accumulated depreciation and depletion, is used in the numerator instead of K_g.

K_g'/L_p: Same as K_g'/L, except L_p is used in the denominator instead of L.

K_g/L_p: Same as K_g/L, except L_p is used in the denominator, instead of L.

K_g'/L_p: Same as K_g'/L, except L_p is used in the denominator.

K_n/L_p: Same as K_g/L_p, except K_n is used in the numerator, instead of K_g.

$\dfrac{[V-(T+D)]}{K_g}$:   The ratio of value added (V) minus property tax (T) and depreciation and depletion charges (D) in 1957 to gross book value of plant and equipment at the beginning of 1957 (K_g) in dollars per dollar.

[1] A nonproduction employee is assumed to work 2,000 man-hours per year.

[2] The rented portion is estimated by dividing the data on rental payments in [8] by 0.05 (i.e., an assumed discount rate of 5 per cent per year).

$$\frac{[V-(T+D)]}{K_g'}:$$ Same as $[V-(T+D)]/K_g$, except K_g' is used in the denominator.

r: The ratio of nonproduction employee man-hours[3] to production worker man-hours in per cent.

R: The ratio of K_n to K_g in per cent.

Food and Kindred Products

State	V/L	V/L$_p$	W$_L$	W$_p$	K$_g$/L	K$'_g$/L	K$_n$/L
Maine............	4.23	5.45	1.69	1.36	2.36	3.48	1.23
Vermont..........	4.82	6.58	2.06	1.92	4.33	4.64	2.28
Massachusetts.....	4.03	6.39	2.19	1.89	2.91	4.00	1.43
New York.........	4.84	7.03	2.35	2.00	3.11	4.32	1.24
New Jersey........	5.97	8.97	2.67	2.42	3.69	4.72	1.94
Pennsylvania......	4.86	7.63	2.26	2.04	3.04	3.88	1.53
Ohio.............	4.49	7.30	2.38	2.07	2.76	3.59	1.46
Indiana..........	4.66	6.81	2.23	1.96	3.05	3.94	1.64
Illinois...........	6.08	8.48	2.59	2.32	3.56	4.51	1.77
Michigan.........	5.37	7.78	2.54	2.18	3.31	4.34	1.79
Wisconsin.........	4.25	5.72	2.24	1.98	3.42	4.26	2.14
Minnesota........	4.93	6.69	2.34	2.14	3.70	4.48	2.02
Iowa.............	4.54	6.36	2.47	2.30	3.25	4.24	1.92
Missouri..........	4.65	6.72	2.37	2.12	3.56	4.79	1.78
South Dakota......	4.20	5.65	2.19	2.06	2.79	3.45	1.46
Nebraska.........	4.74	6.34	2.22	2.08	2.87	4.19	1.45
Kansas...........	4.22	5.90	2.27	2.11	3.42	4.52	1.68
Delaware.........	3.88	4.96	1.85	1.55	3.37	4.02	2.19
Maryland.........	4.07	6.22	2.15	1.79	2.78	3.75	1.21
District of Columbia	3.65	7.24	2.47	1.89	2.81	3.85	0.75
North Carolina....	3.60	6.06	1.66	1.35	2.85	4.17	1.51
South Carolina....	3.34	6.02	1.70	1.34	2.37	3.44	1.23
Georgia..........	4.52	6.44	1.70	1.44	2.30	3.50	1.36
Florida..........	4.43	6.51	1.80	1.47	2.85	5.13	1.46
Kentucky.........	7.54	1.05	2.33	2.05	4.16	4.95	2.37
Tennessee........	4.02	6.50	1.92	1.59	2.33	3.16	1.37
Alabama..........	3.01	4.96	1.59	1.39	1.84	2.60	1.00
Louisiana.........	4.33	6.58	1.75	1.54	3.11	3.89	1.61
Oklahoma........	3.87	6.12	1.95	1.62	2.54	3.55	1.37
Texas............	4.51	7.05	1.86	1.59	2.87	3.86	1.45
Colorado..........	4.68	6.81	2.06	1.87	4.04	4.99	2.07
Utah.............	4.12	5.24	2.05	1.72	3.28	4.45	1.71
Washington.......	4.62	6.69	2.51	2.18	3.44	4.43	1.79
Oregon...........	4.60	6.53	2.24	1.94	2.62	3.81	1.32
California.........	5.70	8.67	2.51	2.29	3.68	5.49	1.96

[3]See n. 1, p. 160.

Food and Kindred Products

State	$\dfrac{K_g}{L_p}$	$\dfrac{K'_g}{L_p}$	$\dfrac{K_n}{L_p}$	$\dfrac{[V-(T+D)]}{K_g}$	$\dfrac{[V-(T+D)]}{K'_g}$	r	R
Maine	3.04	4.49	1.58	1.68	1.14	10.3	52.0
Vermont	5.91	6.33	3.11	1.03	0.97	10.3	52.6
Massachusetts	4.62	6.35	2.27	1.29	0.94	10.9	49.2
New York	4.52	6.27	1.81	1.48	1.07	10.1	40.0
New Jersey	5.54	7.08	2.92	1.54	1.21	10.0	52.7
Pennsylvania	4.77	6.08	2.39	1.52	1.19	9.59	50.1
Ohio	4.48	5.84	2.37	1.53	1.18	10.3	52.9
Indiana	4.46	5.77	2.40	1.44	1.11	10.2	53.9
Illinois	4.97	6.30	2.47	1.63	1.28	9.88	50.7
Michigan	4.80	6.29	2.59	1.52	1.16	10.2	54.1
Wisconsin	4.60	5.74	2.88	1.16	0.93	9.78	62.5
Minnesota	5.02	6.09	2.75	1.23	1.01	10.2	55.7
Iowa	4.55	5.94	2.69	1.31	1.00	10.6	59.1
Missouri	5.14	6.93	2.57	1.23	0.91	9.03	50.0
South Dakota	3.75	4.64	1.96	1.43	1.16	9.78	52.3
Nebraska	3.83	5.60	1.94	1.57	1.07	10.9	51.7
Kansas	4.77	6.32	2.35	1.13	0.85	11.0	49.2
Delaware	4.31	5.14	2.80	1.07	0.90	10.4	65.0
Maryland	4.25	5.74	1.85	1.39	1.03	9.78	44.6
District of Columbia	5.57	7.62	1.46	1.23	0.90	11.0	26.3
North Carolina	4.81	7.03	2.54	1.16	0.79	8.37	52.7
South Carolina	4.28	6.20	2.22	1.28	0.89	8.18	51.9
Georgia	3.28	4.98	1.94	1.87	1.23	8.47	59.1
Florida	4.18	7.53	2.14	1.43	0.80	10.3	51.2
Kentucky	5.82	6.91	3.31	1.73	1.46	8.18	56.8
Tennessee	3.76	5.11	2.21	1.64	1.21	8.28	58.9
Alabama	3.04	4.27	1.66	1.52	1.08	8.56	54.5
Louisiana	4.72	5.89	2.44	1.32	1.06	8.28	51.6
Oklahoma	4.02	5.62	2.17	1.43	1.03	9.78	53.9
Texas	4.48	6.02	2.26	1.47	1.09	9.78	50.4
Colorado	5.87	7.25	3.00	1.08	0.88	11.4	51.2
Utah	4.17	5.66	2.17	1.16	0.86	11.5	52.1
Washington	4.98	6.41	2.59	1.25	0.98	11.4	52.0
Oregon	3.73	5.41	1.87	1.65	1.14	11.1	50.3
California	5.60	8.34	2.98	1.45	0.97	11.4	53.2

Textile Mill Products

State	V/L	V/L$_p$	W$_L$	W$_p$	K$_g$/L	K$'_g$/L	K$_n$/L
Maine............	2.14	2.30	1.66	1.60	1.78	2.06	0.96
Massachusetts.....	2.99	3.41	1.96	1.75	2.69	3.33	1.38
Rhode Island......	2.54	2.93	1.88	1.75	2.41	3.17	1.21
Connecticut.......	2.76	3.19	2.06	1.84	2.53	3.57	1.16
New York.........	3.11	3.74	2.03	1.79	1.49	2.64	0.74
New Jersey........	3.15	3.71	2.21	1.97	2.44	3.49	1.22
Pennsylvania......	2.80	3.22	1.94	1.80	2.01	2.63	0.96
Ohio.............	3.83	4.57	2.21	1.89	2.33	2.67	1.19
Illinois............	3.33	4.07	2.19	1.81	1.61	2.40	0.63
Maryland.........	2.81	3.18	1.65	1.54	2.69	3.31	1.22
Virginia..........	2.77	3.08	1.61	1.56	2.99	3.39	1.55
North Carolina....	2.51	2.71	1.62	1.50	2.42	2.78	1.35
South Carolina....	2.59	2.76	1.65	1.55	3.23	3.44	1.88
Georgia...........	2.36	2.56	1.51	1.44	2.48	2.86	1.38
Tennessee.........	2.54	2.78	1.53	1.42	2.47	2.97	1.28
Alabama..........	2.36	2.51	1.56	1.47	2.56	2.67	1.25
Arkansas..........	2.52	2.71	1.45	1.37	3.94	4.10	2.73
California.........	3.54	4.21	2.09	1.81	2.27	3.54	1.02

State	$\dfrac{K_g}{L_p}$	$\dfrac{K'_g}{L_p}$	$\dfrac{K_n}{L_p}$	$\dfrac{[V-(T+D)]}{K_g}$	$\dfrac{[V-(T+D)]}{K'_g}$	r	R
Maine............	1.91	2.20	1.03	1.13	0.98	10.30	54.22
Massachusetts.....	3.06	3.79	1.57	1.05	0.85	10.90	51.32
Rhode Island......	2.78	3.66	1.40	0.99	0.75	9.41	50.19
Connecticut.......	2.92	4.13	1.34	1.02	0.72	10.30	45.89
New York.........	1.78	3.17	0.89	2.01	1.13	10.10	49.71
New Jersey........	2.87	4.11	1.44	1.22	0.85	9.97	50.17
Pennsylvania......	2.31	3.02	1.10	1.33	1.01	9.59	47.59
Ohio.............	2.77	3.19	1.42	1.57	1.37	10.30	51.01
Illinois............	1.97	2.93	0.78	1.95	1.31	9.88	39.39
Maryland.........	3.04	3.74	1.38	1.01	0.81	9.78	45.50
Virginia..........	3.32	3.77	1.72	0.87	0.77	9.31	51.76
North Carolina....	2.61	3.00	1.46	0.97	0.85	8.37	55.91
South Carolina....	3.45	3.68	2.01	0.74	0.70	8.18	58.38
Georgia...........	2.68	3.09	1.49	0.90	0.78	8.47	55.57
Tennessee.........	2.70	3.25	1.40	0.97	0.80	8.28	51.78
Alabama..........	2.72	2.84	1.33	0.87	0.84	8.56	48.93
Arkansas..........	4.25	4.42	2.94	0.55	0.53	8.37	69.28
California.........	2.70	4.21	1.21	1.47	0.94	11.40	44.91

Apparel and Related Products

State	V/L	V/L_p	W_L	W_p	K_g/L	K'_g/L	K_n/L
Maine............	2.49	2.80	1.52	1.43	1.21	2.01	0.54
Massachusetts.....	2.51	2.87	1.67	1.50	0.37	1.47	0.18
Connecticut.......	2.84	3.02	1.43	1.52	0.31	1.07	0.13
New York.........	3.31	3.92	1.96	1.73	0.35	1.92	0.20
New Jersey........	2.60	2.85	1.77	1.61	0.49	1.45	0.23
Maryland.........	2.61	3.01	1.60	1.44	0.76	1.16	0.42
Michigan.........	2.80	3.24	2.13	1.97	1.26	2.01	0.88
Wisconsin	2.58	3.02	1.67	1.43	0.47	1.02	0.20
Missouri..........	2.21	2.58	1.56	1.43	0.31	1.22	0.13
Delaware.........	4.76	6.65	1.90	1.58	1.44	1.80	0.77
Virginia..........	1.78	1.90	1.38	1.27	0.32	0.57	0.15
North Carolina....	2.02	2.26	1.33	1.24	0.48	0.91	0.28
South Carolina....	2.01	2.17	1.35	1.24	0.40	0.82	0.24
Georgia..........	2.15	2.35	1.37	1.25	0.40	0.85	0.21
Alabama..........	2.09	2.23	1.25	1.16	0.48	0.91	0.26
Mississippi........	1.59	1.71	1.18	1.11	0.27	0.59	0.15
Colorado..........	2.66	3.23	1.55	1.34	0.40	0.92	0.21
California.........	3.21	3.76	1.89	1.66	0.47	1.71	0.23

State	$\dfrac{K_g}{L_p}$	$\dfrac{K'_g}{L_p}$	$\dfrac{K_n}{L_p}$	$\dfrac{[V-(T+D)]}{K_g}$	$\dfrac{[V-(T+D)]}{K'_g}$	r	R
Maine............	1.36	2.26	0.60	2.00	1.20	10.3	44.50
Massachusetts.....	0.42	1.68	0.21	6.74	1.68	10.9	49.93
Connecticut.......	0.33	1.13	0.14	9.16	2.62	10.3	43.04
New York.........	0.42	2.28	0.24	9.30	1.70	10.1	57.68
New Jersey........	0.54	1.59	0.25	5.17	1.76	9.97	46.13
Maryland.........	0.87	1.33	0.49	3.33	2.18	10.2	55.78
Michigan.........	1.47	2.31	1.02	2.10	1.33	10.2	69.58
Wisconsin.........	0.54	1.19	0.23	5.44	2.49	9.78	43.06
Missouri..........	0.36	1.42	0.16	7.09	1.79	9.03	43.88
Delaware.........	2.02	2.51	1.07	3.23	2.59	10.4	53.02
Virginia..........	0.34	0.60	0.16	5.48	3.07	9.31	46.54
North Carolina....	0.54	1.02	0.31	4.08	2.16	8.37	57.53
South Carolina....	0.44	0.91	0.26	4.90	2.39	8.18	60.64
Georgia..........	0.43	0.92	0.23	5.31	2.49	8.47	52.24
Alabama..........	0.51	0.98	0.27	4.27	2.24	8.56	53.51
Mississippi........	0.29	0.63	0.16	5.69	2.64	8.37	53.96
Colorado..........	0.49	1.12	0.26	6.58	2.86	11.4	53.51
California.........	0.55	2.01	0.27	6.62	1.83	11.4	48.24

Lumber and Wood Products

State	V/L	V/L_p	W_L	W_p	K_g/L	K'_g/L	K_n/L
Pennsylvania	2.79	3.22	1.74	1.49	1.67	2.79	0.93
Missouri	2.56	2.97	1.57	1.44	1.08	1.37	0.45
Virginia	1.95	2.15	1.38	1.20	1.11	1.16	0.52
North Carolina	1.78	1.92	1.28	1.17	0.85	1.03	0.42
South Carolina	1.90	2.12	1.22	1.18	2.07	2.18	1.25
Florida	2.24	2.52	1.50	1.36	1.30	1.87	0.61
Tennessee	2.11	2.42	1.36	1.24	1.33	1.48	0.71
Louisiana	2.12	2.31	1.31	1.19	1.76	1.95	0.95
Oklahoma	1.86	2.15	1.41	1.27	2.20	3.98	1.18
Texas	1.89	2.17	1.30	1.20	1.67	2.16	1.05
Montana	4.11	4.59	2.51	2.45	5.26	6.17	2.75
Washington	3.37	3.70	2.53	2.43	3.90	4.45	1.87
Oregon	3.91	4.25	2.70	2.44	4.50	5.26	2.51
California	3.90	4.46	2.61	2.44	3.97	4.79	1.95

State	$\dfrac{K_g}{L_p}$	$\dfrac{K'_g}{L_p}$	$\dfrac{K_n}{L_p}$	$\dfrac{[V-(T+D)]}{K_g}$	$\dfrac{[V-(T+D)]}{K'_g}$	r	R
Pennsylvania	1.93	3.22	1.07	1.56	0.94	9.59	55.37
Missouri	1.25	1.59	0.52	2.15	1.70	9.03	41.90
Virginia	1.23	1.28	0.57	1.63	1.57	9.31	46.46
North Carolina	0.92	1.11	0.45	1.94	1.60	8.37	49.24
South Carolina	2.30	2.42	1.39	0.81	0.77	8.18	60.44
Florida	1.46	2.10	0.69	1.60	1.12	8.18	46.96
Tennessee	1.52	1.70	0.81	1.50	1.34	10.3	53.14
Louisiana	1.91	2.13	1.03	1.12	1.00	8.28	53.97
Oklahoma	2.54	4.61	1.36	0.74	0.41	8.28	53.63
Texas	1.92	2.49	1.20	1.03	0.79	9.78	62.64
Montana	5.87	6.89	3.07	0.68	0.58	10.9	52.27
Washington	4.28	4.89	2.06	0.77	0.67	11.4	48.06
Oregon	4.89	5.72	2.72	0.73	0.62	11.1	55.69
California	4.54	5.47	2.23	0.86	0.72	11.4	49.05

Furniture and Fixtures

State	V/L	V/L$_p$	W$_L$	W$_p$	K$_g$/L	K$'_g$/L	K$_n$/L
New Hampshire....	2.77	3.34	1.82	1.63	0.77	2.00	0.49
Massachusetts.....	3.12	3.77	2.05	1.79	0.94	2.43	0.50
New York.........	3.89	4.83	2.19	1.93	1.23	3.17	0.62
Pennsylvania......	3.25	3.82	2.05	1.83	1.45	2.24	0.75
Ohio.............	4.19	5.34	2.49	2.31	1.67	2.81	0.88
Indiana...........	3.08	3.66	2.05	1.81	1.32	2.10	0.72
Illinois............	3.61	4.62	2.25	1.98	1.45	2.82	0.77
Michigan.........	4.36	5.40	2.39	2.12	1.64	2.46	1.00
Maryland.........	3.55	4.85	2.11	1.89	1.29	3.31	0.67
Virginia..........	3.21	3.82	1.73	1.52	1.25	1.75	0.60
North Carolina....	2.77	3.12	1.69	1.48	1.03	1.41	0.64
South Carolina....	1.92	2.22	1.55	1.46	2.77	3.07	2.11
Georgia...........	2.61	2.96	1.48	1.33	0.90	1.75	0.42
Tennessee.........	2.45	2.75	1.57	1.35	0.94	1.46	0.51
Mississippi........	2.41	2.92	1.60	1.47	1.01	1.76	0.58
Arkansas..........	2.54	2.88	1.59	1.37	1.12	1.56	0.60
Oklahoma........	3.15	3.81	1.81	1.55	1.15	2.54	0.64
Texas............	3.93	4.86	2.26	2.15	1.13	2.94	0.65
California.........	2.95	3.50	1.68	1.37	0.93	1.86	0.53

State	$\dfrac{K_g}{L_p}$	$\dfrac{K'_g}{L_p}$	$\dfrac{K_n}{L_p}$	$\dfrac{[V-(T+D)]}{K_g}$	$\dfrac{[V-(T+D)]}{K'_g}$	r	R
New Hampshire....	0.93	2.42	0.60	3.47	1.34	10.30	63.84
Massachusetts.....	1.14	2.95	0.61	3.19	1.23	10.90	53.57
New York.........	1.52	3.94	0.76	3.07	1.19	10.10	50.19
Pennsylvania......	1.71	2.64	0.89	2.16	1.40	9.59	51.84
Ohio.............	2.13	3.58	1.13	2.42	1.44	10.30	52.97
Indiana...........	1.57	2.50	0.85	2.23	1.40	10.20	54.39
Illinois............	1.85	3.61	0.99	2.41	1.24	9.88	53.48
Michigan.........	2.04	3.04	1.24	2.54	1.70	10.20	61.06
Maryland.........	1.76	4.52	0.91	2.65	1.03	9.78	51.55
Virginia..........	1.49	2.08	0.72	2.48	1.77	9.31	48.29
North Carolina....	1.16	1.59	0.72	2.60	1.89	8.37	62.42
South Carolina....	3.19	3.54	2.43	0.61	0.55	8.18	76.33
Georgia...........	1.02	1.98	0.48	2.81	1.45	8.47	47.00
Tennessee.........	1.06	1.65	0.58	2.51	1.61	8.28	54.64
Mississippi........	1.23	2.13	0.70	2.31	1.33	8.37	57.14
Arkansas..........	1.27	1.77	0.68	2.16	1.54	8.37	54.02
Oklahoma........	1.40	3.07	0.78	2.62	1.19	9.78	55.63
Texas............	1.40	3.63	0.80	3.32	1.28	11.40	57.50
California.........	1.10	2.20	0.63	3.06	1.53	9.78	57.63

Pulp, Paper, and Products

State	V/L	V/L$_p$	W$_L$	W$_p$	K$_g$/L	K$'_g$/L	K$_n$/L
Maine............	4.74	5.51	2.46	2.31	10.30	10.46	6.98
New Hampshire....	4.57	5.49	2.27	2.11	5.04	5.19	2.74
Massachusetts.....	3.88	4.85	2.32	2.01	3.50	4.06	1.77
Connecticut.......	3.87	4.85	2.56	2.32	3.24	4.04	1.78
New York.........	3.95	4.72	2.30	2.04	3.31	4.51	1.74
New Jersey........	4.57	5.72	2.59	2.31	4.31	6.06	2.30
Pennsylvania......	4.66	5.75	2.58	2.29	4.90	5.85	2.61
Ohio.............	4.55	5.67	2.59	2.33	4.15	4.80	2.27
Indiana...........	4.11	5.13	2.43	2.13	3.22	4.07	2.05
Illinois............	4.08	5.23	2.51	2.19	4.47	5.43	1.60
Michigan.........	4.43	5.53	2.67	2.43	4.47	5.43	2.63
Wisconsin.........	5.27	6.29	2.57	2.36	5.78	6.35	3.46
Minnesota........	5.52	8.23	2.73	2.36	5.05	6.50	2.90
Missouri..........	4.50	5.62	2.19	1.93	2.63	3.24	1.62
Virginia..........	5.38	6.28	2.33	2.04	5.66	6.66	3.34
North Carolina....	4.37	5.38	2.43	2.26	7.81	8.49	3.97
South Carolina....	6.02	7.46	2.58	2.35	6.79	7.25	3.42
Georgia..........	6.54	8.02	2.41	2.14	8.92	9.58	5.84
Florida...........	6.69	8.11	2.58	2.47	13.73	14.10	8.83
Kentucky.........	3.51	4.28	2.23	1.83	2.76	3.03	1.78
Tennessee........	5.99	7.31	2.48	2.30	7.82	8.29	4.15
Mississippi........	5.65	6.52	2.39	2.33	7.20	7.23	3.62
Arkansas.........	6.18	7.00	2.43	2.34	7.59	8.03	4.83
Louisiana........	5.65	6.55	2.59	2.45	6.95	7.08	4.30
Texas............	5.89	7.43	2.70	2.42	8.54	10.92	5.73
Colorado..........	4.72	5.92	2.29	1.91	4.06	5.35	2.67
Washington.......	7.68	9.02	2.92	2.70	12.87	13.37	7.86
California.........	5.37	6.63	2.69	2.41	5.60	7.17	3.91

Pulp, Paper, and Products

State	$\dfrac{K_g}{L_p}$	$\dfrac{K'_g}{L_p}$	$\dfrac{K_n}{L_p}$	$\dfrac{[V-(T+D)]}{K_g}$	$\dfrac{[V-(T+D)]}{K'_g}$	r	R
Maine............	11.97	12.15	8.11	0.42	0.41	10.3	67.73
New Hampshire....	6.05	6.22	3.28	0.84	0.81	10.3	54.23
Massachusetts.....	4.38	5.07	2.22	1.04	0.90	10.9	50.64
Connecticut.......	4.05	5.06	2.23	1.11	0.89	10.3	55.14
New York.........	3.95	5.39	2.08	1.13	0.83	10.1	52.56
New Jersey........	5.40	7.59	2.87	0.98	0.70	9.97	53.25
Pennsylvania......	6.05	7.22	3.23	0.89	0.75	9.59	53.28
Ohio.............	5.18	5.99	2.83	1.03	0.89	10.3	54.60
Indiana...........	4.03	5.09	2.56	1.20	0.95	10.2	63.61
Illinois............	3.98	6.13	2.05	1.24	0.80	9.88	51.58
Michigan.........	5.58	6.77	3.28	0.91	0.75	10.2	58.73
Wisconsin.........	6.91	7.59	4.14	0.84	0.77	9.78	59.89
Minnesota........	7.52	9.68	4.32	1.01	0.78	10.2	57.43
Missouri..........	3.28	4.04	2.03	1.57	1.27	9.03	61.70
Virginia..........	6.61	7.78	3.90	0.87	0.74	9.31	58.98
North Carolina....	9.63	10.46	4.89	0.49	0.46	8.37	50.84
South Carolina....	8.41	8.99	4.24	0.82	0.77	8.18	50.41
Georgia...........	10.94	11.75	7.16	0.66	0.61	8.47	65.43
Florida...........	16.65	17.09	10.70	0.41	0.40	10.3	64.29
Kentucky.........	3.37	3.70	2.17	1.20	1.09	8.18	64.49
Tennessee.........	9.55	10.11	5.06	0.70	0.67	8.28	53.06
Mississippi........	8.31	8.34	4.18	0.72	0.71	8.37	50.28
Arkansas..........	8.61	9.10	5.47	0.74	0.70	8.37	63.56
Louisiana.........	8.06	8.21	4.98	0.76	0.74	8.28	61.79
Texas.............	10.78	13.78	7.23	0.62	0.49	9.78	67.11
Colorado..........	5.10	6.71	3.35	1.07	0.82	11.4	65.67
Washington.......	15.13	15.71	9.24	0.52	0.51	11.4	61.05
California.........	6.92	8.85	4.83	0.88	0.69	11.4	69.79

Chemicals and Products

State	V/L	V/L$_p$	W$_L$	W$_p$	K$_g$/L	K$'_g$/L	K$_n$/L
Massachusetts.....	6.17	9.62	2.72	2.48	5.26	6.53	2.84
Connecticut.......	7.00	9.88	2.77	2.33	5.98	6.61	2.95
New York.........	7.93	11.88	2.79	2.32	5.51	6.75	2.78
New Jersey........	8.74	14.11	3.09	2.63	6.34	7.29	2.71
Pennsylvania......	7.95	12.06	2.76	2.35	6.55	7.19	3.01
Ohio.............	7.14	11.42	2.77	2.54	6.84	7.71	3.69
Indiana...........	1.08	16.32	3.44	2.65	7.06	7.59	4.25
Illinois...........	8.29	12.95	2.84	2.39	6.57	7.70	3.97
Michigan.........	7.65	11.63	3.24	2.73	7.67	8.94	3.52
Wisconsin........	6.91	11.51	2.75	2.27	3.66	4.42	1.96
Minnesota........	9.76	14.51	2.53	2.29	6.07	7.54	3.67
Iowa.............	8.27	11.68	2.55	2.13	5.85	7.13	2.68
Missouri..........	7.80	12.43	2.62	2.32	5.85	7.09	3.32
Kansas...........	7.85	12.49	2.84	3.06	8.63	9.12	5.02
Delaware.........	10.09	13.76	3.08	2.65	9.56	10.23	3.09
Maryland.........	6.90	10.00	2.42	2.12	7.03	8.05	3.35
Virginia..........	6.75	9.12	2.72	2.41	8.19	8.65	2.70
West Virginia.....	9.14	12.70	3.31	2.98	12.89	13.15	5.42
North Carolina....	6.12	9.04	2.46	1.97	6.68	7.13	3.21
Georgia...........	5.39	7.32	1.96	1.61	4.74	5.30	2.13
Florida...........	6.89	8.96	2.12	1.89	8.60	8.93	6.36
Kentucky.........	9.82	14.33	3.05	2.74	9.51	9.68	4.85
Tennessee........	6.63	9.36	2.96	2.57	6.64	7.10	3.29
Alabama..........	8.07	11.09	2.43	2.10	13.49	15.74	8.98
Mississippi........	5.78	7.25	1.98	1.64	7.05	7.91	4.05
Arkansas..........	6.76	8.44	2.45	2.27	10.80	12.08	6.71
Louisiana.........	9.02	11.91	3.13	2.78	13.71	15.43	7.85
Texas.............	13.12	18.67	3.14	2.84	19.77	21.51	9.96
Montana..........	3.74	6.10	2.40	2.54	10.65	10.70	4.98
Washington.......	6.22	10.07	3.56	3.09	2.65	3.21	1.53
California.........	7.98	12.33	2.88	2.46	6.37	8.05	3.73

Chemicals and Products

State	$\dfrac{K_g}{L_p}$	$\dfrac{K'_g}{L_p}$	$\dfrac{K_n}{L_p}$	$\dfrac{[V-(T+D)]}{K_g}$	$\dfrac{[V-(T+D)]}{K'_g}$	r	R
Massachusetts.....	8.19	10.19	4.44	1.10	0.89	10.9	54.19
Connecticut.......	8.44	9.33	4.16	1.09	0.98	10.3	49.33
New York.........	8.26	10.12	4.17	1.37	1.12	10.1	50.48
New Jersey........	10.25	11.78	4.37	1.29	1.12	9.97	42.66
Pennsylvania......	9.94	10.92	4.57	1.14	1.04	9.59	45.95
Ohio.............	10.94	12.34	5.90	0.97	0.86	10.3	53.92
Indiana...........	10.71	11.51	6.45	1.44	1.34	10.2	60.23
Illinois...........	10.27	12.04	6.20	1.18	1.01	9.88	60.34
Michigan.........	11.67	12.60	5.36	0.89	0.77	10.2	45.92
Wisconsin.........	6.09	7.37	3.26	1.81	1.49	9.78	53.58
Minnesota........	9.02	11.22	5.46	1.51	1.21	10.2	60.54
Iowa.............	8.26	10.08	3.79	1.27	1.04	10.6	45.83
Missouri..........	9.32	11.30	5.30	1.26	1.04	9.03	56.85
Kansas...........	13.74	14.51	7.99	0.83	0.79	11.0	58.14
Delaware.........	13.04	13.94	4.21	0.96	0.90	10.4	32.31
Maryland.........	10.19	11.67	4.86	0.90	0.78	9.78	47.64
Virginia..........	11.07	11.70	3.65	0.75	0.71	9.31	32.96
West Virginia.....	17.90	18.26	7.53	0.63	0.62	8.28	42.03
North Carolina....	9.87	10.53	4.74	0.83	0.78	8.37	48.02
Georgia...........	6.44	7.21	2.90	1.04	0.93	8.47	44.98
Florida...........	11.18	11.61	8.27	0.71	0.68	10.3	74.01
Kentucky.........	13.89	14.13	7.08	0.94	0.93	8.18	50.97
Tennessee.........	9.38	10.03	4.65	0.93	0.87	8.28	49.62
Alabama..........	18.55	21.64	12.35	0.53	0.45	8.56	66.56
Mississippi........	8.84	9.92	5.09	0.72	0.64	8.37	57.54
Arkansas..........	13.48	15.08	8.38	0.55	0.49	8.37	62.13
Louisiana.........	18.10	20.37	10.36	0.57	0.50	8.28	57.26
Texas.............	28.13	30.61	14.18	0.57	0.52	9.78	50.40
Montana..........	17.36	17.44	8.13	0.28	0.28	10.9	46.82
Washington.......	4.29	5.21	2.48	2.26	1.86	11.4	57.78
California.........	9.84	12.43	5.76	1.15	0.91	11.4	58.58

Petroleum and Coal Products

State	V/L	V/L$_p$	W$_L$	W$_p$	K$_g$/L	K$'_g$/L	K$_n$/L
Massachusetts.....	7.12	10.09	2.96	2.67	13.32	14.99	6.83
New York.........	8.28	12.06	3.29	3.05	13.77	15.20	5.45
New Jersey........	6.70	10.12	3.64	3.30	19.25	20.09	9.81
Pennsylvania......	7.16	9.06	3.37	3.10	20.99	21.89	10.19
Indiana...........	6.78	9.04	3.73	3.64	22.70	22.71	11.26
Illinois............	9.24	12.41	3.41	3.13	17.00	17.72	7.45
Minnesota........	6.82	9.93	2.82	2.59	6.32	8.30	4.02
Missouri..........	7.34	10.37	3.09	2.77	17.27	17.89	9.11
Kansas...........	9.22	12.00	3.22	3.09	17.72	18.17	8.95
Kentucky.........	12.72	19.63	3.32	3.15	16.12	16.36	7.17
Alabama..........	6.28	8.08	2.41	2.26	6.86	7.67	4.90
Arkansas..........	6.29	8.05	2.98	2.81	12.94	13.41	6.72
Louisiana.........	10.26	16.78	3.88	3.61	22.85	24.78	10.80
Oklahoma........	9.97	12.05	2.89	2.81	15.44	15.63	6.83
Texas............	8.92	11.84	3.70	3.40	17.94	19.34	8.11
Wyoming.........	6.47	9.48	3.13	3.17	22.07	24.70	9.47
Utah.............	13.45	18.29	3.01	3.01	22.53	22.53	13.69
California.........	9.55	13.48	3.47	3.15	23.30	24.48	10.77

State	$\dfrac{K_g}{L_p}$	$\dfrac{K'_g}{L_p}$	$\dfrac{K_n}{L_p}$	$\dfrac{[V-(T+D)]}{K_g}$	$\dfrac{[V-(T+D)]}{K'_g}$	r	R
Massachusetts.....	18.92	21.29	9.69	0.45	0.40	10.9	51.24
New York.........	20.06	22.14	7.94	0.52	0.47	10.1	39.57
New Jersey........	29.05	30.32	14.80	0.27	0.26	9.97	50.94
Pennsylvania......	26.54	27.68	12.88	0.28	0.27	9.59	48.52
Indiana...........	30.26	30.27	15.01	0.24	0.24	10.2	49.59
Illinois............	22.83	23.79	10.01	0.46	0.44	9.88	43.83
Minnesota........	9.19	12.08	5.84	0.94	0.72	10.2	63.56
Missouri..........	24.38	25.26	12.87	0.34	0.32	0.93	52.78
Kansas...........	23.06	23.65	11.66	0.44	0.43	11.0	50.54
Kentucky.........	24.87	25.25	11.07	0.69	0.68	8.18	44.49
Alabama..........	88.82	9.86	6.30	0.85	0.76	8.56	71.43
Arkansas..........	16.57	17.17	8.61	0.42	0.40	8.37	51.94
Louisiana.........	37.37	40.54	17.66	0.36	0.33	8.28	47.26
Oklahoma........	18.66	18.88	8.25	0.59	0.58	9.78	44.20
Texas............	23.83	25.69	10.77	0.42	0.39	9.78	45.18
Wyoming.........	32.32	36.16	13.87	0.24	0.22	11.4	42.90
Utah.............	30.63	30.63	18.61	0.53	0.53	11.5	60.76
California.........	32.91	34.57	15.20	0.33	0.31	11.4	46.20

Rubber Products

State	V/L	V/L$_p$	W$_L$	W$_p$	K$_g$/L	K$'_g$/L	K$_n$/L
Massachusetts.....	4.07	5.15	2.59	2.34	2.49	2.94	1.13
Rhode Island......	3.88	4.79	2.43	2.20	2.29	2.80	7.58
Connecticut.......	4.46	5.69	2.62	2.40	3.05	3.80	1.57
New York.........	4.21	5.49	2.58	2.42	3.81	4.59	1.94
Ohio.............	4.80	6.32	3.11	2.89	3.40	3.94	1.42
Indiana..........	4.16	5.21	2.75	2.53	2.77	3.31	1.25
Illinois...........	3.48	4.41	2.22	1.92	2.65	3.06	1.70
Michigan.........	4.96	6.59	3.17	3.04	4.47	5.81	1.68
Wisconsin.........	4.90	5.64	2.87	2.71	3.91	4.55	1.02
Minnesota........	4.74	5.38	2.57	2.37	1.97	5.58	0.73
Iowa.............	6.30	7.65	2.95	2.90	4.80	5.33	2.86
Maryland.........	4.10	4.98	2.25	2.03	1.88	2.59	0.69
North Carolina....	4.83	5.94	2.46	2.35	2.40	2.73	1.40
Tennessee.........	6.47	7.62	2.99	2.90	3.87	4.28	1.66
Alabama..........	7.47	8.48	3.03	2.91	3.53	3.85	2.40
California.........	5.00	6.30	2.87	2.61	3.25	4.27	1.52

State	$\dfrac{K_g}{L_p}$	$\dfrac{K'_g}{L_p}$	$\dfrac{K_n}{L_p}$	$\dfrac{[V-(T+D)]}{K_g}$	$\dfrac{[V-(T+D)]}{K'_g}$	r	R
Massachusetts.....	3.15	3.72	1.42	1.56	1.32	10.90	45.26
Rhode Island......	2.83	3.46	0.93	1.62	1.32	9.41	33.04
Connecticut.......	3.90	4.85	2.01	1.38	1.11	10.30	51.46
New York.........	4.97	5.99	2.53	1.04	0.86	10.10	50.96
Ohio.............	4.48	5.20	1.87	1.33	1.15	10.30	41.87
Indiana..........	3.47	4.15	1.57	1.43	1.19	10.20	45.14
Illinois...........	3.37	3.87	2.15	1.23	1.07	9.88	63.95
Michigan.........	5.94	7.71	2.23	1.02	0.78	10.20	37.61
Wisconsin.........	4.49	5.24	1.17	1.21	1.04	9.78	26.06
Minnesota........	2.24	6.34	0.83	2.30	0.81	10.20	36.93
Iowa.............	5.83	6.48	3.48	1.18	1.07	10.60	59.66
Maryland.........	2.29	3.14	0.84	2.08	1.51	9.78	36.66
North Carolina....	2.95	3.35	1.72	1.92	1.69	8.37	58.13
Tennessee.........	4.56	5.04	1.96	1.56	1.41	8.28	42.85
Alabama..........	4.01	4.37	2.73	2.06	1.89	8.56	68.05
California.........	4.10	5.39	1.92	1.44	1.10	11.40	46.79

Leather and Leather Products

State	V/L	V/L$_p$	W$_L$	W$_p$	K$_g$/L	K$'_g$/L	K$_n$/L
New Hampshire....	2.46	2.74	1.84	1.71	0.52	1.48	0.26
Massachusetts.....	2.86	3.29	2.01	1.81	0.53	1.68	0.25
New York.........	2.79	3.18	1.86	1.72	0.59	1.75	0.25
Pennsylvania......	2.36	2.61	1.67	1.69	0.71	1.76	0.31
Ohio.............	2.90	3.32	2.03	1.81	0.92	1.50	0.52
Illinois............	3.27	3.64	1.91	1.76	0.55	1.20	0.09
Michigan.........	3.90	4.40	2.33	2.14	2.05	2.47	1.21
Wisconsin.........	3.19	3.83	2.08	1.87	1.05	2.03	0.52
Missouri..........	3.01	3.33	1.70	1.56	0.51	1.42	0.26
Delaware.........	3.39	4.24	2.21	2.06	1.72	1.91	0.60
Maryland.........	2.43	2.71	1.66	1.45	1.02	1.66	0.42
Virginia..........	1.93	2.17	1.61	1.55	0.55	1.05	0.26
Georgia...........	2.78	3.01	1.53	1.36	0.24	1.23	0.07
Tennessee.........	3.14	3.37	1.53	1.43	0.39	0.95	0.25
Arkansas..........	2.78	2.91	1.50	1.46	0.44	1.01	0.23

State	K$_g$/L$_p$	K$'_g$/L$_p$	K$_n$/L$_p$	[V − (T+D)]/K$_g$	[V − (T+D)]/K$'_g$	r	R
New Hampshire....	0.58	1.65	0.29	4.60	1.62	10.30	49.95
Massachusetts.....	0.61	1.94	0.28	5.29	1.66	10.90	46.75
New York.........	0.68	1.99	0.29	4.59	1.56	10.10	42.18
Pennsylvania......	0.79	1.95	0.35	3.23	1.31	9.59	43.93
Ohio.............	1.05	1.72	0.59	3.09	1.88	10.30	56.50
Illinois............	0.62	1.33	0.11	5.78	2.67	9.88	17.05
Michigan.........	2.32	2.79	1.37	1.80	1.49	10.20	59.18
Wisconsin.........	1.27	2.44	0.62	2.92	1.52	9.78	49.13
Missouri..........	0.56	1.58	0.28	5.83	2.09	9.03	50.36
Delaware.........	2.15	2.39	0.75	1.92	1.72	10.40	34.87
Maryland.........	1.13	1.86	0.47	2.30	1.40	9.78	41.11
Virginia..........	0.61	1.18	0.29	3.47	1.81	9.31	46.77
Georgia...........	0.26	1.33	0.08	11.58	2.23	8.47	30.20
Tennessee.........	0.42	1.02	0.26	7.96	3.27	8.28	63.19
Arkansas..........	0.46	1.06	0.24	6.06	2.61	8.37	51.78

Stone, Clay, and Glass Products

State	V/L	V/L$_p$	W$_L$	W$_p$	K$_g$/L	K$'_g$/L	K$_n$/L
New Hampshire....	3.73	4.47	2.10	1.93	2.26	2.44	1.05
Massachusetts.....	4.80	6.73	2.78	2.46	3.97	4.71	2.10
Connecticut.......	4.18	5.52	2.32	2.26	3.08	3.56	1.88
New York.........	4.49	5.78	2.65	2.35	3.58	4.70	1.88
Pennsylvania......	5.04	5.98	2.58	2.46	4.30	4.59	2.66
Ohio.............	4.61	5.45	2.51	2.36	3.97	4.29	2.13
Indiana...........	4.41	5.15	2.44	2.24	3.86	4.21	2.21
Illinois............	5.47	6.42	2.61	2.39	3.76	4.16	1.83
Michigan.........	5.36	6.51	2.69	2.39	4.88	5.23	2.50
Wisconsin.........	4.92	6.15	2.41	2.04	3.26	4.22	1.51
Minnesota........	3.80	4.47	2.29	1.96	5.87	6.20	3.54
Missouri..........	5.38	6.37	2.79	2.55	5.53	5.87	2.87
Maryland.........	4.98	5.83	2.39	2.19	7.29	7.97	5.26
Virginia..........	4.67	5.52	1.83	1.68	5.56	6.00	3.09
West Virginia.....	3.61	4.02	2.47	2.37	2.49	2.68	0.90
Georgia...........	3.53	4.08	1.73	1.50	2.56	2.90	0.68
Florida...........	3.76	4.64	1.73	1.53	3.95	4.57	2.20
Kentucky.........	4.06	4.81	2.19	2.06	4.25	4.67	2.03
Tennessee.........	3.21	3.82	2.15	1.90	3.98	4.27	1.87
Alabama..........	4.58	5.34	2.01	1.83	4.59	4.97	1.97
Louisiana.........	5.55	6.61	2.29	2.15	6.76	7.66	4.23
Oklahoma........	4.84	5.46	2.40	2.17	4.39	5.08	2.18
Colorado..........	4.70	5.71	2.28	2.07	6.00	6.52	3.51
Utah.............	6.18	7.44	2.29	2.18	6.94	7.04	3.62
Nevada...........	6.28	7.85	2.44	2.23	1.03	1.05	6.10

Stone, Clay, and Glass Products

State	$\dfrac{K_g}{L_p}$	$\dfrac{K'_g}{L_p}$	$\dfrac{K_n}{L_p}$	$\dfrac{[V - (T+D)]}{K_g}$	$\dfrac{[V - (T+D)]}{K'_g}$	r	R
New Hampshire....	2.71	2.92	1.25	1.55	1.43	10.30	46.3
Massachusetts.....	5.57	6.61	2.94	1.13	0.96	10.90	52.8
Connecticut.......	4.06	4.70	2.49	1.27	1.10	10.30	61.2
New York.........	4.61	6.04	2.42	1.17	0.89	10.10	52.5
Pennsylvania......	5.11	5.46	3.16	1.10	1.03	9.59	61.9
Ohio.............	4.69	5.07	2.51	1.07	0.99	10.30	53.5
Indiana...........	4.50	4.91	2.58	1.07	0.98	10.20	57.2
Illinois............	4.41	4.88	2.15	1.36	1.23	9.88	48.8
Michigan.........	5.92	6.35	3.04	1.00	0.93	10.20	51.2
Wisconsin.........	4.07	5.27	1.89	1.39	1.08	9.78	46.3
Minnesota........	6.91	7.30	4.17	0.56	0.53	10.20	60.3
Missouri..........	6.56	6.96	3.40	0.90	0.85	9.03	51.9
Maryland.........	8.53	9.32	6.15	0.60	0.55	9.78	72.1
Virginia..........	6.58	7.10	3.65	0.78	0.72	9.31	55.6
West Virginia.....	2.77	2.98	1.01	1.39	1.30	8.28	36.2
Georgia...........	2.96	3.35	0.79	1.20	1.06	8.47	26.5
Florida...........	4.87	5.63	2.71	0.82	0.71	10.30	55.8
Kentucky.........	5.05	5.43	2.41	0.87	0.79	8.18	47.7
Tennessee.........	4.74	5.08	2.22	0.67	0.63	8.28	46.9
Alabama..........	5.35	5.81	2.30	0.92	0.85	8.56	42.9
Louisiana.........	8.06	9.13	5.04	0.74	0.65	8.28	62.6
Oklahoma........	4.94	5.72	2.46	1.01	0.88	9.78	49.7
Colorado..........	7.28	7.93	4.26	0.71	0.66	11.40	58.5
Utah.............	9.35	8.47	4.36	0.84	0.82	11.50	52.2
Nevada...........	1.29	1.31	7.63	0.53	0.53	11.40	59.1

Primary Metals Products

State	V/L	V/L$_p$	W$_L$	W$_p$	K$_g$/L	K$'_g$/L	K$_n$/L
Massachusetts.....	4.33	5.31	2.90	2.67	3.45	4.37	1.22
Rhode Island......	4.59	5.69	2.69	2.39	2.53	3.25	1.17
Connecticut.......	4.64	5.33	2.96	2.55	3.87	4.37	1.77
New York.........	5.06	6.15	2.95	2.77	4.75	5.00	1.78
New Jersey........	4.47	5.63	2.95	2.68	3.84	4.29	1.71
Pennsylvania......	5.23	6.54	3.15	3.06	6.60	7.02	2.70
Ohio.............	5.90	6.92	3.22	3.04	6.78	7.16	3.16
Indiana...........	5.84	7.06	3.23	3.05	7.82	8.16	3.40
Illinois............	4.99	6.13	3.08	2.83	5.05	5.38	2.29
Michigan.........	5.00	5.96	3.22	2.99	6.17	6.72	2.11
Wisconsin.........	4.60	5.70	2.95	2.75	2.80	3.33	1.35
Minnesota........	4.45	5.17	2.98	2.71	6.22	7.02	1.38
Iowa.............	6.26	7.79	2.74	2.55	11.70	12.54	7.19
Missouri..........	4.51	5.51	2.87	2.63	4.49	4.69	2.12
Delaware.........	3.32	4.49	2.99	2.84	3.93	4.10	1.56
Maryland.........	5.05	6.01	3.05	2.88	8.94	9.19	4.84
Virginia..........	3.66	4.23	2.27	2.01	4.12	4.31	2.71
West Virginia.....	5.34	6.35	3.29	3.14	8.42	8.56	3.28
Kentucky.........	5.10	5.70	3.44	3.07	10.90	11.06	5.63
Tennessee.........	5.22	6.43	2.57	2.40	5.58	5.74	1.85
Alabama..........	5.71	6.64	3.08	2.89	6.23	6.54	2.22
Louisiana.........	8.81	10.51	2.85	2.63	11.58	11.86	8.49
Oklahoma........	3.82	4.23	2.59	2.45	2.37	2.42	0.88
Texas............	5.79	6.90	2.85	2.62	7.83	8.60	4.83
Arizona...........	3.72	4.49	2.78	2.66	5.01	5.07	2.43
Nevada...........	16.82	24.44	3.03	2.80	6.03	9.72	2.23
Washington.......	7.79	9.40	3.09	2.95	6.22	6.74	3.35
California.........	5.35	6.61	3.01	2.75	5.61	6.63	3.15

Primary Metals Products

State	$\dfrac{K_g}{L_p}$	$\dfrac{K'_g}{L_p}$	$\dfrac{K_n}{L_p}$	$\dfrac{[V-(T+D)]}{K_g}$	$\dfrac{[V-(T+D)]}{K'_g}$	r	R
Massachusetts.....	4.23	5.36	1.49	1.18	0.93	10.90	35.30
Rhode Island......	3.13	4.03	1.45	1.73	1.35	9.41	46.17
Connecticut.......	4.45	5.03	2.03	1.11	0.98	10.30	45.67
New York.........	5.77	6.07	2.16	1.00	0.95	10.10	37.39
New Jersey........	4.84	5.39	2.15	1.09	0.98	9.97	44.48
Pennsylvania......	8.24	8.77	3.38	0.72	0.68	9.59	40.96
Ohio.............	7.95	8.39	3.70	0.80	0.75	10.30	46.54
Indiana..........	9.47	9.88	4.11	0.67	0.65	10.20	43.44
Illinois...........	6.20	6.61	2.82	0.92	0.86	9.88	45.43
Michigan.........	7.35	8.00	3.71	0.71	0.66	10.20	50.40
Wisconsin.........	3.47	4.12	1.67	1.55	1.31	9.78	48.10
Minnesota........	7.23	8.16	1.60	0.65	0.58	10.20	22.15
Iowa.............	14.57	15.60	8.94	0.46	0.43	10.60	61.41
Missouri..........	5.49	5.73	2.60	0.93	0.89	9.03	47.29
Delaware.........	5.32	5.56	2.11	0.72	0.69	10.40	39.68
Maryland.........	10.65	10.96	5.77	0.49	0.48	9.78	54.14
Virginia..........	4.77	4.98	3.13	0.81	0.78	9.31	65.66
West Virginia.....	10.00	10.17	3.89	0.57	0.56	8.28	38.94
Kentucky.........	12.18	12.35	6.29	0.36	0.36	8.18	51.64
Tennessee........	6.87	7.08	2.27	0.88	0.85	8.28	33.09
Alabama..........	7.26	7.61	2.58	0.86	0.82	8.56	35.51
Louisiana.........	13.82	14.15	10.13	0.67	0.66	8.28	73.33
Oklahoma........	2.63	2.68	0.97	1.52	1.49	9.78	37.02
Texas............	9.32	10.24	5.75	0.66	0.60	9.78	48.45
Arizona...........	6.04	6.11	2.93	0.70	0.69	10.60	48.45
Nevada...........	8.76	14.12	3.24	2.61	1.62	11.40	37.04
Washington.......	7.50	8.13	4.04	1.19	1.09	11.40	53.86
California.........	6.93	8.19	3.89	0.88	0.74	11.40	56.19

Fabricated Metal Products

State	V/L	V/L$_p$	W$_L$	W$_p$	K$_g$/L	K'$_g$/L	K$_n$/L
Massachusetts.....	4.19	5.18	2.42	2.08	1.65	2.64	0.79
Rhode Island......	3.49	3.98	2.20	1.86	1.28	2.50	0.65
Connecticut.......	3.72	4.71	2.49	2.22	2.32	2.89	1.15
New York.........	3.95	4.93	2.49	2.20	1.78	3.23	0.86
New Jersey........	4.61	5.84	2.68	2.44	2.36	3.46	1.23
Pennsylvania......	4.54	5.71	2.70	2.47	2.41	3.17	1.08
Ohio.............	4.33	5.52	2.76	2.48	2.61	3.52	1.42
Indiana...........	4.50	4.81	2.74	2.47	2.65	3.07	1.45
Illinois............	4.65	5.80	2.70	2.39	2.47	3.45	1.40
Michigan.........	4.29	5.26	2.83	2.49	2.78	3.49	1.71
Wisconsin.........	4.45	5.73	2.54	2.29	2.66	3.37	1.61
Minnesota........	4.18	5.77	2.33	2.23	2.47	3.14	1.42
Iowa.............	4.84	6.40	2.52	2.25	2.07	3.01	1.19
Missouri..........	4.35	5.75	2.59	2.32	2.18	3.29	1.16
Nebraska.........	3.91	5.04	2.13	1.90	2.04	2.72	1.61
Kansas...........	4.10	5.55	2.35	2.05	1.33	2.58	0.42
Delaware.........	4.06	5.64	2.43	2.15	2.54	3.43	0.89
Maryland.........	4.47	5.82	2.64	2.49	3.44	4.45	2.06
Virginia..........	3.87	5.41	2.28	2.16	1.42	2.14	0.81
West Virginia.....	3.81	4.71	2.41	2.20	2.51	3.11	0.84
North Carolina....	4.01	5.04	2.17	1.83	1.82	2.60	1.13
Florida...........	4.33	5.61	2.10	1.87	2.54	3.97	1.75
Kentucky.........	3.75	4.48	2.68	2.51	2.60	3.02	1.41
Tennessee.........	3.32	4.15	2.14	1.93	2.42	2.89	1.16
Alabama..........	4.53	5.46	2.43	2.12	1.82	2.33	0.97
Mississippi........	4.31	5.33	1.98	1.67	2.21	2.81	1.56
Louisiana.........	4.25	5.40	2.50	2.26	2.01	2.64	1.09
Oklahoma........	4.41	6.18	2.57	2.20	1.56	1.83	0.77
Texas............	3.77	4.85	2.35	2.08	2.24	3.03	1.46
Arizona...........	2.75	3.39	2.45	2.43	0.85	1.30	0.51
Washington.......	4.90	6.43	2.74	2.55	1.82	2.71	0.87
California.........	4.96	6.41	2.71	2.46	2.37	3.87	1.38

Fabricated Metal Products

State	$\dfrac{K_g}{L_p}$	$\dfrac{K'_g}{L_p}$	$\dfrac{K_n}{L_p}$	$\dfrac{[V-(T+D)]}{K_g}$	$\dfrac{[V-(T+D)]}{K'_g}$	r	R
Massachusetts	2.04	3.26	0.98	2.45	1.53	10.90	48.08
Rhode Island	1.46	2.85	0.75	2.62	1.34	9.41	51.08
Connecticut	2.94	3.66	1.46	1.52	1.22	10.30	49.63
New York	2.22	4.04	1.08	2.13	1.17	10.10	48.55
New Jersey	2.98	4.38	1.55	1.86	1.27	9.97	52.07
Pennsylvania	3.04	4.00	1.37	1.81	1.37	9.59	44.91
Ohio	3.32	4.50	1.81	1.57	1.16	10.30	54.59
Indiana	3.41	3.97	1.87	1.62	1.39	10.20	54.86
Illinois	3.08	4.31	1.75	1.79	1.28	9.88	56.70
Michigan	3.41	4.28	2.10	1.41	1.13	10.20	61.50
Wisconsin	3.42	4.34	2.08	1.57	1.24	9.78	60.68
Minnesota	3.40	4.33	1.96	1.60	1.25	10.20	57.51
Iowa	2.74	3.98	1.58	2.22	1.53	10.60	57.48
Missouri	2.88	4.35	1.54	1.91	1.26	9.03	53.45
Nebraska	2.62	3.50	2.07	1.79	1.34	10.90	78.79
Kansas	1.81	3.49	0.58	2.91	1.51	11.00	31.80
Delaware	3.54	4.76	1.24	1.53	1.13	10.40	34.98
Maryland	4.48	5.79	2.68	1.21	0.94	9.78	59.73
Virginia	1.98	2.99	1.13	2.63	1.74	9.31	56.91
West Virginia	3.10	3.84	1.04	1.44	1.16	8.28	33.37
North Carolina	2.29	3.27	1.42	2.08	1.46	8.37	61.78
Florida	3.29	5.14	2.26	1.61	1.03	10.30	68.79
Kentucky	3.11	3.61	1.68	1.37	1.18	8.18	54.09
Tennessee	3.03	3.62	1.45	1.29	1.08	8.28	47.98
Alabama	2.19	2.81	1.18	2.40	1.87	8.56	53.57
Mississippi	2.73	3.47	1.92	1.84	1.45	8.37	70.40
Louisiana	2.55	3.35	1.39	2.01	1.53	8.28	54.32
Oklahoma	2.19	2.56	1.08	2.70	2.30	9.78	49.60
Texas	2.89	3.90	1.88	1.60	1.18	9.78	65.07
Arizona	1.05	1.60	0.63	3.10	2.03	10.60	60.46
Washington	2.38	3.56	1.14	2.56	1.71	11.40	48.00
California	3.07	5.01	1.78	1.97	1.21	11.40	58.14

Machinery except Electrical

State	V/L	V/L$_p$	W$_L$	W$_p$	K$_g$/L	K'$_g$/L	K$_n$/L
New Hampshire....	4.59	5.97	2.22	2.05	1.66	2.18	0.83
Vermont..........	3.97	5.21	2.63	2.37	2.25	2.69	1.06
Massachusetts.....	4.18	5.79	2.72	2.45	2.29	2.93	1.07
Rhode Island......	3.68	4.94	2.50	2.22	2.86	3.54	1.24
Connecticut.......	4.53	5.76	2.78	2.58	2.70	3.62	1.21
New York.........	4.57	6.37	2.80	2.45	2.57	3.53	1.43
New Jersey........	4.44	6.17	2.83	2.54	2.57	3.32	1.31
Pennsylvania......	4.44	6.04	2.80	2.52	1.93	2.61	0.70
Ohio.............	4.62	6.35	2.81	2.72	2.49	3.14	1.11
Indiana...........	4.66	6.10	2.77	2.46	2.39	3.00	1.27
Illinois............	4.82	6.47	2.89	2.60	2.63	3.43	1.40
Michigan.........	4.73	6.11	3.16	2.88	2.65	3.46	1.43
Wisconsin.........	5.00	6.96	2.95	2.68	2.49	3.28	1.21
Minnesota........	3.89	5.54	2.38	2.09	1.35	2.05	0.74
Iowa.............	5.00	6.12	3.06	2.52	2.73	2.92	1.12
Missouri..........	4.33	5.83	2.57	2.33	1.95	3.06	1.04
Maryland.........	4.19	6.05	2.64	2.18	2.40	2.79	1.38
Virginia..........	4.43	5.63	2.36	2.03	2.19	3.31	1.68
Kentucky.........	6.50	8.30	2.71	2.46	4.35	4.89	3.58
Alabama..........	4.19	5.52	2.53	2.22	2.52	3.20	1.42
Oklahoma........	4.27	6.01	2.63	2.23	2.10	2.95	1.01
Texas............	5.30	7.18	2.75	2.31	2.27	3.30	1.23
Colorado..........	4.47	5.71	2.59	2.35	2.43	3.26	1.08
Washington.......	4.42	6.07	2.94	2.73	2.14	2.73	1.12
California.........	4.39	6.14	2.81	2.54	1.96	3.43	1.15

Machinery except Electrical

State	$\frac{K_g}{L_p}$	$\frac{K'_g}{L_p}$	$\frac{K_n}{L_p}$	$\frac{[V-(T+D)]}{K_g}$	$\frac{[V-(T+D)]}{K'_g}$	r	R
New Hampshire....	2.16	2.84	1.08	2.65	2.02	10.30	49.84
Vermont..........	2.95	3.52	1.38	1.69	1.41	10.30	46.94
Massachusetts.....	3.17	4.05	1.48	1.75	1.36	10.90	46.81
Rhode Island......	3.83	4.75	1.67	1.19	0.96	9.41	43.54
Connecticut.......	3.44	4.61	1.54	1.59	1.18	10.30	44.73
New York.........	3.58	4.92	2.00	1.70	1.24	10.10	55.80
New Jersey........	3.57	4.61	1.83	1.64	1.27	9.97	51.11
Pennsylvania......	2.63	3.55	0.95	2.20	1.62	9.59	36.04
Ohio.............	3.42	4.31	1.53	1.76	1.39	10.30	44.75
Indiana...........	3.13	3.92	1.66	1.84	1.47	10.20	53.12
Illinois............	3.52	4.59	1.88	1.74	1.33	9.88	53.26
Michigan.........	3.42	4.48	1.85	1.67	1.28	10.20	53.92
Wisconsin.........	3.47	4.56	1.68	1.90	1.45	9.78	48.39
Minnesota........	1.92	2.91	1.06	2.75	1.81	10.20	54.99
Iowa.............	3.35	3.58	1.37	1.70	1.59	10.60	40.99
Missouri..........	2.62	4.12	1.40	2.13	1.36	9.03	53.32
Maryland.........	3.46	4.02	1.99	1.67	1.44	9.78	57.48
Virginia..........	2.78	4.21	2.14	1.94	1.28	9.31	76.93
Kentucky.........	5.55	6.24	4.57	1.39	1.24	8.18	82.31
Alabama..........	3.32	4.22	1.88	1.58	1.24	8.56	56.55
Oklahoma........	2.96	4.15	1.42	1.93	1.38	9.78	48.00
Texas............	3.07	4.46	1.67	2.21	1.53	9.78	54.17
Colorado..........	3.11	4.17	1.38	1.73	1.29	11.40	44.31
Washington.......	2.94	3.75	1.55	1.98	1.55	11.40	52.62
California.........	2.74	4.79	1.61	2.11	1.21	11.40	58.67

Electrical Machinery

State	V/L	V/L$_p$	W$_L$	W$_p$	K$_g$/L	K'$_g$/L	K$_n$/L
New Hampshire....	3.44	4.57	1.94	1.71	1.39	1.91	0.76
Massachusetts.....	3.77	5.14	2.27	2.02	1.29	1.94	0.63
Connecticut.......	4.63	6.52	2.41	2.09	1.43	2.34	0.69
New York.........	4.35	6.01	2.62	2.23	1.49	2.65	0.75
New Jersey........	4.30	5.95	2.72	2.37	1.81	2.67	0.95
Pennsylvania......	5.31	7.57	2.68	2.41	1.93	2.39	1.04
Ohio.............	4.78	6.38	2.67	2.45	1.92	2.51	0.85
Indiana..........	4.54	5.69	2.64	2.39	2.05	2.63	1.05
Illinois...........	4.25	5.85	2.56	2.23	1.54	2.34	0.90
Wisconsin........	4.66	6.62	2.75	2.53	1.67	2.32	0.90
Iowa.............	3.54	4.75	2.28	1.91	0.98	2.07	0.46
Missouri..........	3.87	5.22	2.52	2.22	2.15	2.87	1.15
Maryland.........	4.40	7.14	2.98	2.36	1.15	1.96	0.67
North Carolina....	4.54	6.90	2.31	1.92	2.34	3.04	1.62
Georgia..........	6.14	7.51	2.48	2.19	4.22	5.08	2.42
Florida...........	3.38	4.62	2.25	1.75	0.58	1.74	0.37
Kentucky.........	4.67	5.63	2.19	1.97	2.13	2.38	1.03
Alabama..........	3.64	4.18	2.02	1.88	1.83	1.95	0.90
Mississippi........	4.00	4.51	1.78	1.46	1.63	1.77	1.08
Oklahoma.........	6.31	8.11	2.02	1.92	1.88	2.00	1.24
Texas............	3.71	5.21	2.51	2.01	1.19	2.25	0.66
California.........	4.51	6.51	2.69	2.48	1.14	2.35	0.68

Electrical Machinery

State	$\dfrac{K_g}{L_p}$	$\dfrac{K'_g}{L_p}$	$\dfrac{K_n}{L_p}$	$\dfrac{[V-(T+D)]}{K_g}$	$\dfrac{[V-(T+D)]}{K'_g}$	r	R
New Hampshire....	1.84	2.54	1.01	2.36	1.71	10.30	55.05
Massachusetts.....	1.76	2.64	0.86	2.82	1.88	10.90	48.90
Connecticut.......	2.02	3.29	0.97	3.11	1.91	10.30	48.09
New York.........	2.05	3.65	1.04	2.83	1.59	10.10	50.37
New Jersey........	2.50	3.70	1.31	2.29	1.55	9.97	52.44
Pennsylvania......	2.75	3.40	1.48	2.67	2.16	9.59	53.63
Ohio.............	2.57	3.36	1.14	2.38	1.82	10.30	44.40
Indiana..........	2.57	3.29	1.32	2.11	1.65	10.20	51.19
Illinois...........	2.12	3.23	1.23	2.66	1.75	9.88	58.05
Wisconsin........	2.38	3.29	1.27	2.64	1.91	9.78	53.54
Iowa.............	1.31	2.78	0.61	3.49	1.65	10.60	46.47
Missouri..........	2.90	3.87	1.56	1.72	1.28	9.03	53.71
Maryland.........	1.86	3.18	1.08	3.70	2.18	9.78	57.81
North Carolina....	3.56	4.62	2.47	1.83	1.41	8.37	69.35
Georgia..........	5.16	6.21	2.96	1.31	1.09	8.47	57.31
Florida..........	0.79	2.37	0.51	5.70	1.89	10.30	64.91
Kentucky.........	2.57	2.87	1.24	2.12	1.90	8.18	48.15
Alabama..........	2.10	2.23	1.03	1.87	1.76	8.56	49.18
Mississippi........	1.84	2.00	1.22	2.37	2.18	8.37	66.57
Oklahoma........	2.42	2.58	1.60	3.28	3.08	9.78	66.03
Texas............	1.67	3.15	0.93	2.96	1.57	9.78	55.60
California.........	1.65	3.38	0.97	3.81	1.85	11.40	59.21

Transportation Equipment

State	V/L	V/L$_p$	W$_L$	W$_p$	K$_g$/L	K$'_g$/L	K$_n$/L
Maine............	4.20	4.56	2.46	2.29	2.03	2.83	1.02
Massachusetts.....	4.23	6.14	2.82	2.59	1.73	2.23	0.73
Connecticut.......	4.17	5.57	2.83	2.58	1.29	1.82	0.54
New York.........	3.73	4.95	2.96	2.74	1.90	2.51	0.96
New Jersey........	5.66	8.04	3.00	2.83	2.17	2.78	1.06
Pennsylvania......	4.93	6.29	3.00	2.81	2.62	3.08	1.18
Ohio.............	4.53	6.20	3.06	2.84	2.62	3.31	1.55
Indiana...........	4.92	6.66	3.04	2.84	3.40	4.27	1.90
Illinois............	6.15	8.18	3.03	2.77	3.25	3.67	1.90
Michigan.........	5.41	6.92	2.96	2.91	3.96	4.24	2.02
Wisconsin.........	5.52	6.63	2.82	2.70	2.64	3.26	1.27
Iowa.............	3.55	4.46	2.71	2.40	1.38	1.84	0.81
Missouri..........	5.68	7.69	2.88	2.52	1.70	2.43	0.92
Kansas...........	4.40	5.74	2.68	2.49	0.40	1.04	0.16
Maryland.........	4.13	5.99	2.93	2.68	0.88	1.40	0.40
Virginia..........	5.07	5.56	2.90	2.81	1.69	1.99	0.78
West Virginia.....	4.56	5.59	2.69	2.89	3.05	3.30	1.52
Georgia..........	5.09	6.70	3.00	2.56	0.91	1.61	0.51
Florida...........	2.58	2.93	2.04	1.87	1.08	2.22	0.61
Kentucky.........	9.14	10.42	2.76	2.50	2.38	2.71	1.59
Alabama..........	3.28	3.99	2.33	2.43	0.48	0.92	0.24
Louisiana.........	4.00	4.61	2.60	2.43	1.11	1.82	0.59
Oklahoma........	2.11	2.71	2.75	2.64	0.26	0.66	0.11
Texas............	3.63	4.79	3.02	2.79	0.56	1.32	0.30
Washington.......	4.63	7.24	3.01	2.61	0.79	1.81	0.45
California.........	4.73	7.07	3.10	2.70	0.90	2.03	0.45

Transportation Equipment

State	$\dfrac{K_g}{L_p}$	$\dfrac{K'_g}{L_p}$	$\dfrac{K_n}{L_p}$	$\dfrac{[V-(T+D)]}{K_g}$	$\dfrac{[V-(T+D)]}{K'_g}$	r	R
Maine............	2.02	3.07	1.11	1.99	1.42	10.30	50.32
Massachusetts.....	2.52	3.24	1.06	2.34	1.82	10.90	42.24
Connecticut.......	1.72	2.43	0.72	3.12	2.21	10.30	41.81
New York........	2.52	3.33	1.27	1.86	1.41	10.10	50.17
New Jersey........	3.08	3.95	1.51	2.53	1.97	9.97	48.83
Pennsylvania......	3.34	3.93	1.50	1.82	1.55	9.59	44.88
Ohio.............	3.59	4.54	2.12	1.62	1.28	10.30	58.95
Indiana...........	4.60	5.78	2.56	1.34	1.06	10.20	55.77
Illinois...........	4.32	4.89	2.53	1.79	1.58	9.88	58.63
Michigan.........	5.06	5.42	2.58	1.26	1.17	10.20	50.97
Wisconsin.........	3.17	3.92	1.52	2.01	1.63	9.78	48.03
Iowa.............	1.73	2.31	1.02	2.46	1.84	10.60	58.63
Missouri..........	2.30	3.29	1.25	3.25	2.27	9.03	54.47
Kansas...........	0.52	1.35	0.21	1.09	4.21	11.00	39.97
Maryland.........	1.28	2.02	0.58	4.59	2.89	9.78	45.82
Virginia..........	1.85	2.18	0.86	2.93	2.49	9.31	46.36
West Virginia.....	3.74	4.05	1.86	1.43	1.32	8.28	49.88
Georgia...........	1.20	2.12	0.67	5.47	3.09	8.47	55.68
Florida...........	1.23	2.53	0.70	2.21	1.08	10.30	56.54
Kentucky.........	2.72	3.09	1.82	3.72	3.27	8.18	66.87
Alabama..........	0.59	1.12	0.29	6.71	3.50	8.56	50.22
Louisiana.........	1.28	2.10	0.68	3.51	2.14	8.28	53.27
Oklahoma........	0.34	0.85	0.14	7.89	3.15	9.78	39.97
Texas............	0.75	1.75	0.40	6.29	2.68	9.78	53.36
Washington.......	1.24	2.83	0.71	5.70	2.50	11.40	57.35
California.........	1.35	3.03	0.68	5.06	2.25	11.40	50.33

Instruments and Related Products

State	V/L	V/L$_p$	W$_L$	W$_p$	K$_g$/L	K$'_g$/L	K$_n$/L
Massachusetts.....	4.59	6.47	2.51	2.16	1.44	2.04	0.73
New York.........	5.60	8.07	3.16	2.70	2.82	3.75	1.37
New Jersey........	4.19	6.32	2.93	2.62	1.73	2.65	0.96
Pennsylvania......	4.24	6.36	2.59	2.25	1.50	2.06	0.81
Ohio.............	3.47	5.28	2.31	1.99	1.46	1.79	0.86
Indiana...........	3.94	5.07	2.25	2.08	1.24	1.85	0.65
Michigan.........	4.40	6.04	2.83	2.58	1.06	1.89	0.61
Iowa.............	3.60	5.63	2.43	2.18	1.08	1.55	0.55
Maryland.........	3.98	5.20	2.85	2.08	1.59	2.60	0.93
North Carolina....	2.92	3.89	2.06	1.74	0.83	1.40	0.40
Tennessee.........	4.06	5.40	2.41	2.24	2.15	2.69	1.02
Colorado..........	4.16	6.03	2.26	2.14	1.50	1.98	1.04

State	$\dfrac{K_g}{L_p}$	$\dfrac{K'_g}{L_p}$	$\dfrac{K_n}{L_p}$	$\dfrac{[V-(T+D)]}{K_g}$	$\dfrac{[V-(T+D)]}{K'_g}$	r	R
Massachusetts.....	2.03	2.87	1.03	3.09	2.18	10.90	50.94
New York.........	4.06	5.41	1.98	1.92	1.44	10.10	48.71
New Jersey........	2.60	3.99	1.45	2.32	1.51	9.97	55.70
Pennsylvania......	2.25	3.09	1.22	2.74	2.01	9.59	53.93
Ohio.............	2.22	2.72	1.32	2.29	1.87	10.30	59.12
Indiana...........	1.59	2.38	0.83	3.05	2.04	10.20	52.12
Michigan.........	1.46	2.59	0.84	4.01	2.26	10.20	57.76
Iowa.............	1.68	2.43	0.85	3.26	2.26	10.60	50.80
Maryland.........	2.13	3.49	1.25	2.33	1.42	9.78	58.76
North Carolina....	1.11	1.86	0.54	3.40	2.03	8.37	48.46
Tennessee.........	2.85	3.58	1.35	1.83	1.46	8.28	47.36
Colorado..........	2.17	2.87	1.50	2.64	1.99	11.40	69.31

APPENDIX II

Estimated Marginal Physical and Revenue Products of Labor and Capital by Industry and by State, 1957.*

Table II.1. Interindustry and Interstate Comparison of Estimated Marginal Physical Product of Production Workers per Dollar of Wage Cost in the United States.[a]

	Maine	N.H.	Vt.	Mass.	R.I.	Conn.	N.Y.	N.J.	Pa.
Food and Kindred Products	1.28		1.09	1.11			1.11	1.17	1.16
Apparel and Related Products	1.17			1.18		1.19	1.35	1.04	
Paper and Products	1.31	1.43		1.32		1.14	1.26	1.35	1.37
Chemicals and Products				1.40		1.50	1.79	1.87	1.75
Petroleum and Coal Products				1.08			1.09	0.84	0.79
Stone, Clay, and Glass Products		1.57		1.90		1.66	1.66		1.60
Fabricated Metal Products				1.32	1.13	1.12	1.19	1.27	1.22
Machinery except Electrical		1.38	1.04	1.15	1.01	1.06	1.22	1.14	1.10
Electrical Machinery		1.10		1.05		1.28	1.11	1.03	1.29
Transportation	0.84			1.02		0.91	0.75	1.18	0.91

	Ohio	Ind.	Ill.	Mich.	Wis.	Minn.	Iowa	Mo.
Food and Kindred Products	1.13	1.10	1.14	1.13	0.90	1.00	0.89	0.95
Apparel and Related Products		1.24		0.98	1.24			1.02
Paper and Products	1.33	1.32	1.31	1.25	1.46	1.91		1.60
Chemicals and Products	1.58	2.16	1.88	1.49	1.75	2.22	1.95	1.78
Petroleum and Coal Products		0.69	1.08			1.06		0.98
Stone, Clay, and Glass Products	1.57	1.55	1.79	1.84	2.00	1.55		1.61
Fabricated Metal Products	1.18	1.24	1.28	1.12	1.32	1.37	1.51	1.31
Machinery except Electrical	1.10	1.17	1.16	1.00	1.20	1.25	1.63	1.12
Electrical Machinery	1.07	0.97	1.08		1.07		1.02	0.96
Transportation Equipment	0.92	0.98	1.22	1.00	1.01		0.79	1.21

*See Chapter IV, Section (6).

[a] Computed on the basis of the production functions presented in Table 2, Chapter IV.

Table II.1 (continued).

	S. Dak.	Nebr.	Kans.	Del.	Md.	D.C.	Va.	W. Va.
Food and Kindred Products.	0.86	0.99	0.92	1.03	1.09	1.25		
Apparel and Related Products...............				2.52			0.86	
Paper and Products........							1.69	
Chemicals and Products.....			1.48	1.84	1.62		1.28	1.36
Petroleum and Coal Products			1.11					
Stone, Clay, and Glass Products...............					1.77		2.13	1.04
Fabricated Metal Products..		1.40	1.44	1.39	1.24		1.33	1.13
Machinery except Electrical.					1.28		1.25	
Electrical Machinery.......					1.24			
Transportation Equipment..			1.00		0.92		0.79	0.74

	N.C.	S.C.	Ga.	Fla.	Ky.	Tenn.	Ala.	Miss.	Ark.
Food and Kindred Products..........	1.30	1.29	1.31	1.41	1.48	1.18	1.05		
Apparel and Related Products..........	1.00	0.95	1.03				1.06	0.84	
Paper and Products..	1.30	1.74	2.05	1.79	1.28	1.74		1.53	1.64
Chemicals and Products..........	1.47		1.46	1.67	1.66	1.17	1.71	1.42	1.19
Petroleum and Coal Products..........					1.56		0.91		0.73
Stone, Clay, and Glass Products.....			1.70	2.06	1.43	1.24	1.83		
Fabricated Metal Products..........	1.46			1.58	0.95	1.14	1.36	1.69	
Machinery except Electrical........					1.44		1.08		
Electrical Machinery.	1.48		1.40	1.08	1.17		0.91	1.27	
Transportation Equipment........			1.01	0.66	1.58		0.63		

Table II.1 (continued).

	La.	Okla.	Texas	Mont.	Wyo.	Colo.	Ariz.	Utah
Food and Kindred Products.	1.23	1.18	1.38			1.21		1.02
Apparel and Related Products...............						1.51		
Paper and Products........	1.46		1.68			1.69		
Chemicals and Products.....	1.37		2.26	0.87				
Petroleum and Coal Products	1.17	1.16	0.95		0.86			1.77
Stone, Clay, and Glass Products...............	1.89	1.67				1.69		2.43
Fabricated Metal Products..	1.27	1.49	1.49				0.74	
Machinery except Electrical.		1.24	1.44			1.20		
Electrical Machinery.......		1.73	1.06					
Transportation Equipment..	0.72	0.42	0.71					

	Nev.	Wash.	Ore.	Calif.
Food and Kindred Products........................		1.02	1.11	1.26
Apparel and Related Products......................				1.41
Paper and Products...............................		1.83		1.51
Chemicals and Products...........................		1.20		1.84
Petroleum and Coal Products.......................				1.24
Stone, Clay, and Glass Products....................	2.50			
Fabricated Metal Products.........................		1.33		1.38
Machinery except Electrical.......................		1.10		1.19
Electrical Machinery..............................				1.08
Transportation Equipment.........................		1.22		1.15

Table II.2. Interindustry and Interstate Comparison of Estimated Marginal Revenue Product of Nonproduction Employees per Dollar of Salary Cost in the United States.[a]

	Maine	N.H.	Vt.	Mass.	R.I.	Conn.	N.Y.	N.J.	Pa.
Food and Kindred Products.........	0.98		0.83	0.85			0.85	0.89	0.89
Apparel and Related Products.........	0.93			0.93		0.94	1.07	0.83	
Paper and Products..	0.79	0.87		0.80		0.70	0.77	0.82	0.84
Chemicals and Products.........						0.68	0.81	0.84	0.79
Petroleum and Coal Products.........				0.75			0.76	0.59	0.55
Stone, Clay, and Glass Products.....		0.74		0.89		0.78	0.78		0.75
Fabricated Metal Products.........				0.94	0.81	0.80	0.85	0.91	0.88
Machinery except Electrical........		1.06	0.80	0.88	0.78	0.82	0.94	0.88	0.85
Electrical Machinery.		0.87		0.83		1.02	0.88	0.82	1.02
Transportation Equipment........	0.67			0.82		0.73	0.60	0.94	0.73

	Ohio	Ind.	Ill.	Mich.	Wis.	Minn.	Iowa	Mo.
Food and Kindred Products.	0.86	0.84	0.87	0.87	0.69	0.76	0.68	0.73
Apparel and Related Products...............		0.98		0.78	0.98			0.81
Paper and Products........	0.81	0.80	0.80	0.76	0.89	1.16		0.97
Chemicals and Products.....	0.72	0.98	0.85	0.68	0.79	1.00	0.88	0.80
Petroleum and Coal Products		0.48	0.75			0.74		0.68
Stone, Clay, and Glass Products...............	0.74	0.73	0.84	0.86	0.94	0.72		0.75
Fabricated Metal Products..	0.84	0.89	0.92	0.80	0.95	0.98	1.08	0.94
Machinery except Electrical.	0.85	0.90	0.89	0.77	0.93	0.96	0.90	0.86
Electrical Machinery.......	0.85	0.77	0.86		0.85		0.81	0.76
Transportation Equipment..	0.74	0.79	0.98	0.80	0.81	0	0.63	0.97

[a]Computed on the basis of the production functions presented in Table 2, Chapter IV, Section (4).

Table II.2 (continued).

	S. Dak.	Nebr.	Kans.	Del.	Md.	D.C.	Va.	W. Va.
Food and Kindred Products.	0.65	0.76	0.70	0.79	0.83	0.96		
Apparel and Related Products..............				2.00			0.68	
Paper and Products........							1.03	
Chemicals and Products.....			0.67	0.83	0.73		0.58	0.61
Petroleum and Coal Products			0.77					
Stone, Clay, and Glass Products..........					0.83		1.00	0.49
Fabricated Metal Products..		1.00	1.03	1.00	0.88		0.95	0.81
Machinery except Electrical.					0.99		0.97	
Electrical Machinery.......					0.99			
Transportation Equipment..			0.80		0.74		0.64	0.59

	N.C.	S.C.	Ga.	Fla.	Ky.	Tenn.	Ala.	Miss.
Food and Kindred Products.	1.00	0.98	1.00	1.08	1.13	0.90	0.80	
Apparel and Related Products..............	0.79	0.75	0.81				0.84	0.67
Paper and Products........	0.79	1.06	1.25	1.09	0.78	1.06		0.93
Chemicals and Products.....	0.67		0.66	0.75	0.75	0.53	0.77	0.64
Petroleum and Coal Products					1.09		0.64	
Stone, Clay, and Glass Products..............			0.79	0.96	0.67	0.58	0.86	
Fabricated Metal Products..	1.04			1.13	0.68	0.81	0.98	1.21
Machinery except Electrical.					1.11		0.83	
Electrical Machinery.......	1.17		1.11	0.86	0.93		0.72	1.01
Transportation Equipment..			0.81	0.53	1.27		0.51	

Table II.2 (continued).

	Ark.	La.	Okla.	Texas	Mont.	Wyo.	Colo.	Ariz.
Food and Kindred Products.		0.94	0.90	1.05			0.93	
Apparel and Related Products...............							1.19	
Paper and Products........	1.00	0.89		1.02			1.03	
Chemicals and Products.....	0.54	0.62		1.02	0.39			
Petroleum and Coal Products	0.51	0.81	0.81	0.66		0.60		
Stone, Clay, and Glass Products...............		0.89	0.78				0.92	
Fabricated Metal Products..		0.91	1.07	0.88				0.53
Machinery except Electrical.			0.96	1.11			0.92	
Electrical Machinery.......			1.37	0.85				
Transportation Equipment..		0.58	0.34	0.57				

	Utah	Nev.	Wash.	Ore.	Calif.
Food and Kindred Products...................	0.78		0.78	0.84	0.86
Apparel and Related Products................					1.12
Paper and Products.........................			1.11		0.92
Chemicals and Products......................			0.54		0.83
Petroleum and Coal Products.................	1.23				0.86
Stone, Clay, and Glass Products...............	1.14	1.17			
Fabricated Metal Products...................			0.95		0.99
Machinery except Electrical..................			0.85		0.92
Electrical Machinery........................					0.86
Transportation Equipment...................			0.97		0.92

Table II.3. Interindustry and Interstate Comparison of Estimated Marginal Physical Products of Employment Per Dollar of Salary and Wage Cost in the United States.[a]

	Maine	N.H.	Vt.	Mass.	R.I.	Conn.	N.Y.	N.J.
Lumber and Wood Products.								
Rubber Products..........				1.34	1.36	1.45	1.39	
Leather and Leather Goods..		1.13		1.21			1.28	
Primary Metal Industries....				1.43	1.64	1.50	1.64	1.45
Instruments and Related								
Products...............				1.22			1.18	0.95

	Pa.	Ohio	Ind.	Ill.	Mich.	Wis.	Minn.	Iowa
Lumber and Wood Products.	1.27							
Rubber Products..........		1.31	1.29	1.33	1.33	1.46	1.57	1.82
Leather and Leather Goods..	1.19	1.22		1.45	1.42	1.30		
Primary Metal Industries....	1.59	1.75	1.73	1.55	1.49	1.50	1.43	2.19
Instruments and Related								
Products...............	1.10	1.00	1.17		1.04			0.99

	Mo.	S. Dak.	Nebr.	Kans.	Del.	Md.	D.C.	Va.
Lumber and Wood Products.	1.29							1.12
Rubber Products..........						1.55		
Leather and Leather Goods..	1.50				1.30	1.24		1.02
Primary Metal Industries....	1.50				1.07	1.59		1.55
Instruments and Related								
Products...............						0.91		

	W. Va.	N.C.	S.C.	Ga.	Fla.	Ky.	Tenn.	Ala.
Lumber and Wood Products.		1.10	1.24		1.19		1.23	
Rubber Products..........		1.67					1.84	2.10
Leather and Leather Goods..				1.55			1.74	
Primary Metal Industries....	1.56					1.42	1.95	1.78
Instruments and Related								
Products...............		0.95					1.12	

[a]Computed on the basis of the production functions presented in Table 2, Chapter IV.

Table II.3 (continued).

	Miss.	Ark.	La.	Okla.	Texas	Mont.	Wyo.	Colo.
Lumber and Wood Products.			1.28	1.04	1.15	1.30		
Rubber Products...........								
Leather and Leather Goods..		1.57						
Primary Metal Industries....			2.96	1.41	1.95			
Instruments and Related Products...............								1.23

	Ariz.	Utah	Nev.	Wash.	Ore.	Calif.
Lumber and Wood Products............				1.06	1.15	1.19
Rubber Products......................						1.48
Leather and Leather Goods.............						
Primary Metal Industries...............	1.28		5.33	2.42		1.70
Instrument and Related Products........						

Table II.4. Interindustry and Interstate Comparison of Estimated Marginal Revenue Products of Employment per Dollar of Salary and Wage Cost in the United States, 1957.[a]

(In 1957 dollars)

	Maine	N.H.	Vt.	Mass.	R.I.	Conn.	N.Y.	N.J.
Lumber and Wood Products.								
Rubber Products...........				0.85	0.87	0.92	0.89	
Leather and Leather Goods..		0.82		0.87			0.92	
Primary Metal Industries....				0.70	0.80	0.73	0.80	0.71
Instruments and Related Products...............				0.98			0.95	0.77

	Pa.	Ohio	Ind.	Ill.	Mich.	Wis.	Minn.	Iowa
Lumber and Wood Products.	0.86							
Rubber Products...........		0.84	0.82	0.85	0.85	0.93	1.00	1.16
Leather and Leather Goods..	0.96	0.88		1.05	1.03	0.94		
Primary Metal Industries....	0.78	0.85	0.84	0.76	0.72	0.73	0.70	1.06
Instruments and Related Products...............	0.88	0.80	0.94		0.83			0.80

[a]Computed on the basis of the production functions presented in Table 2, Chapter IV.

Table II.4 (continued).

	Mo.	S. Dak.	Nebr.	Kans.	Del.	Md.	D.C.	Va.
Lumber and Wood Products.	0.88							0.76
Rubber Products..........						0.99		
Leather and Leather Goods..	1.09				0.94	0.90		0.74
Primary Metal Products.....	0.73				0.52	0.77		0.75
Instruments and Related Products...............						0.73		

	W. Va.	N.C.	S.C.	Ga.	Fla.	Ky.	Tenn.	Ala.
Lumber and Wood Products.		0.75	0.84		0.81		0.83	
Rubber Products..........		1.07					1.18	1.34
Leather and Leather Goods..				1.12			1.26	
Primary Metal Industries....	0.76					0.69	0.95	0.87
Instruments and Related Products...............		0.76					0.90	

	Miss.	Ark.	La.	Okla.	Texas	Mont.	Wyo.	Colo.
Lumber and Wood Products.			0.87	0.71	0.78	0.88		
Rubber Products..........								
Leather and Leather Goods..		1.13						
Primary Metal Industries....			1.44	0.69	0.95			
Instruments and Related Products...............								0.98

	Ariz.	Utah	Nev.	Wash.	Ore.	Calif.
Lumber and Wood Products............				0.72	0.78	0.80
Rubber Products.....................						0.95
Leather and Leather Goods.............						
Primary Metal Industries...............	0.62		2.59	1.18		0.83
Instruments and Related Products.......						

Table II.5. Interindustry and Interstate Comparison of Estimated Marginal Physical Product (Net of Depreciation and Property Taxes) of Capital Per Dollar Invested in the United States, 1957.[a]

(In 1957 dollars)

	Maine	N.H.	Vt.	Mass.	R.I.	Conn.	N.Y.	N.J.
Food and Kindred Products.	1.36		1.12	1.23			1.81	1.54
Apparel and Related Products.	0.69			0.73		1.25	0.62	0.78
Lumber and Wood Products.								
Paper and Products.	0.24	0.57		0.64		0.57	0.55	0.48
Chemicals and Products.				0.55		0.73	0.78	1.02
Petroleum and Coal Products				0.25			0.39	0.19
Rubber Products.				0.90	1.28	0.69	0.45	
Leather and Leather Goods.		0.74		0.83			0.73	
Stone, Clay, and Glass Products.		0.46		0.29		0.28	0.28	
Primary Metal Industries.				0.62	0.65	0.51	0.65	0.52
Fabricated Metal Products.				0.55	0.43	0.44	0.42	0.43
Machinery except Electrical.		2.12	1.55	1.49	1.10	1.48	1.21	1.24
Electrical Machinery.		1.62		2.18		2.39	2.00	1.64
Transportation Equipment.	1.45			2.37		3.50	1.64	2.29
Instruments and Related Products.				2.39			1.71	1.55

	Pa.	Ohio	Ind.	Ill.	Mich.	Wis.	Minn.	Iowa
Food and Kindred Products.	1.53	1.43	1.35	1.77	1.39	0.94	1.22	1.11
Apparel and Related Products.			0.86		0.42	1.19		
Lumber and Wood Products.	0.54							
Paper and Products.	0.52	0.61	0.53	0.56	0.48	0.49	0.54	
Chemicals and Products.	0.83	0.58	0.81	0.59	0.65	0.90	0.67	0.83
Petroleum and Coal Products	0.20		0.19	0.39			0.34	
Rubber Products.		0.96	0.88	0.45	0.68	1.28	0.57	0.60
Leather and Leather Goods.	0.59	0.45		2.63	0.26	0.50		
Stone, Clay, and Glass Products.	0.28	0.31	0.28	0.41	0.29	0.33	0.13	
Primary Metal Industries.	0.47	0.43	0.42	0.48	0.32	0.63	0.69	0.16
Fabricated Metal Products.	0.58	0.40	0.46	0.41	0.33	0.37	0.38	0.45
Machinery except Electrical.	2.49	1.65	1.38	1.35	1.22	1.63	1.85	1.77
Electrical Machinery.	1.94	2.13	1.70	1.70		1.91		2.66
Transportation Equipment	1.88	1.25	1.11	1.33	1.24	1.88		1.55
Instruments and Related Products.	2.05	1.61	1.97		2.6			2.39

[a]Computed on the basis of the production functions presented in Table 2, Chapter IV.

Table II.5 (continued).

	Mo.	S. Dak.	Nebr.	Kans.	Del.	Md.	D.C.	Va.
Food and Kindred Products.	1.24	1.41	1.43	1.13	0.88	1.58	2.63	
Apparel and Related Products.	0.93				1.20			1.43
Lumber and Wood Products.	1.13							0.95
Paper and Products.	0.71							0.50
Chemicals and Products.	0.64			0.49	1.25	0.61		0.97
Petroleum and Coal Products	0.21			0.32				
Rubber Products.						1.41		
Leather and Leather Goods.	0.95				0.53	0.47		0.61
Stone, Clay, and Glass Products.	0.28					0.13		0.21
Primary Metal Products.	0.44				0.48	0.25		0.25
Fabricated Metal Products.	0.42		0.29	0.83	0.59	0.29		0.54
Machinery except Electrical.	1.49					1.13		0.92
Electrical Machinery.	1.23					2.36		
Transportation Equipment	2.67			1.18		4.30		2.71
Instruments and Related Products.						1.21		

	W. Va.	N.C.	S.C.	Ga.	Fla.	Ky.	Tenn.	Ala.
Food and Kindred Products.		0.95	1.03	1.33	1.03	1.70	1.28	1.20
Apparel and Related Products.		0.85	0.90	1.07				0.97
Lumber and Wood Products.		0.92	0.40		0.74		0.78	
Paper and Products.		0.36	0.64	0.36	0.24	0.54	0.50	
Chemicals and Products.	0.69	0.59		0.71	0.31	0.71	0.71	0.24
Petroleum and Coal Products						0.53		0.30
Rubber Products.		0.85					1.11	0.91
Leather and Leather Goods.				0.63			0.98	
Stone, Clay, and Glass Products.	0.65			0.61	0.19	0.26	0.22	0.33
Primary Metal Industries.	0.44					0.18	0.70	0.68
Fabricated Metal Products.	0.70	0.40			0.25	0.42	0.43	0.61
Machinery except Electrical.						0.68		1.06
Electrical Machinery.		1.01		0.88	2.55	1.73		1.44
Transportation Equipment.	1.26			4.14	1.33	2.31		5.16
Instruments and Related Products.		2.26					1.72	

Table II.5 (continued).

	Miss.	Ark.	La.	Okla.	Texas	Mont.	Wyo.	Colo.
Food and Kindred Products.			1.32	1.18	1.38			1.13
Apparel and Related Products................	1.13							1.07
Lumber and Wood Products.			0.62	0.26	0.43	0.40		
Paper and Products........	0.63	0.43	0.48		0.26			0.41
Chemicals and Products.....	0.40	0.30	0.34		0.42	0.23		
Petroleum and Coal Products		0.26	0.29	0.51	0.35		0.20	
Rubber Products...........								
Leather and Leather Goods..		0.97						
Stone, Clay, and Glass Products................			0.17	0.29				0.17
Primary Metal Industries....			0.21	0.90	0.23			
Fabricated Metal Products..	0.35		0.49	0.77	0.31			
Machinery except Electrical.				1.45	1.54			1.43
Electrical Machinery........	1.26			1.70	1.77			
Transportation Equipment..			2.43	6.72	4.53			
Instruments and Related Products................								1.40

	Ariz.	Utah	Nev.	Wash.	Ore.	Calif.
Food and Kindred Products............		1.03		1.21	1.44	1.24
Apparel and Related Products..........						0.78
Lumber and Wood Products............				0.51	0.42	0.54
Paper and Products...................				0.34		0.34
Chemicals and Products...............				1.09		0.52
Petroleum and Coal Products...........		0.30				0.26
Rubber Products.....................						0.68
Leather and Leather Goods.............						
Stone, Clay, and Glass Products.........		0.25	0.15			
Primary Metal Industries...............	0.36		1.35	0.50		0.30
Fabricated Metal Products.............	0.50			0.58		0.36
Machinery except Electrical............				1.28		1.26
Electrical Machinery..................						2.11
Transportation Equipment.............				4.08		4.08
Instruments and Related Products........						

Table II.6. Interindustry and Interstate Comparison of Estimated Marginal Revenue Product (Net of Depreciation and Property Taxes) of Capital per Dollar Invested in the United States, 1957.[a]

(In 1957 dollars)

	Maine	N.H.	Vt.	Mass.	R.I.	Conn.	N.Y.	N.J.
Food and Kindred Products.	1.04		0.85	0.94			1.38	1.18
Apparel and Related Products.	0.54			0.58		0.99	0.49	0.62
Lumber and Wood Products.								
Paper and Products.	0.15	0.35		0.39		0.35	0.34	0.29
Chemicals and Products.				0.25		0.33	0.35	0.46
Petroleum and Coal Products				0.18			0.27	0.13
Rubber Products.				0.58	0.82	0.44	0.29	
Leather and Leather Goods.		0.53		0.60			0.53	
Stone, Clay, and Glass Products.		0.21		0.14		0.13	0.13	
Primary Metal Industries.				0.30	0.32	0.25	0.32	0.25
Fabricated Metal Products.				0.39	0.31	0.32	0.30	0.31
Machinery except Electrical.		1.63	1.20	1.15	0.85	1.14	0.93	0.96
Electrical Machinery.		1.28		1.73		1.90	1.58	1.31
Transportation Equipment.	1.17			1.90		2.80	1.31	1.84
Instruments and Related Products.				1.91			1.37	1.24

	Pa.	Ohio	Ind.	Ill.	Mich.	Wis.	Minn.	Iowa
Food and Kindred Products.	1.17	1.09	1.03	1.35	1.06	0.72	0.93	0.85
Apparel and Related Products.			0.68		0.33	0.94		
Lumber and Wood Products.	0.37							
Paper and Products.	0.32	0.37	0.32	0.34	0.29	0.30	0.33	
Chemicals and Products.	0.38	0.26	0.37	0.27	0.30	0.41	0.30	0.38
Petroleum and Coal Products	0.14		0.13	0.27			0.23	
Rubber Products.		0.61	0.56	0.28	0.43	0.81	0.37	0.38
Leather and Leather Goods.	0.42	0.33		1.90	0.19	0.36		
Stone, Clay, and Glass Products.	0.13	0.15	0.13	0.19	0.13	0.16	0.63	
Primary Metal Industries.	0.23	0.21	0.21	0.23	0.16	0.31	0.34	0.08
Fabricated Metal Products.	0.41	0.28	0.33	0.29	0.24	0.26	0.27	0.32
Machinery except Electrical.	1.92	1.27	1.06	1.04	0.94	1.26	1.43	1.36
Electrical Machinery.	1.54	1.69	1.35	1.35		1.52		2.11
Transportation Equipment.	1.50	1.00	0.89	1.07	1.00	1.51		1.24
Instruments and Related Products.	1.65	1.29	1.58		1.65			1.92

[a]Computed on the basis of the production functions presented in Table 2, Chapter IV, Section (4).

Table II.6 (continued).

	Mo.	S. Dak.	Nebr.	Kans.	Del.	Md.	D.C.	Va.
Food and Kindred Products.	0.95	1.08	1.09	0.86	0.67	1.21	2.01	
Apparel and Related Products.	0.74				0.95			1.14
Lumber and Wood Products.	0.76							0.65
Paper and Products.	0.43							0.30
Chemicals and Products.	0.29			0.22	0.57	0.28		0.44
Petroleum and Coal Products	0.15			0.22				
Rubber Products.						0.90		
Leather and Leather Goods.	0.68				0.38	0.34		0.44
Stone, Clay, and Glass Products.	0.13					0.59		0.98
Primary Metal Products.	0.22				0.23	0.12		0.12
Fabricated Metal Products.	0.30		0.21	0.60	0.42	0.21		0.38
Machinery except Electrical.	1.15					0.87		0.71
Electrical Machinery.	0.98					1.88		
Transportation Equipment.	2.14			9.45		3.45		2.17
Instruments and Related Products.						0.97		

	W. Va.	N.C.	S.C.	Ga.	Fla.	Ky.	Tenn.	Ala.
Food and Kindred Products.		0.72	0.79	1.02	0.79	1.30	0.98	0.92
Apparel and Related Products.		0.67	0.71	0.85				0.76
Lumber and Wood Products.		0.63	0.27		0.51		0.53	
Paper and Products.		0.22	0.39	0.22	0.15	0.33	0.30	
Chemicals and Products.	0.31	0.26		0.32	0.14	0.32	0.32	0.11
Petroleum and Coal Products						0.37		0.21
Rubber Products.		0.54					0.71	0.58
Leather and Leather Goods.				1.90			0.71	
Stone, Clay, and Glass Products.	0.30			0.28	0.87	0.12	0.10	0.15
Primary Metal Industries.	0.21					0.09	0.34	0.33
Fabricated Metal Products.	0.50	0.29			0.18	0.29	0.31	0.43
Machinery except Electrical.						0.52		0.82
Electrical Machinery.		0.80		0.70	2.03	1.37		1.14
Transportation Equipment.	1.01			3.32	1.07	1.86		4.14
Instruments and Related Products.		1.81					1.38	

Table II.6 (continued).

	Miss.	Ark.	La.	Okla.	Texas	Mont.	Wyo.	Colo.
Food and Kindred Products.			1.01	0.90	1.06			0.86
Apparel and Related Products	0.89							0.85
Lumber and Wood Products.			0.42	0.18	0.29	0.27		
Paper and Products	0.38	0.26	0.30		0.16			0.25
Chemicals and Products	0.18	0.14	0.15		0.19	0.10		
Petroleum and Coal Products		0.18	0.20	0.36	0.24		0.14	
Rubber Products								
Leather and Leather Goods		0.70						
Stone, Clay, and Glass Products			0.79	0.13				0.81
Primary Metal Industries			0.10	0.44	0.11			
Fabricated Metal Products	0.25		0.35	0.55	0.22			
Machinery except Electrical.				1.12	1.19			1.10
Electrical Machinery	1.00			1.35	1.40			
Transportation Equipment			1.95	5.39	3.63			
Instruments and Related Products								1.12

	Ariz.	Utah	Nev.	Wash.	Ore.	Calif.
Food and Kindred Products		0.79		0.93	1.10	0.95
Apparel and Related Products						0.62
Lumber and Wood Products				0.35	0.28	0.37
Paper and Products				0.21		0.21
Chemicals and Products				0.49		0.24
Petroleum and Coal Products		0.21				0.18
Rubber Products						0.43
Leather and Leather Goods						
Stone, Clay, and Glass Products		0.12	0.70			
Primary Metal Industries	0.18		0.66	0.24		0.15
Fabricated Metal Products	0.36			0.41		0.26
Machinery except Electrical				0.99		0.97
Electrical Machinery						1.67
Transportation Equipment				3.27		3.28
Instruments and Related Products						

APPENDIX III

Results of a Sample Study of Manufacturing Production Functions in New York State

The review of literature presented in Chapter II led the authors to conclude that estimates of production functions can best be obtained from data for individual establishments. While the Bureau of the Census has such tabulations at its disposal, they were unavailable to us. Moreover, they lack certain data of critical importance. As explained in Chapter II, Section (2), the level of technology in operation in the different manufacturing establishments can be indicated in relative terms by (1) the ratio of the value of machinery and tools to the value of structures and buildings (suggesting the degree of elaborateness of the technical processes in use); (2) the ratio of net book value of capital assets to gross book value (indicating the "average age" of the assets and hence the "'vintage' of technology"); and (3) the ratio of technical and professional workers to all employees (again indicating the degree of complexity of the technology in use). The census returns required information on annual capital expenditure for new equipment and for new plant separately, but not on the total amounts of equipment and of plant in existence separately. Except for the data on the total book value of equipment and plant as a whole for the single year 1957, the Census Bureau has not been collecting data on the book value of plant and equipment for four decades. The census returns also did not require data on technical and professional workers.

The authors therefore decided to collect sample observations from manufacturing establishments in New York State. We had reason to be optimistic about the success of the projected sample survey. A great deal of the information needed is similar to that required by the federal *Census of Manufactures*. All manufacturing establishments[1] in New York State have filed the 1954 and 1958 census returns; and many of them are also in the sample of establishments which have been reporting to the Census Bureau on an annual basis in the non-census

---

[1]Except those created after the respective censuses or closed down before they were taken.

years. Although we requested some additional data beyond that required in the census questionnaires, the total number of our questions was substantially smaller. Essentially, we sought figures for the following items for 1956–1960: value of shipment, inventories, materials, and energy consumed; maintenance expenditure; certain categories of employment and payroll; book value and depreciation of plant and of equipment separately; and costs of longterm borrowing. The non-census items required are the separate data for book value and depreciation of plant and equipment, the number of technical and professional employees, and interest rates and other costs on long term debt.

In spite of these favorable considerations, the response we received was much worse than we had anticipated. The sample has yielded some evidence on the correctness of our assumption that the ratio of equipment to plant is a good proxy variable for the level of technology in operation in a given establishment. However, the evidence was not conclusive, the main reason being, we believe, the small number of completed returns received. Except for the limited light it has thrown on this aspect of the problem, this attempt to collect sample observations must be considered a failure.[2] Through telephone conversations and correspondence, three main reasons were found to be responsible for the poor response. First, the required data involved some confidential information not required in census and other reports to government. Business firms were generally unwilling or reluctant to reveal these data to private investigators because there is no legal protection against disclosure, even though they had no question about our good faith in keeping the information confidential. Second, the large and growing number of private and public surveys in which these firms were asked to cooperate have now become a burden which they are increasingly unwilling to shoulder. Finally, in spite of the effort we made to explain the purpose and nature of the study in terms readily understandable to laymen, the technical nature of the project was such that many did not really grasp its meaning and practical usefulness.

Because of the poor sample response, we report our findings concerning it only briefly.

The *Industrial Directory of New York State, 1958,* published by the Department of Commerce of New York State, lists all the manufacturing establishments in the state, classified according to the federal

---

[2] The cost of the sample survey was borne by Cornell University. The NSF grant was not used to finance this part of the work.

Standard Industrial Classification Manual and by size classes of employees. It was the most recent one available, and was used as the statistical frame for our survey.

In carrying out the sample study, we sought reliable measurements of the regression relationships among output, labor, capital, and certain other variables. On the assumption that the "state of nature" is rather unfavorable to this kind of undertaking, we first estimated the size of the sample that would yield estimates of regression coefficients whose respective standard errors are no larger than one-third of the absolute values of the coefficients themselves. The unfavorable state of nature was reflected by the high intercorrelations among the explanatory variables. On the basis of certain plausible assumptions about these intercorrelations, the sample size that would yield estimates of regression coefficients with at least the required precision was estimated at 50 for each regression. Preliminary computations on the basis of certain assumed distributions of establishments by size[3] for a number of industries indicated that the precision in the estimated regression relationships achieved by apportioning the sample observations approximately evenly throughout the size range is close to that attainable by more elaborate methods.[4] For most industries, this results in the inclusion in the sample of roughly equal numbers of establishments from the following three size groups: those employing 100 or more workers, those employing 50 to 99 workers, and those employing 49 or fewer workers.

We had no knowledge of the rate of nonresponse for a survey of this kind, and the rate was expected to vary by industry, location, and size class. For estimating aggregates or averages, procedures exist to determine the optimum number of questionnaires to be sent out and the optimum number of field interviews to be made to visit a sample of nonrespondents sufficient to give the necessary precision at minimum cost. This optimum number can be estimated even when the nonresponse rates are unknown.[5] However, a comparison of the cost of survey by questionnaire with that by interview, and an analysis of the distribution of establishments by size, led very readily to a decision regarding the number of questionnaires to be sent out.

[3]Distribution by size is known only for the number of workers employed. It is unknown for value added, capital, and other variables.

[4]For a more efficient and elaborate method, see Kiefer and Wolfowitz [42] and Kiefer [41].

[5]See M. H. Hansen, W. N. Hurwitz, and W. G. Madow [32] and M. H. Hansen and W. N. Hurwitz [31].

A study of the *1958 Census of Manufactures* for New York State indicates that it is desirable and feasible to make estimates for some 58 industries at the three-digit level. The 58 three-digit industries are not only the more important ones in terms of value of production, but are those in which the number of establishments in each substantially exceeds the critical minimum of 50 required for attaining the desired precision in the estimated production functions. The minimum number of returns required is therefore 2,900. There were about 2,700 establishments in 1958 employing more than 100 employees each within the State of New York. The cost saving of a mail questionnaire over a field canvass is so great that it is obvious that the questionnaires should be sent out to all 2,700 large establishments. In addition, there were about 3,400 units employing between 50 and 99 people in 1958. Mail questionnaires should obviously be sent to all of these also. In addition, the plan was to mail questionnaires to a random selection of 3,000 establishments in the 1 to 50 employee range. The total number of questionnaires planned to be mailed out came to 9,100. We anticipated that if, out of a total of 9,100 establishments, the rate of nonresponse were as large as about two-thirds then, under ideal circumstances in which the nonresponse spreads out evenly across the industries, no field interviews would be required. Conceding that the result would fall short of this ideal, the expense of a supplemental field canvass did not appear to be formidable. It turned out that our judgment on the rate of nonresponse was wrong.

In using the *Industrial Directory of New York State, 1958* as the statistical frame, a number of technical difficulties were encountered in deciding upon the industrial classes to which certain establishments should fall and in determining branch products and addresses. The preparation of the questionnaires for mailing took a much longer time than planned. A total of 8,775 questionnaires, a somewhat smaller number than the 9,100 planned, were mailed in September 1962. The 1958 directory was used because a more recent one was not available. Roughly 15 per cent of the questionnaires mailed out were returned by the post office because the addresses could not be located. Other firms returned the questionnaire explaining that they were no longer in business or that they had moved out of New York State. The number of outright refusals to participate also was high. A very large number simply neglected the inquiry. The number of completed returns received up to the end of November 1962 amounted to the shockingly low rate of 1.5 per cent of those sent out.

This unexpectedly low rate of response became known when our work on the census data, as reported in the text of this book, was yielding satisfactory and interesting results. It was decided that a personal approach to the senior officials in charge of accounts in the various establishments would improve the response rate. A long-distance call from an experienced interviewer in the university would, it was thought, stand a better chance of reaching senior officials concerned than a visit by a student interviewer. A sample of the nonrespondents was so approached by telephone. The conversations clarified and confirmed the reasons given earlier for the poor response, but no completed returns were received even from those who agreed on the telephone to do their best and to whom we sent a follow-up letter after the telephone call.

Following the disappointing results of the telephone sample, an effort was made to select a random sample from the nonrespondents and to find out the names of the officials in charge of finance or accounts. Flexowriter was used to address the questionnaire personally to them. About 1,400 questionnaires then were sent out, including those addressed to small establishments with a revised letter specifically designed for these firms. The result was again extremely poor. Only 50 completed returns were received. It became clear that obstacles to sample studies of this type, involving a request for business information not usually disclosed to outsiders, could not be overcome except by making efforts far beyond our resources and power.

With less than two hundred returns at our disposal and with many of them lacking information for all years of 1956–1960, there was obviously no possibility of getting really satisfactory estimates. In the meantime, the promising results of our study of the census data encouraged us to concentrate on that part of our project. The sample returns were then used mainly to throw light on an important point which cannot be dealt with in the analysis of the census data. This has to do with representing the level of technology by the ratio of the value of equipment to the value of plant.[6]

The equations fitted to the sample data are as follows:

Version 1:

$$\log V = a + b \log L + e \log R' \log K_g;$$

[6]See Chapter II, Section (2). Since in none of the returns was the question on the number of technical and professional employees answered satisfactorily, our sample does not enable us to construct the third proxy variable, discussed in Chapter II, for the level of technology in operation in a given establishment: the ratio of techni-

Version 2:

$$\log V = a + b \log L_p + c \log L_n + e \log R' \log K_g.$$

The variables included are as follows:

V: Value added in a given establishment in thousands of 1957 dollars.[7]

L: Employment (both production workers and nonproduction employees) in a given establishment in thousands of man-hours.[8]

L_p: Employment of production workers in a given establishment in thousands of man-hours.

L_n: Employment of nonproduction employees in a given establishment in thousands of man-hours.[9]

R': Ratio of the gross value of equipment to the gross value of plant in 1957 dollars[10] in per cent at the beginning of the year in a given establishment.

K_g: The gross value of plant and equipment in thousands of 1957 dollars at the beginning of the year in a given establishment.[11]

Two sets of regressions have been computed. The first includes data for all the five years of 1956–1960. As 1958 is a recession year and data on a number of items for 1960 are unsatisfactory, another set of regressions has been run with the data for these two years omitted.[12] Because of the small number of completed returns received, functions have been computed for only 16 two-digit industries. The results of the single equation least-squares regressions are given in the table below.

The estimated functions appear to be reasonably satisfactory for nine industries: food products; textiles (Version 2 only); paper products; rubber products (Version 1 only); stone, clay, and glass products;

---

cal and professional employees to production (manual) workers. In most of the returns received, production workers are given separately from all other employees, but it was apparently difficult for the establishment to separate technical and professional staff from other nonproduction employees.

[7] Data for years other than 1957 are deflated by indexes constructed to approximate the changes in the prices of inputs and outputs of the different industries.

[8] A nonproduction employee is assumed to work 2,000 man-hours a year.

[9] See n. 8.

[10] Data for the other years are deflated by indexes constructed from the price deflators given in the National Income Number (July issue) of the *Survey of Current Business* for adjusting the current values of privately owned structures and equipment in manufacturing establishments to a constant cost basis.

[11] See n. 10.

[12] In some of the returns, complete information has not been given for all the five years. The number of observations (given in the table) for these two sets of regressions are therefore not in the ratio of five to three.

machinery except electrical (Version 1 only); transportation equipment; instruments; and miscellaneous manufactured products. In addition, the regression coefficient of the variable in which we are especially interested in this sample study (i.e., log R' log K_g) takes on reasonable magnitudes also in Version 1 of the estimated functions for the textile industry and of the furniture and fixtures industry and, in Version 2, of the rubber products industry, even though the other coefficients in these functions are unsatisfactory. This limited evidence tends to indicate that the variable log R' log K_g would have been a satisfactory proxy variable for the level of technology if a larger number of observations had been available.

Production Functions for 16 Manufacturing Industries in New York State

Food and Kindred Products
Version 1

Years	*No. of observations*			R^2
56–60	133	$\log V = 0.398 \log L + 0.304 \log R' \log K_g$		
		(0.044)	(0.030)	0.787
56, 57, 59	76	0.380	0.307	
		(0.057)	(0.040)	0.792

Version 2

56–60	133	$\log V = 0.596 \log L_p + 0.365 \log L_n + 0.068 \log R' \log K_g$				
		(0.083)	(0.037)	(0.042)		0.847
56, 57, 59	76	0.490	0.363	0.104		
		(0.117)	(0.051)	(0.061)		0.832

Textile Mill Products
Version 1

56–60	29	$\log V = -0.081 \log L + 0.341 \log R' \log K_g$		
		(0.193)	(0.077)	0.655
56, 57, 59	15	0.079	0.263	
		(0.220)	(0.085)	0.753

Version 2

56–60	29	$\log V = 0.659 \log L_p + 0.037 \log L_n + 0.214 \log R' \log K_g$			
		(0.213)	(0.170)	(0.079)	0.750
56, 57, 59	15	0.734	0.240	0.086	
		(0.221)	(0.168)	(0.080)	0.877

APPENDIX III

Lumber and Wood Products
Version 1

$Years$	$No.\ of$ $observations$		R^2
56–60	20	$\log V = 1.500 \log L - 0.251 \log R'\log K_g$	
		(0.123) (0.073)	0.965
56, 57, 59	12	1.388 -0.201	
		(0.165) (0.098)	0.964

Version 2

56–60	20	$\log V = 1.149 \log L_p + 0.092 \log L_n - 0.428 \log R'\log K_g$		
		(0.276) (0.350) (0.068)		0.983
56, 57, 59	12	1.374 -0.273 -0.426		
		(0.460) (0.570) (0.104)		0.983

Furniture and Fixtures
Version 1

56–60	28	$\log V = 0.095 \log L + 0.556 \log R'\log K_g$	
		(0.245) (0.132)	0.949
56, 57, 59	16	0.209 0.511	
		(0.332) (0.167)	0.960

Version 2

56–60	28	$\log V = 0.896 \log L_p + 0.429 \log L_n - 0.079 \log R'\log K_g$		
		(0.214) (0.206) (0.183)		
56, 57, 59	16	0.921 0.487 -0.117		
		(0.327) (0.285) (0.261)		0.976

Pulp, Paper and Products
Version 1

56–60	63	$\log V = 0.325 \log L + 0.191 \log R'\log K_g$	
		(0.141) (0.055)	0.750
56, 57, 59	38	0.334 0.194	
		(0.158) (0.062)	0.786

Version 2

56–60	63	$\log V = 0.960 \log L_p + 0.418 \log L_n + 0.128 \log R'\log K_g$		
		(0.046) (0.234) (0.081)		0.770
56, 57, 59	38	0.930 0.431 0.130		
		(0.053) (0.026) (0.090)		0.808

Chemicals and Products

Version 1

Years	No. of observations		R^2
56–60	50	$\log V = 1.298 \log L - 0.092 \log R' \log K_g$	
		(0.169) (0.085)	0.760
56, 57, 59	29	1.316 − 0.112	
		(0.222) (0.150)	0.779

Version 2

56–60	50	$\log V = 1.120 \log L_p + 0.573 \log L_n - 0.241 \log R' \log K_g$	
		(0.170) (0.157) (0.063)	0.884
56, 57, 59	29	1.220 0.632 − 0.295	
		(0.200) (0.182) (0.080)	0.911

Rubber Products

Version 1

56–60	23	$\log V = 0.546 \log L + 0.155 \log R' \log K_g$	
		(0.084) (0.035)	0.951
56, 57, 59	13	0.618 0.129	
		(0.084) (0.036)	0.969

Version 2

56–60	23	$\log V = 0.032 \log L_p + 0.528 \log L_n + 0.151 \log R' \log K_g$	
		(0.118) (0.106) (0.040)	0.951
56, 57, 59	13	− 0.087 0.669 0.144	
		(0.111) (0.107) (0.042)	0.971

Leather and Leather Goods

Version 1

56–60	22	$\log V = 1.308 \log L - 0.044 \log R' \log K_g$	
		(0.204) (0.067)	0.713
56, 57, 59	13	1.020 − 0.075	
		(0.236) (0.064)	0.690

Version 2

56–60	22	$\log V = 0.850 \log L_p - 0.155 \log L_n + 0.021 \log R' \log K_g$	
		(0.217) (0.405) (0.054)	0.844
56, 57, 59	13	0.756 0.035 − 0.042	
		(0.159) (0.261) (0.037)	0.910

210

APPENDIX III

Stone, Clay, and Glass Products
Version 1

Years	No. of observations		R^2
56–60	48	$\log V = 0.653 \log L + 0.227 \log R' \log K_g$ (0.108) (0.027)	0.833
56, 57, 59	28	0.558 0.224 (0.130) (0.032)	

Version 2

			R^2
56–60	48	$\log V = 0.605 \log L_p + 0.126 \log L_n + 0.165 \log R' \log K_g$ (0.072) (0.092) (0.019)	0.935
56, 57, 59	28	0.501 0.138 0.185 (0.109) (0.133) (0.026)	0.921

Primary Metal Industries
Version 1

56–60	25	$\log V = 1.451 \log L - 0.043 \log R' \log K_g$ (0.108) (0.041)	0.954
56, 57, 59	15	1.363 − 0.013 (0.076) (0.028)	0.986

Version 2

56–60	25	$\log V = 0.071 \log L_p + 1.397 \log L_n - 0.054 \log R' \log K'_g$ (0.121) (0.143) (0.046)	0.954
56, 57, 59	15	0.099 1.277 − 0.026 (0.081) (0.103) (0.030)	0.988

Fabricated Metal Products
Version 1

50–60	69	$\log V = 0.679 \log L + 0.020 \log R' \log K_g$ (0.076) (0.054)	0.667
56, 57, 59	39	0.722 − 0.032 (0.098) (0.067)	0.682

Version 2

56–60	69	$\log V = 0.942 \log L_p + 0.392 \log L_n - 0.154 \log R' \log K'_g$ (0.093) (0.055) (0.038)	0.871
56. 57. 59	39	0.815 0.439 − 0.159 (0.158) (0.092) (0.057)	0.824

Machinery, except Electrical

Version 1

Years	No. of observations		R^2
56–60	80	$\log V = 0.745 \log L + 0.151 \log R' \log K_g$	
		(0.045) (0.025)	0.964
56, 57, 59	46	0.726 0.160	
		(0.051) (0.028)	0.973

Version 2

56–60	80	$\log V = 0.532 \log L_p + 0.555 \log L_n - 0.007 \log R' \log K_g$	
		(0.080) (0.046) (0.031)	0.977
56, 57, 59	46	0.443 0.566 0.030	
		(0.100) (0.054) (0.037)	0.982

Electrical Machinery

Version 1

56–60	42	$\log V = 0.954 \log L - 0.010 \log R' \log K_g$	
		(0.125) (0.073)	0.918
56, 57, 59	24	0.855 0.054	
		(0.164) (0.096)	0.931

Version 2

56–60	42	$\log V = 0.454 \log L_p + 0.769 \log L_n - 0.148 \log R' \log K_g$	
		(0.054) (0.078) (0.047)	0.971
56, 57, 59	24	0.462 0.754 -0.134	
		(0.060) (0.085) (0.055)	0.982

Transportation Equipment

Version 1

56–60	54	$\log V = 0.755 \log L + 0.168 \log R' \log K_g$	
		(0.051) (0.030)	0.925
56, 57, 59	32	0.716 0.180	
		(0.048) (0.029)	0.955

Version 2

56–60	54	$\log V = 0.722 \log L_p + 0.228 \log L_n + 0.070 \log R' \log K_g$	
		(0.095) (0.078) (0.025)	0.965
56, 57, 59	32	0.593 0.292 0.100	
		(0.083) (0.066) (0.021)	0.984

APPENDIX III

Instruments and Related Products
Version 1

Years	No. of observations		R^2
56–60	53	$\log V = 0.448 \log L + 0.144 \log R' \log K_g$ (0.079)　　　　(0.044)	0.640
56, 57, 59	29	0.596　　　　0.118 (0.112)　　　　(0.060)	0.707

Version 2

56–60	53	$\log V = 0.093 \log L_p + 0.392 \log L_n + 0.123 \log R' \log K_g$ (0.148)　　　(0.119)　　　(0.056)	0.643
56, 57, 59	29	0.089　　　0.546　　　0.096 (0.191)　　　(0.155)　　　(0.077)	0.710

Miscellaneous Manufactures
Version 1

56–60	51	$\log V = 0.448 \log L + 0.248 \log R' \log K_g$ (0.073)　　　　(0.042)	0.866
56, 57, 59	29	0.517　　　　0.233 (0.091)　　　　(0.051)	0.899

Version 2

56–60	51	$\log V = 0.313 \log L_p + 0.425 \log L_n + 0.127 \log R' \log K_g$ (0.078)　　　(0.064)　　　(0.047)	0.899
56, 57, 59	29	0.384　　　0.455　　　0.095 (0.110)　　　(0.078)　　　(0.058)	0.932

APPENDIX IV

Rejected Estimates for the Textile and the Furniture and Fixture Industries

As has been explained we have not been able to obtain plausible estimates for the textile mill products and the furniture and fixtures industries.[1] All four versions of the estimated functions[2] have been analyzed and rejected on the ground that plausible and reasonably reliable estimates of the productivities of labor and capital cannot be obtained from them. These results are given below so that research workers in this field need not repeat this effort.

Textile Mills Products

Version 1

$(I,A,1) \log V = 0.238 \log q \log L_p + 0.572 L_N + 0.149 \log R \log K_g$
$\qquad\qquad (0.123) \qquad\qquad\quad (0.112) \qquad (0.031) \qquad\qquad R^2 = 0.979$

$(I,A,2) \qquad\qquad 0.198 \qquad\qquad\quad +0.573 \quad +0.161$
$\qquad\qquad\quad (0.174) \qquad\qquad\qquad\qquad\qquad\qquad\qquad\qquad 0.962$

$(I,B,1) \qquad\qquad 0.276 \log q \log L_p + 0.542 L_N + 0.164 \log R \log K'_g$
$\qquad\qquad\quad (0.125) \qquad\qquad\quad (0.117) \qquad (0.037) \qquad\qquad\qquad 0.978$

$(I,B,2) \qquad\qquad 0.241 \qquad\qquad\quad +0.540 \quad +0.177$
$\qquad\qquad\quad (0.172) \qquad\qquad\quad (0.168) \quad (0.049) \qquad\qquad\qquad 0.961$

Version II

$(II,A,1) \log V = 0.435 \log L_p + 0.480 \log L_N + 0.057 \log R \log K_g$
$\qquad\qquad\quad (0.119) \qquad (0.092) \qquad (0.041) \qquad\qquad\qquad 0.987$

$(II,A,2) \qquad\qquad 0.420 \qquad +0.474 \qquad +0.065$
$\qquad\qquad\quad (0.188) \qquad (0.150) \qquad (0.064) \qquad\qquad\qquad 0.969$

$(II,B,1) \qquad\qquad 0.474 \log L_p + 0.461 \log L_N + 0.049 \log R \log K'_g$
$\qquad\qquad\quad (0.117) \qquad (0.092) \qquad (0.047) \qquad\qquad\qquad 0.986$

$(II,B,2) \qquad\qquad 0.458 \qquad +0.457 \qquad +0.058$
$\qquad\qquad\quad (0.180) \qquad (0.146) \qquad (0.071) \qquad\qquad\qquad 0.970$

[1]See n. 14, Chapter IV.
[2]For a discussion of the four versions, see Chapter IV, Section (2).

Version III

(III,A,1) $\log V = 0.926 \log L - 0.026 \log R \log K_g$
(0.113) (0.050) $R^2 = 0.972$

(II,A,2) 0.875 $- 0.004$
(0.154) (0.068) 0.951

(III,B,1) $0.930 \log L - 0.031 \log R \log K'_g$
(0.114) (0.058) 0.972

(III,B,2) 0.880 $- 0.008$
(0.155) (0.078) 0.951

Version IV

(IV,A,1) $\log V = 0.841 \log L + 0.027 \log K_g$
(0.165) (0.142) 0.971

(IV,A,2) 0.745 $+ 0.106$
(0.219) (0.187) 0.956

(IV,B,1) $0.807 \log L + 0.067 \log K'_g$
(0.175) (0.174) 0.971

(IV,B,2) 0.706 $+ 0.164$
(0.225) (0.223) 0.958

Furnitures and Fixtures
Version I

(I,A,1) $\log V = 0.662 \log q \log L_p + 0.446 \log L_N - 0.023 \log R \log K_g$
(0.172) (0.163) (0.044) $R^2 = 0.926$

(I,A,2) 0.697 $+ 0.494$ $- 0.044$
(0.423) (0.466) (0.065) 0.654

(I,B,1) $0.651 \log q \log L_p + 0.531 \log L_N - 0.085 \log R \log K'_g$
(0.159) (0.171) (0.065) 0.933

(I,B,2) 0.668 $+ 0.670$ $- 0.163$
(0.376) (0.583) (0.257) 0.664

Version II

(II,A,1) $\log V = 0.386 \log L_p + 0.706 \log L_N - 0.056 \log R \log K_g$
(0.149) (0.152) (0.058) $R^2 = 0.899$

(II,A,2) 0.400 $+ 0.838$ $- 0.100$
(0.379) (0.480) (0.224) 0.617

(II,B,1) 0.347 $+ 0.790$ $- 0.111 \log R \log K'_g$
(0.127) (0.167) (0.079) 0.905

(II,B,2) 0.323 $+ 1.006$ $- 0.198$
(0.263) (0.593) (0.290) 0.623

Version III

(III,A,1) $\log V = 0.885 \log L - 0.016 \log R \log K_g$

    (0.186)   (0.077)   0.805

(III,A,2)   0.249 $+ 0.202$

    (0.540)   (0.197)   0.534

(III,B,1) $0.808 \log L + 0.036 \log R \log K'_{g'}$

    (0.159)   (0.096)   0.806

(III,B,2)   0.314 $+ 0.261$

    (0.397)   (0.207)   0.511

Version IV

(IV,A,1) $\log V = 0.730 \log L + 0.110 \log K_g$

    (0.220)   (0.173)   0.809

(IV,A,2) $- 0.084$ $+ 0.674$

    (0.491)   (0.357)   0.678

(IV,B,1)   0.605 $+ 0.359 \log K'_g$

    (0.167)   (0.199)   0.837

(IV,B,2)   0.172 $+ 0.781$

    (0.297)   (0.327)   0.710

Bibliography

[1] Abramovitz, A. M. "Resource and Output Trends in the United States Since 1870." *American Economic Review* (Papers and Proceedings): May 1956.

[2] Arrow, K., H. B. Chenery, B. Minhas, and R. M. Solow. "Capital-Labor Substitution and Economic Efficiency." *Review of Economics and Statistics:* August 1961.

[3] Bronfenbrenner, M. "Production Functions: Cobb-Douglas, Interfirm Intrafirm." *Econometrica:* January 1944.

[4] Bronfenbrenner, M., and P. H. Douglas. "Cross-Section Studies in the Cobb-Douglas Function." *Journal of Political Economy:* December 1939.

[5] Brown, Murray, and Alfred Conrad. "Fundamental Economic Variables in a Generalized System of Production." Netherlands Economic Institute: July 1962.

[6] Bureau of the Census. *Annual Survey of Manufactures, 1956.*

[7] ————. *Annual Survey of Manufactures, 1957.*

[8] ————. *Supplementary Employee Costs, Cost of Maintenance and Repair, Insurance, Rent, Taxes, and Depreciation and Book Value of Depreciable Assets: 1957; 1958 Census of Manufactures.*

[9] ————. *1958 Census of Manufactures, "New York."*

[10] Chenery, H. B., and P. G. Clark. *Interindustry Economics.* New York: 1959.

[11] Chernoff, H., and H. Rubin. "Asymptotic Properties of Limited Information Estimates under Generalized Conditions" in W. Hood and T. C. Koopmans, editors. *Studies in Econometric Methods.* New York: 1953.

[12] Cobb, C. W., and P. H. Douglas. "A Theory of Production." *American Economic Review:* (March Supplement) 1928.

[13] Daly, P. O., E. Olson, and P. H. Douglas. "The Production Function for Manufacturing in the United States, 1904." *Journal of Political Economy:* February 1943.

[14] Denison, E. F. *The Sources of Economic Growth in the United States and the Alternatives Before Us.* New York: Committee for Economic Development, 1962.

[15] Department of Commerce of the State of New York. *The Industrial Directory of New York State.* 1958.

[16] Douglas, P. H. *The Theory of Wages.* New York: 1943.

[17] Douglas, P. H., and G. T. Gunn. "The Production Function for American Manufacturing for 1914." *Journal of Political Economy:* August 1942.

[18] Durand, D. "Some Thoughts on Marginal Productivity with Special Reference to Professor Douglas' Analysis." *Journal of Political Economy:* December 1937.

[19] Edelberg, V. "An Econometric Model of Production and Distribution." *Econometrica:* July 1936.

[20] Ferber, R. *Statistical Techniques in Market Research:* New York, 1949.

[21] Fisher, W. "Estimation in the Linear Decision Model." *International Economic Review:* January 1962.

[22] Frankel, M. "The Production Function in Allocation and Growth: A Synthesis." *The American Economic Review:* December 1962.

[23] Friedman, M. *A Theory of the Consumption Function.* Princeton: 1957.

[24] Goldsmith, R. W. *A Study of Saving in the United States.* New York: 1955.

[25] Gordon, R. A. "Differential Changes in the Prices of Consumers' and Capital Goods." *The American Economic Review:* December 1961.

[26] Griliches, Zvi. "The Sources of Measured Productivity Growth: United States Agriculture, 1940–60." *The Journal of Political Economy:* August 1963.

[27] ———. "Specification Bias in Estimates of Production Functions." *Journal of Farm Economics:* February 1957.

[28] Grunfeld, Y., and Z. Griliches. "Is Aggregation Necessarily Bad?" *The Review of Economics and Statistics:* February 1960.

[29] Gunn, G. T., and P. H. Douglas. "The Production Function for American Manufacturing in 1919." *American Economic Review:* March 1941.

[30] ———. "The Production Function for Australian Manufacturing." *Quarterly Journal of Economics:* November 1941.

[31] Hansen, M. H., and W. N. Hurwitz. "The Problem of Nonresponse in Sample Surveys." *Journal of the American Statistical Association:* December 1946.

[32] Hansen, M. H., W. N. Hurwitz, and W. G. Madow. *Sample Survey Methods and Theory.* New York: 1953.

[33] Heady, E. O., and J. L. Dillon. *Agricultural Production Functions.* Ames: 1961.

[34] Hildreth, C. "Combining Cross Section Data and Time Series Data." *Cowles Commission Discussion Paper:* May 1950.

[35] ———. "Preliminary Considerations Regarding Time Series and/or Cross Section Studies." *Cowles Commission Discussion Paper. Statistics:* July 1949.

[36] Hoch, I. "Estimation of Production Function Parameters Combining Times Series and Cross Section Data." *Econometrica:* January 1962.

[37] ———. "Simultaneous Equation Bias in the Context of the Cobb-Douglas Production Function." *Econometrica:* October 1958.

[38] Hogan, W. P. "Technical Progress and Production Function." *Review of Economics and Statistics:* November 1958.

[39] Hood, W. C., and J. C. Koopmans. *Studies in Econometric Method.* New York: 1953.

[40] Kendrick, J. W. "Productivity Trends: Capital and Labor." *Review of Economics and Statistics:* August 1956.

[41] Kiefer, J. "Optimum Designs in Regression Problems, II." *Annals of Mathematical Statistics:* March 1961.

[42] Kiefer, J., and J. Wolfowitz. "Optimum Design in Regression Problems." *Annals of Mathematical Statistics:* June 1959.

[43] Klein, L. R. *Econometrics.* Evanston: 1953.

[44] ———. "Macroeconomics and the Theory of Rational Behavior." *Econometrica:* April 1946.

[45] Klein, L. R., and A. S. Goldberger. *An Econometric Model of the United States, 1929–1952.* Amsterdam: 1955.

[46] Klock, T., and L. B. M. Mennes. "Simultaneous Equations Estimation Based on Principal Components of Predetermined Variables." *Econometrica:* January 1960.

219

[47] Koopmans, T. C., and W. Hood. "The Estimation of Simultaneous Linear Economic Relationships." in W. Hood, and T. C. Koopmans, eds., *Studies in Econometric Methods:* New York, 1953.

[48] Marschak, J., and W. H. Andrews. "Random Simultaneous Equations and the Theory of Production." *Econometrica:* October 1944.

[49] Massell, B. F. "Capital Formation and Technological Change in U. S. Manufacturing." *Review of Economics and Statistics:* May 1960.

[50] ————. "A Disaggregated View of Technical Change." *Review of Economics and Statistics:* December 1961.

[51] May, K. "Structure of Production Function of the Firm." *Econometrica:* October 1949.

[52] Menderhausen, H. "On the Significance of Professor Douglas' Production Function." *Econometrica:* April 1938.

[53] Mundlak, Y. "Estimation of Production and Behavior Functions from a Combination of Cross Section and Time-Series Data." *Measurement in Economics.* Stanford: 1963.

[54] Nataf, A. "Sur la Possibilite de Construction de certains Macro-modeles." *Econometrica:* October 1950.

[55] Nerlove, M. "Identification and Estimation of the Cobb-Douglas Production Functions" processed, December 1958, revised, May 1959.

[56] ————. *Distributive Lags and Demand Analysis.* Washington, D.C.: 1958.

[57] ————. "On Measurement of Relative Economic Efficiency." processed, 1960.

[58] ————. "Returns to Scale in Electric Supply." *Measurement in Economics.* Stanford: 1963.

[59] Phelps Brown, E. H. "The Meaning of the Fitted Cobb-Douglas Function." *The Quarterly Journal of Economics:* November 1957.

[60] Raiffa, H., and R. Schlaifer. *Applied Statistical Decision Theory.* Boston: 1961.

[61] Reder, M. W. "An Alternative Interpretation of the Cobb-Douglas Production Function." *Econometrica:* July-October 1943.

[62] Schmookler, J. "The Changing Efficiency of the American Economy: 1869–1938." *Review of Economics and Statistics:* August 1952.

[63] Shen, T. Y. "A Multivariate Model of Production." processed, 1961.

[64] Smith, V. E. "The Statistical Production Function." *The Quarterly Journal of Economics:* August 1945.

[65] Solow, R. M. "Investment and Technical Progress." *Mathematical Methods in the Social Sciences, 1959.* Stanford: 1960.

[66] ————. "Reply to the Note by Hogan." *Review of Economics and Statistics:* November 1958.

[67] ————. "Technical Change and the Aggregate Production Function." *Review of Economics and Statistics:* August 1957.

[68] ————. "Technical Progress, Capital Formation, and Economic Growth." *The American Economic Review:* May 1962.

[69] Strotz, R. H. "Interdependence as a Specification Error." *Econometrica:* April 1960.

[70] Strotz, R. H., and H. Wold. "Recursive *vs* Nonrecursive Systems: An Attempt at Synthesis." *Econometrica:* April 1960.

[71] Theil, H. "Alternative Approaches to the Aggregation Problem." *Logic, Methodology and Philosophy of Science:* 1961.

[72] ————. *Economic Forecasts and Policy* (2nd ed.). Amsterdam: 1961.

[73] ————. *Linear Aggregation of Economic Relations.* Amsterdam: 1954.

[74] ————. "On the Bayesian Approach to Regression Analysis." Report 6206. Netherland School of Economics: March 1962.

[75] Valavanis-Vail, S. "An Econometric Model of Growth, U. S. A., 1869–1953." *American Economic Review:* May 1955.

[76] Verhulst, M. J. J. "The Pure Theory of Production Applied to the French Gas Industry." *Econometrica:* October 1948.

[77] Wall, B. "A Cobb-Douglas Function for United States Manufacturing and Mining." *Econometrica* (Abstract): April 1948.

[78] Walters, A. A. "Production and Cost Functions: An Econometric Survey." *Econometrica:* January-April 1963.

Index

A

Abramovitz, A. M., 106, 217
Aggregation, problems of, 21–23, 125–129, 130–133
Andrews, W. H., 21, 24, 25, 27, 28, 44–45, 220
Annual Survey of Manufactures, 1956, 71, 217
Annual Survey of Manufactures, 1957, 71, 217
Arrow, K., 29, 30–41, 111, 217

B

Bayesian approach, 62
Bronfenbrenner, M., 20, 21, 24, 25, 106, 217
Brown, Murray, 29, 217
Bureau of the Census, 71, 205, 217

C

Capital
   capital-labor ratio, 160–180
   marginal physical product, 187–201
   marginal revenue product, 187–201
   measurement, 28, 133–135
Chenery, H. B., 29, 30–41, 111, 217
Chernoff, H., 63, 217
Clark, P. G., 217
Cobb, C. W., 1–2, 19, 20, 217
Conrad, Alfred, 29, 217

D

Daly, P. O., 217
Demand for labor, 53–57
   equilibrium demand, 53–57
   Nerlove's approach to the speed of adjustment, 53, 56–57
   see also Labor
Demand for output, 45–49, 136–137
Denison, E. F., 10, 218
Dillon, J. L., 19, 21, 219

Douglas, P. H., 1–2, 19, 20, 21, 24, 27, 106, 217, 218, 219
Durand, D., 21, 218

E

Edelberg, V., 20, 218

F

Ferber, R., 116, 120, 218
Fisher, W., 61, 218
Frankel, M., 29, 218
Friedman, M., 57, 218

G

Goldberger, A. S., 20, 27, 219
Goldsmith, R. W., 218
Gordon, R. A., 134, 218
Griliches, Zvi, 26, 29, 106, 131, 218
Grunfeld, Y., 131, 218
Gunn, G. T., 21, 218, 219

H

Hansen, M. H., 204, 219
Heady, E. O., 19, 21, 219
Hildreth, C., 219
Hoch, I., 29, 42, 219
Hogan, W. P., 219
Hood, W. C., 64, 219, 220
Hurwitz, W. N., 204, 219

I

Identification problem, 26–27
   Hoch, 42–43
   Marshak and Andrews, 27
   Nerlove, 29, 53
Income shares, 111–113
Industrial Directory of the State of New York, The, 203, 205, 218

K

Kendrick, J. W., 106, 219
Kiefer, J., 204, 219

Klein, L. R., 19, 20, 21, 22, 23, 27, 126, 127, 133, 219
Klock, T., 219
Koopmans, J. C., 64, 219, 220

L

Labor
labor-capital ratio, 160–180
labor-output ratio, 160–186
marginal physical product, 187–201
marginal revenue product, 187–201
quality, 57–58, 138

M

Madow, W. G., 219
Marshak, J., 21, 24, 25, 27, 28, 44–45, 220
Massell, B. F., 30, 220
May, K., 21, 220
Menderhausen, H., 21, 220
Mennes, L. B. M., 219
Minhas, B., 29, 30–41, 111, 217
Mundlak, Y., 29, 220

N

Nataf, A., 22, 23, 126, 129, 133, 220
Nerlove, M., 1–3, 19, 29, 57, 220
New York State, *see* Production functions

O

Olson, E., 217
Optimum, Pareto, 122–125

P

Phelps Brown, E. H., 21, 25, 220
Production functions
aggregate functions, 125–130
Cobb-Douglas functions, 20
critical comments, 21–28
constant elasticity functions, summary and critical comments, 30–41
in development of economic thought, 3–4
for individual industries, 70–103, 214–220
New York State, 202–213

statistical functions obtained, summary, 105
Productivity
of labor and capital by state and industry, 138–159
Profit maximization, 114–122

R

Raiffa, H., 62, 220
Reder, M. W., 21, 220
Rubin, H., 63, 217

S

Schlaifer, R., 62, 220
Schmookler, J., 106, 221
Shen, T. Y., 29, 221
Simultaneous equation model, 58–59
Nerlove, 53
Smith, V. E., 21, 221
Solow, R. M., 28, 29–30, 30–41, 41–42, 106, 108, 111, 134, 217, 221
Strotz, R. H., 221
Supply of capital and labor, 137–138

T

Technology
"compensated change" in capital, 51–52
importance, 105–106
scale effect and technology, 106–107
treatment of technological change, 27–28, 41–42, 49–53
Theil, H., 22, 25, 26, 27, 62, 73, 126, 133, 221

V

Valavanis-Vail, S., 20, 221
Verhulst, M. J. J., 221

W

Wall, B., 20, 27, 221
Walters, A. A., 19, 29, 221
"Weighted-output" approach, 106, 108, 111
Wold, H., 221
Wolfowitz, J., 204, 219